Microsoft Windows Communication Foundation 4.0 Cookbook for Developing SOA Applications

Over 85 easy recipes for managing communication between applications

Steven Cheng

BIRMINGHAM - MUMBAI

Microsoft Windows Communication Foundation 4.0 Cookbook for Developing SOA Applications

First published: October 2010

Production Reference: 1141010

Published by Packt Publishing Ltd.
32 Lincoln Road
Olton
Birmingham, B27 6PA, UK.

ISBN 978-1-849680-76-9

www.packtpub.com

Cover Image by Vinayak Chittar (vinayak.chittar@gmail.com)

Credits

Author
Steven Cheng

Reviewers
Frank Xu Lei
Kris van der Mast
Dong Qi

Acquisition Editor
Rashmi Phadnis

Development Editor
Dhwani Devater

Technical Editor
Vinodhan Nair

Copy Editor
Janki Mathuria

Indexer
Rekha Nair
Monica Ajmera Mehta

Editorial Team Leader
Gagandeep Singh

Project Team Leader
Lata Basantani

Project Coordinator
Jovita Pinto

Proofreader
Sandra Hopper

Graphics
Geetanjali Sawant

Production Coordinators
Alwin Roy
Adline Swetha Jesuthas

Cover Work
Alwin Roy

Foreword

In the process of development and integration of enterprise applications and systems, SOA is a flexible set of design principles and is becoming more and more popular.

Windows Communication Foundation (WCF) is a framework for building service-oriented applications, which are based on .NET.

WCF 4 comes with a wide range of specific features as follows:

- Simplified configuration
- Standard endpoints
- IIS hosting without an SVC file
- WS-Discovery
- Routing service (previously included with Dublin)
- REST caching and Help page
- Workflow services
- Non-destructive queue receive
- Simple byte stream encoding
- ETW tracing

Besides giving an introduction of the basic WCF concepts (such as endpoint, contract, binding, and address), this book also covers advanced topics such as security, extensions of Runtime, and diagnostics. By the way, this book also introduces the new features of WCF 4.0. Every section is excellent and is based on a real WCF application. It also provides a lot of sample code to help the readers understand how to implement it. It's really a good handbook for WCF learners.

Thanks Steven for your hard work on this book.

Frank Xu Lei

MVP of Connected System Developer

About the Author

Steven Cheng is a senior support engineer at Microsoft Global Technical Support Center, where he has been supporting Microsoft software development technologies for more than five years. Currently, as a community leader, he is working actively in the MSDN newsgroup and forum communities.

Steven Cheng's technical specialties cover many popular areas of Microsoft development technologies, including .NET framework, ASP.NET, XML Web Service, Windows Communication Foundation, SharePoint development, and so on. His blog can be found at `http://blogs.msdn.com/stcheng`.

The publication of this book could not have been possible without the efforts put in by a large number of individuals. I would like to thank my colleague Andrew Zhu, who has helped me during the entire book authoring lifecycle. And thanks to my friends, Mian Li and Le Fei, who have given me lots of suggestions on the book recipes.

Lastly, I offer my regards and blessings to all of those who supported me in any respect during the completion of this book.

About the Reviewers

Frank Xu Lei is the Microsoft MVP of Connected System Developer. He is also the moderator of Microsoft's Chinese WCF Forum. He has translated the book Inside Windows Communication Foundation into Chinese.

He always focuses on Distributed Applications Development and EAI, based on .NET. Besides this, he is also a fan of NBA and sometimes, he goes to KTV with his friends. You can visit his blog at www.frankxulei.com.

Dong Qi is an experienced .NET developer and has four years experience in .NET development. He worked at Microsoft as a development support engineer in the MSDN team. He now works at the Agree company as a .NET developer for Agree's frontend finance products. Agree is a leading financial consulting, software, and service provider company in China. He has written on .NET debugging and .NET security.

Kris van der Mast, an active and dedicated moderator at the official ASP.NET forums, is a Microsoft MVP and ASP Insider. He's a well-known community member of several Belgian user groups. Kris is also a speaker for user groups in Belgium and abroad. You can find his blog at http://blog.krisvandermast.com.

Kris currently works for Ordina Belgium, a consultancy company, as a senior .NET developer and architect. He also provides courses to clients in his specialization and technical interest—web technologies.

Table of Contents

Preface

Windows Communication Foundation 4.0 (WCF 4.0) is a .NET-based application programming interface for building and running connected systems. It enables secure and reliable communication among systems within an organization or across the Internet. This book deals with the difficult issues faced by a .NET developer while working with WCF.

What this book covers

Chapter 1, Working with Contracts, shows how we can use Contract in WCF service development, including use cases of ServiceContract, DataContract, MessageContract, FaultContract, and so on.

Chapter 2, Endpoint, Binding, and Behavior, focuses on the basic building blocks of a WCF service, including endpoint, binding, and behavior. The recipes in this chapter demonstrate how to create various kinds of services by using the proper combination of these building blocks.

Chapter 3, Hosting and Configuration, covers several common and useful WCF service-hosting scenarios, such as hosting a WCF service in a Windows service, IIS web applications, and a WSS 3.0 site.

Chapter 4, Service Discovery and Proxy Generation, covers how to discover and consume WCF services. Recipes here demonstrate various scenarios of generating a WCF service proxy and introduces the service discovery feature in WCF 4.0.

Chapter 5, Channel and Messaging, digs into the channel layer of WCF programming and shows how to build WCF server and client applications through channel-layer components.

Chapter 6, Dealing with Data in Service, covers various data exchange and communication scenarios in WCF development. Recipes here include how to transfer XML and raw binary data or ADO.NET DataTable objects in service operations.

Chapter 7, Security, demonstrates how to utilize the built-in WCF security features such as service authentication, authorization, identity impersonation, message protection, and so on.

Chapter 8, Concurrency, introduces some typical cases about managing the concurrency and performance behaviors of a WCF service, such as how to use throttling settings and how to use Visual Studio testing tools for service performance tuning.

Chapter 9, Extending WCF Runtime, focuses on how to extend the existing components in the WCF programming model, such as customizing the default ServiceHost, using MessageInspector or MessageEncoder to intercept messages, customizing the service authorization logic, and so on.

Chapter 10, RESTful and AJAX-enabled WCF Services, provides several recipes on WCF REST service programming, including building a standard REST service, building an AJAX-enabled REST service, and consuming a remote REST service from an AJAX client.

Chapter 11, Interoperability, shows how to make a WCF service or client work with non-WCF or even non-.NET platform-based applications (such as a WebRequest client, legacy MSMQ client, or Microsoft Office client).

Chapter 12, Diagnostics, introduces some useful tools and skills for troubleshooting and diagnostics in WCF service development, including how to capture WCF messages, how to debug a Windows service host, how to use WCF performance counters, and so on.

Chapter 13, Miscellaneous WCF Development Tips, provides some additional skills and cases in WCF service development such as how to generate and manage test X.509 certificates and how to build an RSS feed and routing services.

What you need for this book

Though all the samples in this book are C# based, you don't have to be a very experienced C# developer. What is required is that you have a development machine with Visual Studio 2010 (Professional or Ultimate edition) and IIS installed, since the sample code is provided as Visual Studio 2010 solutions and some of them use IIS as host.

Who this book is for

If you work with Windows Communication Foundation 4.0 and want to be efficient when working with WCF features such as interoperability, proxy generation, and security, you will find this book very useful. With this book, you will be able to find quick and handy solutions for various kinds of service development scenarios using Microsoft Windows Communication Foundation 4.0. To follow the recipes, you will need to be comfortable with the .NET framework, C# programming, and the basics of SOA and how to develop them.

Conventions

In this book, you will find a number of styles of text that distinguish between different kinds of information. Here are some examples of these styles, and an explanation of their meaning.

Code words in text are shown as follows: "There is also a corresponding `WebInvokeAttribute` for a HTTP POST request."

A block of code is set as follows:

```
[ServiceContract]
public interface IDataService
{
    [OperationContract]
    string GetData();
}
```

When we wish to draw your attention to a particular part of a code block, the relevant lines or items are set in bold:

```
[ServiceContract(Namespace="WCF.REST")]
public interface IDataService
{
    [OperationContract]
    [WebGet(ResponseFormat= WebMessageFormat.Json)]
    SimpleData GetData();
}
```

Any command-line input or output is written as follows:

```
certmgr -c -r localmachine -s my
```

New terms and **important words** are shown in bold. Words that you see on the screen, in menus or dialog boxes for example, appear in the text like this: "Selecting **Add Service Reference** will launch a dialog where one can control the configuration options on how the WCF service proxy gets generated".

Warnings or important notes appear in a box like this.

Tips and tricks appear like this.

Reader feedback

Feedback from our readers is always welcome. Let us know what you think about this book—what you liked or may have disliked. Reader feedback is important for us to develop titles that you really get the most out of.

To send us general feedback, simply send an e-mail to `feedback@packtpub.com`, and mention the book title via the subject of your message.

If there is a book that you need and would like to see us publish, please send us a note in the **SUGGEST A TITLE** form on `www.packtpub.com` or e-mail `suggest@packtpub.com`.

If there is a topic that you have expertise in and you are interested in either writing or contributing to a book, see our author guide on `www.packtpub.com/authors`.

Customer support

Now that you are the proud owner of a Packt book, we have a number of things to help you to get the most from your purchase.

> **Downloading the example code for this book**
>
> You can download the example code files for all Packt books you have purchased from your account at `http://www.PacktPub.com`. If you purchased this book elsewhere, you can visit `http://www.PacktPub.com/support` and register to have the files e-mailed directly to you.

Errata

Although we have taken every care to ensure the accuracy of our content, mistakes do happen. If you find a mistake in one of our books—maybe a mistake in the text or the code—we would be grateful if you would report this to us. By doing so, you can save other readers from frustration and help us improve subsequent versions of this book. If you find any errata, please report them by visiting `http://www.packtpub.com/support`, selecting your book, clicking on the **errata submission form** link, and entering the details of your errata. Once your errata are verified, your submission will be accepted and the errata will be uploaded on our website, or added to any list of existing errata, under the Errata section of that title. Any existing errata can be viewed by selecting your title from `http://www.packtpub.com/support`.

Piracy

Piracy of copyright material on the Internet is an ongoing problem across all media. At Packt, we take the protection of our copyright and licenses very seriously. If you come across any illegal copies of our works, in any form, on the Internet, please provide us with the location address or website name immediately so that we can pursue a remedy.

Please contact us at copyright@packtpub.com with a link to the suspected pirated material.

We appreciate your help in protecting our authors, and our ability to bring you valuable content.

Questions

You can contact us at questions@packtpub.com if you are having a problem with any aspect of the book, and we will do our best to address it.

1
Working with Contracts

In this chapter, we will cover:

- ▶ Defining a one-way Contract
- ▶ Making `DataContract` forward-compatible
- ▶ Generate `DataContract` from XML Schema
- ▶ Using XMLSerializer to control message serialization
- ▶ Using `MessageContract` to control the SOAP Message
- ▶ Adding a custom `SoapHeader` via Contract
- ▶ Returning custom exception data through `FaultContract`

Introduction

Contracts often occur in business affairs to restrict the operations between the operators that are working with each other. For distributed communication services, Contracts also play a very important role in making sure that the service consumers can co-operate with the service providers correctly. Looking around, we can see the term **SOA (Service-Oriented Architecture)** being widely used. Technically speaking, **SOAP (Simple Object Access Protocol)** can be explained as a set of components that can be invoked, and whose interface descriptions can be published and discovered. From an SOA perspective, with Contracts properly defined, service consumers can get an idea of how to work with the target service without knowing how the service is actually implemented.

As a unified communication programming platform, WCF provides complete support for Contract-related design in various parts of WCF service development. These include **ServiceContract, OperationContract, DataContract, MessageContract, FaultContract**, and so on. ServiceContract and OperationContract are used to represent a Service and its operations' definition (such as the operation collection and operation signatures). DataContract is used to represent an agreement of the data that will be exchanged between the service client and server. If the service designer wants to take full control over the data envelope transferred between client and server, they can use MessageContract to control the underlying service messages. WCF also provides FaultContract for the service designer to declaratively associate custom **Exception** types to certain service operations, and the corresponding fault content will be returned when an error occurs.

This chapter provides seven recipes on how to work with various contracts in WCF service development. These include defining a one-way service operation that helps you get familiar with standard ServiceContract and OperationContract declaration. Next, we will cover how to use **FaultContractAttribute** to associate a custom SOAP fault data type with certain service operations that need a customized error format. With the third, fourth, and fifth recipes, we will focus on DataContract designing topics, such as DataContract versioning, using XMLSerializer for the DataContract types serialization, and the contract-first approach for DataContract generation. The last two recipes describe how to use MessageContract to perform low-level manipulation on the service operations message formatting, such as returning arbitrary XML data as message content and adding a custom SOAPHeader through MessageContract class members.

Defining a one-way Contract

One-way (also called diagram-style) operation is a common pattern in distributed communication programming and is also one of the three supported message exchange patterns in WCF. When using the one-way message exchange pattern, a client sends a message using a fire-and-forget exchange (refer to the next screenshot). A fire-and-forget exchange is one that requires out-of-band confirmation of successful delivery. The message might be lost in transit and never reach the service. If the send operation completes successfully at the client end, it does not guarantee that the remote endpoint has received the message. In those cases where the client only wants to send information to the server side, without taking care of the execution result, we can consider defining our WCF service operation as one-way style.

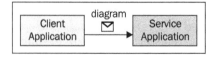

How to do it...

1. Create the service interface or class type and add methods into it.

2. Mark the interface/class type with `ServiceContractAttribute` and mark the methods with `OperationContractAttribute`.

3. Set the `IsOneWay` property of the `OperationContractAttribute` to `true`.

   The following code snippet shows the complete one-way `OperationContract` definition:

```
[ServiceContract]
interface IMyContract
{
[OperationContract(IsOneWay=true)]
void OneWayMethod()
{
    // Do some work here
}
}
```

How it works...

When `OperationContract` is marked with `IsOneWay=true`, the runtime will detect this and know that this service operation needs to be handled as one-way style. One-way operation cannot carry a return value but can only pass input parameters to the service. After the client sends out the service request, the client will wait until it gets the response that the request message has reached the service side. However, the response here is not the return value, but the protocol level ACK, which indicates that the request has reached the service (but gives no idea of whether or how the request has been processed).

We can get further understanding on one-way operation via the following question:

What is the difference between a standard void (no return value) operation and a one-way operation?

Suppose you have the following `ServiceContract` implemented:

```
[ServiceContract]
public interface IHelloService
{
    [OperationContract(IsOneWay=false)]
    void DoWork();
    [OperationContract(IsOneWay = true)]
    void DoWorkAsOneWay();
}
```

By invoking the two operations from the client and capturing the HTTP message, we can get different response messages as shown in the next two screenshots. The first screenshot shows the response of the `DoWork` operation, while the next shows the response of the `DoWorkAsOneWay` operation.

```
HTTP/1.1 200 OK
Content-Length: 366
Content-Type: application/soap+xml; charset=utf-8
Server: Microsoft-HTTPAPI/2.0
Date: Tue, 24 Nov 2009 14:37:10 GMT

<s:Envelope xmlns:s="http://www.w3.org/2003/05/soap-envelope"
  <s:Header>
    <a:Action s:mustUnderstand="1">http://tempuri.org/IHelloS
    <a:RelatesTo>urn:uuid:705900a8-eaba-48e4-b6a9-5e84268048b
  </s:Header>
  <s:Body>
    <DoWorkResponse xmlns="http://tempuri.org/"/>
  </s:Body>
```

```
HTTP/1.1 202 Accepted
Content-Length: 0
Server: Microsoft-HTTPAPI/1.0
Date: Tue, 17 Nov 2009 10:10:00 GMT

<s:Envelope xmlns:s="http://www.w3.org/2003/05/soap-envelope" xmlns:
  <s:Header>
```

As you can see, the normal void operation will return HTTP 200 status code and the complete SOAP Response in the body, while the one-way operation will only return a HTTP 202 Accepted status header. This indicates that the one-way operation call gets finished as long as the server side received the request, while the normal void operation (standard request/reply) will wait for the server side to execute and return the response data. Understanding this can help us to make better decisions about whether to use one-way operation or not.

There's more...

In addition to one-way operation, there are two other message exchange patterns that are widely used in WCF services. They are the **Request-response** pattern and the **Duplex** pattern.

The Request-response pattern is very similar to the standard function call that has an input parameter and return value. In a Request-response pattern-based WCF service operation call, a message is sent and a reply is received. The pattern consists of request-response pairs, as shown in the next figure.

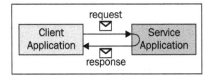

The Duplex exchange pattern allows an arbitrary number of messages to be sent by a client and received in any order. This pattern is like a phone conversation, where each word being spoken is a message (refer to the following screenshot).

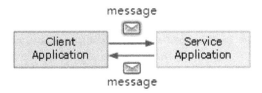

See also

▸ *Capture a raw http request/response of WCF service call* in *Chapter 12*

▸ *Complete source code for this recipe can be found in the* \Chapter 1\recipe1\ *folder*

Make DataContract forward-compatible

WCF uses a serialization engine called DataContractSerializer by default, to serialize and deserialize data. If we want to add new complex data types (that will be transferred in service operations) in a WCF service, we need to define it as a DataContract type so as to make it friendly to the DataContractSerializer engine. A .NET serialization system supports **backward-compatibility** on custom data types naturally. However, sometimes we also need **forward-compatibility** for data types used in a WCF service. Suppose that you have a service that exchanges some custom data types between clients. If one side updates the custom data type (adds some fields or properties) or uses a newer version, it is important to make sure that the other side (without using the updated version of data) can still work correctly with the updated data type instances.

1. Make the custom data type (we will use in our service communication) implement the `IExtensibleDataObject` interface.

```
[DataContract]
    public class FCQuestion : IExtensibleDataObject
    {
        [DataMember]
        public string Subject { get; set; }
        [DataMember]
        public string Answer { get; set; }

        public ExtensionDataObject ExtensionData
        {
            get;
            set;
        }
    }
```

2. Make sure you haven't enabled the `IgnoreExtensionDataObject` property on `ServiceBehaviorAttribute` applied on your WCF service (this property is disabled by default).

   You can have a look at the article *ServiceBehaviorAttribute. IgnoreExtensionDataObject Property* for more information and is available at:

   ```
   http://msdn.microsoft.com/en-us/library/system.servicemodel.
   servicebehaviorattribute.ignoreextensiondataobject.aspx
   ```

After the `DataContract` type implements the `IExtensibleDataObject` interface, an `ExtensionDataObject` property is added; this property plays an important role in forward-compatible serialization. WCF will use `DataContractSerializer` for `DataContract` type serialization/deserialization. When `DataContractSerializer` finds that a certain type (used for operation parameters or return value) has implemented the `IExtensibleDataObject` interface, it will store any data (this is obtained from the message stream during deserialization) that doesn't have corresponding property/fields in the type definition into the `ExtensionDataObject` property so that these data will not get lost. And if the deserialized instance (with some unknown data stored in `ExtensionDataObject`) is serialized into the message later, `DataContractSerializer` will write out `ExtensionDataObject` into the message stream again. This ensures that the data in the new version of `DataContract` can be consumed by the service/client with the old type definition correctly, instead of raising unexpected type, mismatching, or serialization exceptions.

The following modified data type can be consumed by the service/client that has the old definition, as explained earlier, without synchronizing the `DataContract` type definition:

```
[DataContract]
    public class FCQuestion : IExtensibleDataObject
    {
        [DataMember]
        public string Subject { get; set; }
        [DataMember]
        public string Answer { get; set; }
        [DataMember]
        public string Comment { get; set; }

        public ExtensionDataObject ExtensionData
        {              get; set;          }
    }
```

There's more...

Currently, using the `IExtensibleDataObject` interface can make the `DataContractSerializer` preserve unknown data properties/fields when deserializing/serializing custom data types. However, the `ExtensionDataObject` property is an opaque object to developers and we do not have means to manually read the data stored in it. In case we want to manually extract the additional unknown property/fields, we can consider directly accessing the underlying SOAP message via `MessageInspector` or other extension points.

See also

▶   *Altering an operation message via MessageInspector* in *Chapter 9.*

▶   *Complete source code for this recipe can be found in the* `\Chapter 1\recipe2\` *folder*

Generate DataContract from an XML Schema

In the contract-first development approach, one of the most important steps is to generate the data types used in the service from **XML Schemas**, which represent the contract. As a unified distributed communication development platform, it is quite common to support such kind of `DataContract` generation in WCF development.

Getting ready

If you are not yet familiar with the contract-first development approach, you can get a quick overview of it from Aaron Skonnard's MSDN article *Contract-First Service Development* at `http://msdn.microsoft.com/en-us/magazine/cc163800.aspx`.

How to do it...

1. Compose the XML schema that represents the `DataContract` types that will be used in our WCF service. The next screenshot shows a simple sample schema that contains a simple enum and a complex data type definition:

```xml
<xs:schema targetNamespace="http://wcftest.org/datacontract"
           xmlns:xs="http://www.w3.org/2001/XMLSchema">
  <xs:element name="TestData">
    <xs:complexType>
      <xs:all>
        <xs:element name ="StringProperty" type="xs:string" />
        <xs:element name="DateProperty" type="xs:date" />
        <xs:element name="EnumProperty" type="tns:LevelEnum"/>
      </xs:all>
    </xs:complexType>
  </xs:element>
  <xs:simpleType name="LevelEnum">
    <xs:restriction base="xs:string">
      <xs:enumeration value="Low">
        <xs:annotation>
          <xs:appinfo>
            <EnumerationValue    ="" >2</EnumerationValue>
          </xs:appinfo>
        </xs:annotation>
      </xs:enumeration>
      <xs:enumeration value="Middle">
        <xs:annotation>
          <xs:appinfo>
            <EnumerationValue
```

2. Use WCF ServiceModel Metadata Utility Tool (Svcutil.exe) to generate `DataContract` type source code based on the XML Schema composed in step 1. Following is the sample command on how to use the Svcutil.exe tool:

```
svcutil.exe /target:code /dataContractOnly
  /serializer:DataContractSerializer /importXmlTypes
  TestDataContractSchema.xsd
```

The generated `DataContract` is as follows:

```
public enum LevelEnum : int
    {
        [System.Runtime.Serialization.EnumMemberAttribute()]
        Low = 2,
        ............... .
    }
        ............. . .
    [System.Runtime.Serialization.DataContractAttribute(Name=
        "TestData", Namespace="http://wcftest.org/datacontract")]
    public partial class TestData : object,
        System.Runtime.Serialization.IExtensibleDataObject
    {
        ..................... .


        [System.Runtime.Serialization.DataMemberAttribute
                                    (IsRequired=true, Order=2)]
        public wcftest.org.datacontract.LevelEnum EnumProperty
        {               }
    }
```

3. Use the generated `DataContract` in our WCF service as operation parameters or return type.

```
[ServiceContract]
    public interface ITestService
    {
        [OperationContract]
        TestData GetData();
    }
```

How it works...

The contract-first development approach is contract/schema driven; the developers need to author the metadata/contract of the service/data. For the previous example, `TestDataContractSchema.xsd` provides the contract definition of two types that will be used in our WCF service.

Svcutil.exe is a very powerful tool provided in the .NET 3.5 SDK. If you're familiar with ASP .NET ASMX Web Service development, you will find it similar to the wsdl.exe tool. You can generate a WCF client proxy and export metadata from service code. Here we just use it to generate serialization code from the given XML Schema. In the previous sample, we specify `DataContractSerializer` as the serialization type (you can also use `XMLSerializer` instead, if you prefer XML serialization-oriented code) .

By capturing the service operation's underlying SOAP message on wire (refer to the next screenshot), we can find that the return value's XML payload conform to the XML Schema we provided as the generation source (`TestDataContractSchema.xsd`):

```
<GetDataResult xmlns:a="http://wcftest.org/datacontract"
               xmlns:i="http://www.w3.org/2001/XMLSchema-instance">

  <a:StringProperty>some string data</a:StringProperty>
  <a:DateProperty>2009/11/18</a:DateProperty>
  <a:EnumProperty>Middle</a:EnumProperty>

</GetDataResult>
```

There's more...

The `DataContract` we generated here includes two typical class types—a composite type and a simple enum type. In most scenarios, people will define much more complicated data types in their services, and WCF `DataContractSerializer` does provide enough support for mapping between an XML Schema-based contract and .NET code-based types. You can get more information on type mapping in the MSDN document *Data Contract Schema Reference,* available at:

http://msdn.microsoft.com/en-us/library/ms733112.aspx.

See also

▸ *Creating a typed service client* in *Chapter 4*

▸ *Complete source code for this recipe can be found in the* \Chapter 1\recipe3\ *folder*

Using XMLSerializer to control message serialization

By default, WCF runtime uses `DataContractSerializer` to perform data serialization and deserialization. However, in some cases, we will prefer using `XMLSerializer`, which will give developers more control over the serialized XML content or will work more closely with some POX clients (like ASMX Web Service client).

How to do it...

1. First, we should make our data type ready for XMLSerializer. This can be done by adding XML serialization attributes on our data types. The following User class has been decorated with several XML serialization attributes (XmlRootAttribute for top-level type and XmlElementAttribute for type members).

```
[XmlRoot(ElementName="UserObject",Namespace=
  "http://wcftest.org/xmlserializer")]
    public class User
    {
        [XmlElement(ElementName="FName")]
        public string FirstName { get; set; }
        [XmlElement(ElementName = "LName")]
        public string LastName { get; set; }
        [XmlElement(ElementName = "IsEnabled")]
        public bool Enabled { get; set; }
    }
```

2. Then, we need to apply XmlSerializerFormatAttribute on the ServiceContract type used in our service (see the ITestService interface shown as follows):

```
[ServiceContract]
[XmlSerializerFormat(Style=OperationFormatStyle.Document)]
public interface ITestService
{
    [OperationContract]
    void SendUser(User user);
}
```

How it works...

When we apply the XmlSerializerFormatAttribute on the ServiceContract, the WCF runtime will use `XMLSerializer` as the default Serializer to serialize data and deserialize SOAP messages. Also, the auto-generated service metadata will output the data type schema based on the class's XML serialization attributes. For the `User` class mentioned in the previous code example, service metadata will use the schema as shown in the next screenshot to represent its XML format:

```xml
<xs:schema elementFormDefault="qualified"
          targetNamespace="http://wcftest.org/xmlserializer"
          xmlns:xs="http://www.w3.org/2001/XMLSchema"
          xmlns:tns="http://wcftest.org/xmlserializer">

  <xs:complexType name="User">
    <xs:sequence>
      <xs:element minOccurs="0" maxOccurs="1" name="FName" type="xs:string"/
      <xs:element minOccurs="0" maxOccurs="1" name="LName" type="xs:string"/
      <xs:element minOccurs="1" maxOccurs="1" name="IsEnabled" type="xs:bool
    </xs:sequence>
  </xs:complexType>
</xs:complexType>
```

By capturing the underlying SOAP message, we can find that the XML content of the serialized `User` object conforms to the metadata schema defined earlier, which is controlled by those XML serialization attributes applied on the `user` class (refer to the next screenshot):

```xml
<s:Envelope xmlns:s="http://schemas.xmlsoap.org/soap/envelope/"
  <s:Body>
  ...
    <user xmlns:a="http://wcftest.org/xmlserializer">
      <a:FName>Foo</a:FName>
      <a:LName>Bar</a:LName>
      <a:IsEnabled>false</a:IsEnabled>
    </user>
```

See also

  ▶ *Complete source code for this recipe can be found in the* `\Chapter 1\recipe4\`
     folder

Using MessageContract to control the SOAP message

`DataContract` can help us design the data types used in a WCF service. However, this only covers the data members (variables and parameters used in operation) serialized in the underlying SOAP message. Sometimes we also need to control the structure and format of the entire SOAP message.

WCF introduces a `MessageContract` concept, which helps service developers to model the structure and format of the entire message of a given service operation. Actually, we can take `MessageContract` type as a special `DataContract` type, which is marked by the `MessageContractAttribute`. This recipe will show you how we can define a typical `MessageContract` for our WCF service operation to control the format of the underlying SOAP XML message.

How to do it...

1. Define a custom data type that represents the entire SOAP message body content. Use `MessageContractAttribute` to decorate the type and `MessageBodyMemberAttribute` to mark class members that will be embedded in the SOAP message body. The following code demonstrates a sample `MessageContract` pair—one is for operation request and the other for operation response.

```
[MessageContract(WrapperName="Hello",WrapperNamespace=
"http:// wcftest.org/messagecontract")]
public class HelloRequest
{
    [MessageBodyMember(Name="Who")]
    public string User { get; set; }
}
[MessageContract(WrapperName="HelloResponse",WrapperNamespace=
"http://wcftest.org/messagecontract")]
public class HelloResponse
{
    [MessageBodyMember(Name="Reply")]
    public string ReplyContent { get; set; }
}
```

2. After defining the `MessageContract` types for request/response operation, we need to use them as the input parameter (the only input parameter) and return value of the operation's implementation (see the following `SayHello` operation):

```
[OperationContract]
HelloResponse SayHello(HelloRequest req);
```

In the `SayHello` operation, `HelloRequest` is the only input parameter and `HelloResponse` represents the return value.

How it works...

Types marked with `MessageContractAttribute` can be used to represent the entire SOAP envelope body. The serialization of such types still follows the rules for normal `DataContract` types.

Also, it is important that operations which use `MessageContract` to control the SOAP envelope only have a single input parameter and return value. This is because only that input parameter will be serialized as the entire SOAP request body, and the return value will be serialized as the entire SOAP response body.

By capturing the SOAP request/response on wire, we can find that the serialized SOAP message content conforms to the `MessageContract` definition (refer to the next two screenshots):

```
<s:Envelope xmlns:s="http://schemas.xmlsoap.org/soap/envelope/">
  <s:Body>
    <Hello xmlns="http://wcftest.org/messagecontract">
      <Who xmlns="http://tempuri.org/">WCF User</Who>
    </Hello>
  </s:Body>
</s:Envelope>
```

```
<s:Envelope xmlns:s="http://schemas.xmlsoap.org/soap/envelope/">
<s:Body>
  <HelloResponse xmlns="http://wcftest.org/messagecontract">
    <Reply xmlns="http://tempuri.org/">Hello WCF User</Reply>
  </HelloResponse>
</s:Body>
</s:Envelope>
```

See also

- ▶ *Creating a service via ChannelListener* in *Chapter 5*
- ▶ *Complete source code for this recipe can be found in the* `\Chapter 1\recipe5\` *folder*

Adding a custom SoapHeader via Contract

The **SOAP** message (used by an XML Web Service and WCF service) is a standard XML document consisting of a root `Envelope` tag, which in turn consists of a required `Body` element and an optional `Header` element. Each sub element under the optional `Header` is called a **SoapHeader,** which plays a similar role as the other headers, uses a certain network protocol's transmit package.

A SoapHeader is often used in SOAP messages to carry some application protocol-level data in addition to the SOAP body. WCF has used many built-in SoapHeaders for certain protocols it supports (WS-Security, WS-Reliability, and so on). For some user scenarios, we will also need to add a custom SoapHeader into the WCF service message so as to exchange additional information (mostly for communication purposes).

How to do it...

1. We need to define a custom type, which represents the SoapHeader that will be serialized in the service message. Here is a sample `DataContract` type that represents a custom header used for custom authentication:

```
[DataContract]
    public class MyUsernameToken
    {
        [DataMember]
        public string Username { get; set; }
        [DataMember]
        public string Password { get; set; }
    }
```

2. Next, we can apply the custom `Header` type into our service operation's `MessageContract`. What we should do here is mark the `MessageContract` member (of the `Header` type) with `MessageHeaderAttribute`.

```
[MessageContract]
    public class HelloRequest
    {
        [MessageHeader]
        public MyUsernameToken AuthUser { get; set; }

        [MessageBodyMember]
        public string User { get; set; }
    }
    [MessageContract]
    public class HelloResponse
    {
        [MessageBodyMember]
        public string Reply { get; set; }
    }
```

3. At the end, we need to use the `MessageContract` type as the only input parameter/ return value of the particular service operation.

How it works...

The MessageHeaderAttribute helps mark the particular type member (of `MessageContract` type) as the SoapHeader that will be embedded in the resulting SOAP Envelope. Also, since the header is added in `MessageContract` at design-time, the WCF auto-generated metadata will include the SoapHeader information, as shown in the following screenshot:

```
<wsdl:binding name="BasicHttpBinding_ITestService"

  <soap:binding transport="http://schemas.xmlsoap.org/soap/http"/>
  <wsdl:operation name="SayHello">
    <soap:operation soapAction="http://tempuri.org/ITestService/SayHello" s
    <wsdl:input name="HelloRequest">
      <soap:header message="tns:HelloRequest_Headers" part="AuthUser" use="
      <soap:body use="literal"/>
    </wsdl:input>
```

If you use Visual Studio or Svcutil.exe to generate the client proxy class, the generated proxy type will automatically map the SoapHeaders to operation parameters. Thus, when invoking the service operation, we can simply pass SoapHeader data as the operation parameter. The following code demonstrates how the auto-generated service proxy invokes the operation with the custom SoapHeader assigned.

```
private static void CallService()
{
    TestProxy.TestServiceClient client = new
        TestProxy.TestServiceClient();

    TestProxy.MyUsernameToken utoken = new
        TestProxy.MyUsernameToken{ Username="Foo", Password="Bar"};
    string reply = client.SayHello(utoken, "WCF user");

    Console.WriteLine(reply);
}
```

By capturing the underlying SOAP message, we can find that the `MyUsernameToken` header type is serialized as a SoapHeader within the `<Header>` section.

```
<s:Envelope xmlns:s="http://schemas.xmlsoap.org/soap/envelope/">
  <s:Header>
    <h:AuthUser xmlns:h="http://tempuri.org/" xmlns:i="http://www.w3.org/2001/XM
      <Password xmlns="http://schemas.datacontract.org/2004/07/TestService">Bar<
      <Username xmlns="http://schemas.datacontract.org/2004/07/TestService">Foo<
    </h:AuthUser>
  </s:Header>
  <s:Body>
    <HelloRequest xmlns="http://tempuri.org/">
      <User>WCF user</User>
    </HelloRequest>
  </s:Body>
</s:Envelope>
```

There's more...

WCF supports various means to add custom SoapHeader a into service messages. This recipe demonstrates using a custom type and `MessageContract` to add a custom SoapHeader statically. In addition to this, we can also use code to programmatically add SoapHeaders into service messages.

See also

- *Using MessageContract to control the SOAP message*

- *Adding a dynamic SoapHeader into a message in Chapter 05*

- *Securing a dynamic SoapHeader in Chapter 07*

- *Complete source code for this recipe can be found in the* `\Chapter 1\recipe6\` *folder*

Return custom exception data through FaultContract

In an XML Web Service and WCF service, the server side will return any unhandled exception as `SoapFault` in the returned message. For WCF service operations, exceptions are returned to the client through two steps:

- Map exception conditions to custom SOAP faults
- Services and client send and receive SOAP faults as exceptions

By default, WCF will return the simple error message or complete exception information (including **Callstack**) as the Fault content. However, sometimes we want to encapsulate the raw exception information or return some user-friendly error to the client side. To support this kind of customized exception-information format, WCF has provided the `FaultContract` and `FaultException` features. `FaultException` is a new exception type that uses Generic to help WCF service encapsulate various kinds of custom error data objects in a unified way. `FaultContract` is used to formally specify the type of `FaultException` that will be returned from the target WCF service operation, so that the client consumers can properly handle and parse it.

How to do it...

1. First, create the custom error type that will be returned to the service client as exception information. The custom error type is defined as a standard `DataContract` type.

2. Then, apply the custom error type to the service operation (which will return this custom error type) through a FaultContractAttribute.

3. The following code shows a sample custom error type and the service operation that applies it:

```
[DataContract]
    public class UserFriendlyError
    {
        [DataMember]
        public string Message
        { get;set; }
    }

[ServiceContract]
    public interface ICalcService
    {
        [OperationContract]
        int Divide(int lv, int rv);

        [OperationContract]
        [FaultContract(typeof(UserFriendlyError))]
        int DivideWithCustomException(int lv, int rv);
    }
```

4. Finally, we need to add our exception handling code in the service operation's implementation and return the custom error type through the `FaultException<T>` type (see `DivideWithCustomException` method shown as follows):

```
public int Divide(int lv, int rv)
{
```

```
            if (rv == 0) throw new Exception("Divided by Zero is
                      not allowed!");
            return lv / rv;
                }

        public int DivideWithCustomException(int lv, int rv)
        {
            if (rv == 0) throw new
                FaultException<UserFriendlyError>(
                new UserFriendlyError() { Message = "Divided by
                Zero is not allowed!" }
                );
            return lv / rv;
        }
```

How it works...

The `FaultContractAttribute` applied on the service operation will make the runtime generate corresponding metadata entries in the WSDL document (as shown in the next screenshot). Thus, the generated client proxy knows how to handle this custom error type.

```xml
<wsdl:operation name="DivideWithCustomException">
    … … … … … … … … … … … …
  <wsdl:fault wsaw:Action=" … … … … . . "
            name="UserFriendlyErrorFault"
            message="tns:ICalcService_DivideWithCustomException_UserFriendlyError
</wsdl:operation>
```

When invoking the operation, we can add code to handle the specific `FaultException` and get user-friendly error information from the `Exception.Detail` property.

```
    try
    {
        //call the operation with invalid parameter
    }
    catch (FaultException<UserFriendlyError> fex)
    {
        Console.WriteLine("Error: {0}", fex.Detail.Message);
    }
```

If we use Fiddler or message logging to inspect the underlying SOAP message, we can also find the custom error data in XML-serialized format:

```
<s:Envelope xmlns:s="http://schemas.xmlsoap.org/soap/envelope/">
  <s:Body>
    <s:Fault>
      <faultcode>s:Client</faultcode>
      <faultstring >The creator of this fault did not specify a Rea
      <detail>
        <UserFriendlyError xmlns="http://schemas.datacontract.org/2
          <Message>Divided by Zero is not allowed!</Message>
        </UserFriendlyError>
      </detail>
    </s:Fault>
  </s:Body>
```

There's more...

Since the custom error type used by `FaultContract` supports any valid `DataContract` type, we can define various kinds of custom exception data content (from simple primitive types to complex nested classes).

See also

- ▸ *Generating DataContract from XML Schema*
- ▸ *Capturing a WCF request/response message via Fiddler tool* in *Chapter 12*
- ▸ *Complete source code for this recipe can be found in the* `\Chapter 1\recipe7\` *folder*

2
Endpoint, Binding, and Behavior

In this chapter, we will cover:

- ▸ Configuring Default Endpoints
- ▸ Setting up two-way communication over MSMQ
- ▸ Building a Publish-Subscribe service with dual binding
- ▸ Creating a multiple-endpoint service
- ▸ Implementing a POX HTTP service
- ▸ Defining a `CustomBinding` without a timestamp header
- ▸ Suppressing `mustUnderstand` validation on unknown SoapHeaders
- ▸ Sharing a physical address between multiple endpoints

Introduction

WCF services are exposed through service endpoints, which provide the basic access point for client to utilize the functionality offered by a given WCF service. Service endpoints consist of **ABC** and a set **of behaviors**. What is ABC? Well, **A** stands for **Address**, which tells service consumers "Where is the service?", **B** stands for **Binding**, which describes "How to talk to the service?" and **C** stands for **Contract**, which shows "What functionality can the service provide?"

WCF provides plenty of built-in bindings (such as **BasicHttpBinding**, **NetTcpBinding**, **NetMsmqBinding**, and so on), which can help developers host service endpoints over various transport protocols. Behaviors also play an important role in WCF. By using behaviors, we can gain further manipulation over the WCF service at service or endpoint level.

This chapter provides eight recipes on using the built-in binding and behaviors to build various service endpoints, which represent some of the useful scenarios in general WCF service development. We will start from the Default Endpoint feature introduced in WCF 4.0. Then, we will use two built-in bindings (NetMsmqBinding and WSDualHttpBinding) to demonstrate how to build a two-way communication and build a Publish-Subscribe pattern service through system bindings. The fourth recipe shows how WCF allows a single service to expose multiple endpoints layered on heterogeneous transport and message settings. The fifth recipe demonstrates how to build a POX-style WCF service that can talk with the application, which only supports plain XML-based message communication. The last three recipes come from some common and tricky scenarios in service endpoint customization. The sixth recipe shows how to disable the replay detection and remove a timestamp header in a WCF-generated SOAP message, the seventh recipe demonstrates how to make a WCF service/client tolerant to anonymous SoapHeaders, and the final recipe provides an example of how to make multiple WCF endpoints share a single transport address.

Configuring Default Endpoints

When programming with WCF, we will often need to create some simple WCF services for testing our `ServiceContracts`. These services often use very simple and typical endpoint and binding definitions. However, every time we need to set up such a service, we have to define the same endpoint and binding settings again and again, which really adds much duplicated work. Fortunately, WCF 4.0 introduces the Default Endpoint feature which saves us from defining common endpoint/binding settings repeatedly.

How to do it...

The steps for using a default endpoint are quite straightforward:

1. Create a new **Console Application** project in Visual Studio 2010 targeting .NET Framework 4.0.

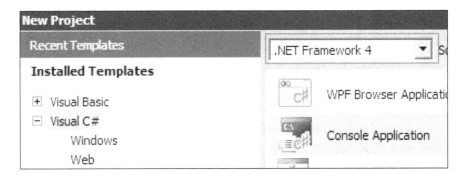

2. Add the `ServiceContract` in the service project and implementation types we need in the service project. We can use any valid `ServiceContract` and its corresponding implementation class here. For example, the following `IHelloService` service containing a single `SayHello` operation is used in our sample service application here:

```
[ServiceContract]
    public interface IHelloService
    {
        [OperationContract]
        string SayHello(string user);
    }
```

3. Add service configuration entries for the service type (defined in step 2) in the `app.config` file. We do not need to define any endpoint and binding configuration here. The following screenshot demonstrates the necessary service configuration elements:

```
<services>
  <service behaviorConfiguration="DefaultHttpService.HelloServiceBehavior"
      name="DefaultHttpService.HelloService">
    <host>
      <baseAddresses>
        <add baseAddress="http://localhost:8732/HelloService/" />
      </baseAddresses>
    </host>
  </service>
</services>
```

4. Start a `ServiceHost` and specify the service type we want to run (see the following code):

```
using (ServiceHost host = new ServiceHost(typeof(HelloService)))
{
host.Open();
Console.ReadLine();
}
```

How it works...

In the previous service definition and hosting code, we haven't added any endpoint and binding configuration. The magic behind scene is the Default Endpoints feature. When we start a WCF 4.0 service host, if the runtime cannot find any endpoint defined (via app. config or code), it will automatically create a default endpoint for each ServiceContract implemented for the service class. The default endpoints will choose the proper binding based on its endpoint address (the URL scheme) by looking up a **protocolMapping** list predefined in the system configuration store (within the .NET 4 Machine.config.comments file). The following screenshot shows the protocolMapping list:

```
<system.serviceModel>
  <protocolMapping>
    <add scheme="http" binding="basicHttpBinding"/>
    <add scheme="net.tcp" binding="netTcpBinding"/>
    <add scheme="net.pipe" binding="netNamedPipeBinding"/>
    <add scheme="net.msmq" binding="netMsmqBinding"/>
  </protocolMapping>
</protocolMapping>
```

For our previous example, since the endpoint address uses the HTTP scheme (derives from the **baseAddress**), the runtime will choose the BasicHttpBinding according to the protocolMapping list.

By using the DumpEndpoint function, we can confirm that Default Endpoint with BasicHttpBinding has been correctly set up in the previous case (refer to the next screenshot).

```
host.Open();
DumpEndpoint(host.Description.Endpoints);
.............. .
}
private static void DumpEndpoint(ServiceEndpointCollection endpoints)
{
    foreach (ServiceEndpoint sep in endpoints)
    {
        Console.Write("Address:{0}\nBinding:{1}\nContract:{2}\n",
            sep.Address, sep.Binding.Name, sep.Contract);
        Console.WriteLine("Binding Stack:");
        foreach (BindingElement be in
          sep.Binding.CreateBindingElements())
        {
            Console.WriteLine(be.ToString());
        }
    }
}
```

The next screenshot shows the auto-configured default endpoint in the sample service.

```
C:\Windows\system32\cmd.exe
Address:http://localhost:8732/HelloService/
Binding:BasicHttpBinding
Contract:System.ServiceModel.Description.ContractDescription
Binding Stack:
System.ServiceModel.Channels.TextMessageEncodingBindingElement
System.ServiceModel.Channels.HttpTransportBindingElement
```

There's more...

In addition to Default Endpoint, WCF 4.0 also provides the **Default Binding** feature which can save the life of developers who want to define a common binding setting for multiple endpoints. For example, we define the following anonymous binding configuration, which does not have an explicit name. Any endpoint that uses BasicHttpBinding will adopt the setting in this anonymous binding configuration.

```
<bindings>
  <basicHttpBinding>
    <binding messageEncoding="Mtom"/>
    <!-- notice no name attribute -->
  </basicHttpBinding>
</bindings>
```

See also

▶ *Complete source code for this recipe can be found in the* \Chapter 2\recipe1\ *folder*

Setting up two-way communication over MSMQ

For a long time, MSMQ has been a great message-based communication component on the Microsoft platform. And the Microsoft .NET framework has also provided managed programming interfaces for developers to develop distributed applications based on MSMQ. However, it is still a bit complicated and time consuming for developers to build a complete distributed service through the raw or encapsulated MSMQ programming interface. As the new unified communication development platform on Windows, WCF provides more convenient means for developing a distributed service over the underlying MSMQ component.

Getting ready

If you are not yet familiar with **Microsoft Message Queuing** (**MSMQ**), you can get useful information on the following site:

`http://msdn.microsoft.com/en-us/library/ms711472(VS.85).aspx`

Also, the MSDN library has provided detailed reference on the .NET Framework `System.Messaging` namespace that encapsulates the raw MSMQ programming interfaces (visit `http://msdn.microsoft.com/en-us/library/system.messaging.aspx`).

How to do it...

To make the WCF client and service perform two-way communication over MSMQ, we need to set up two MSMQ-based endpoints—one for the service to receive client requests and the other for the client to get responses.

1. Define the `ServiceContract` that will be used for the MSMQ-based services. The following code snippet shows the sample `ServiceContract` (one for the service and another for the client):

    ```
    [ServiceContract]
    public interface INotificationReceiver
    {
    [OperationContract(IsOneWay = true)]
        void Notify(long id, string msg, DateTime time);
    }

    [ServiceContract]
    public interface INotificationSender
    {
    [OperationContract(IsOneWay=true)]
        void Ack(long id);
    }
    ```

     All the service operations over MSMQ should be marked as one-way style.

2. Create the MSMQ queues on the client and server machines. There are two means for us to create the queues. One way is to use the MMC snap-in. There are various ways to start up this snap-in, but the easiest is to open the Windows **Computer Management** utility in **Administrative Tools**, expand the **Services and Applications** section of the tree view on the left, and select the **Message Queuing** node. This is also a great way to verify that MSMQ is installed on a particular machine. The next screenshot shows the standard UI of the MSMQ snap-in.

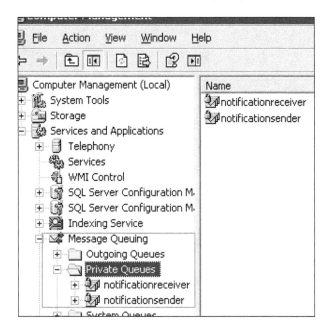

Another way is to create the queue programmatically, is as shown in the following code. In the sample service here, we will create the MSMQ queues in code:

```
private static void Init()
{
    // Ensure the message queue exists
    string qName =
            ConfigurationManager.AppSettings["ReceiverQueue"];

    if (MessageQueue.Exists(qName)) MessageQueue.Delete(qName);
        MessageQueue q = MessageQueue.Create(qName, false);
}
```

3. After the message queues have been created, we can start configuring the service and client endpoints and map them to the underlying MSMQ queues. For the receiver side, the service endpoint should use NetMsmqBinding and set the address in `net.msmq://` format. The following screenshot shows a sample service endpoint configuration:

```
<service name="NotificationService.NotificationReceiver">
  <!-- endpoint for receiving notification from client-->
  <endpoint address="net.msmq://localhost/private/NotificationReceiver"
          binding="netMsmqBinding" bindingConfiguration="simpleQueueBinding"
          contract="NotificationService.INotificationReceiver" >
  </endpoint>
```

The `private` in the endpoint address indicates that the MSMQ queue is a private queue and `NotificationReceiver` is the queue name.

The sender side will need to configure the client endpoint that uses the same configuration as the service endpoint at the receiver side, which is done as follows:

```
<!-- endpoint for sending notification to server-->
<client>
  <endpoint name="receiverEndpoint"
          address="net.msmq://localhost/private/NotificationReceiver"
          binding="netMsmqBinding" bindingConfiguration="simpleQueueBinding"
          contract="NotificationService.INotificationReceiver"></endpoint>
</client>
```

After the endpoints are correctly configured, we can host and consume the MSMQ-based service like any normal WCF service.

How it works...

Since MSMQ physically only supports one-way message delivery, we need to host a MSMQ-based WCF service on both the client and service machine so as to establish the two-way communication.

Also, WCF **NetMSMQBinding** is a WCF natural binding, which completely hides the underlying MSMQ processing details; developers only need to concentrate on the `ServiceContract` and service endpoint configuration, instead of the raw `System.Messaging` programming interfaces. However, in some cases, if you need to establish communication between raw MSMQ application and WCF-based application, there is another built-in binding called **MsmqIntegrationBinding**, which is suitable for such scenarios.

There's more...

You can have a look at the article *How to: Exchange Messages with WCF Endpoints and Message Queuing Applications* at `http://msdn.microsoft.com/en-us/library/ms789008.aspx` for more information.

See also

▶ *Complete source code for this recipe can be found in the* `\Chapter 2\recipe2\` *folder*

Building a Publish-Subscribe service with dual binding

Publish-Subscribe is a common design pattern that is widely used in client/server communication applications. In WCF service development, the Publish-Subscribe pattern will also help in those scenarios where the service application will expose data to certain groups of clients that are interested in the service and the data is provided to clients as a push model actively (instead of polling by the client). This recipe will demonstrate how to implement the Publish-Subscribe pattern in a WCF service through dual binding.

Getting ready

The Publish-Subscribe pattern is widely adopted in various application development scenarios and there are many different kinds of descriptions for this pattern. Refer to the following links for more information:

▶ Publish/subscribe

`http://en.wikipedia.org/wiki/Publish/subscribe`

▶ Observer pattern

`http://en.wikipedia.org/wiki/Observer_pattern`

How to do it...

To implement the Publish-Subscribe pattern, we need to put particular customization in various parts of the WCF service development, including a `ServiceContract` design, binding configuration, and service hosting/consuming code. Let's go through the following steps to build a typical list-based Publish-Subscribe service:

1. The first thing to do is to design a `ServiceContract` that supports Publish-Subscribe pattern. The following `IPublicBillboard` interface represents a sample contract for publishing some announcements to client applications that are interested in the service.

```
[ServiceContract(SessionMode=SessionMode.Required,
    CallbackContract=typeof(IClientReceiver))]
    public interface IPublicBillboard
    {
        [OperationContract(IsInitiating=true)]
        void Subscribe();

        [OperationContract(IsTerminating=true)]
        void Unsubscribe();

        [OperationContract(IsOneWay=true)]
        void Announce(string msg);
    }

    public interface IClientReceiver
    {
        [OperationContract(IsOneWay = true)]
        void GetAnnouncement(string msg);
    }
```

In the previous `ServiceContract`, in addition to the main contract interface, we also need to supply a `CallbackContract` type, which is used for the service to notify the client proactively. Also, a session has been enabled here so that the service can conveniently identify client callback channels through their `sessionId`.

2. When implementing the `ServiceContract`, `Subscribe` will cache the callback channel via the client `sessionId` so that it can notify the client later (by invoking the callback channel).

```
[ServiceBehavior(InstanceContextMode=InstanceContextMode.Single)]
    public class PublicBillboard : IPublicBillboard
    {
        object _syncobj = new object();
        Dictionary<string, IClientReceiver> _receivers = new
                Dictionary<string, IClientReceiver>();
```

```
public void Subscribe()
{
    string sessionId = OperationContext.Current.SessionId;

    lock (_syncobj)
    {
        if (_receivers.Keys.Contains(sessionId))
        {
            _receivers.Remove(sessionId);
        }

        _receivers.Add(sessionId,
OperationContext.Current.GetCallbackChannel<IClientReceiver>());
    }
}
```

The `Subscribe` method mentioned earlier, gets the client `sessionId` from `OperationContext` and caches the client's callback channel by this `sessionId`. If there is already a callback interface with the same `sessionId` cached, the code will remove the existing one first.

3. In the service endpoint configuration, it is important to select a duplex binding. The sample service here uses WSDualHttpBinding through a configuration file.

```
<service behaviorConfiguration="BillboardService.PublicBillboardBehavior"
        name="BillboardService.PublicBillboard">

<endpoint address=""
        binding="wsDualHttpBinding" bindingConfiguration="PSBinding"
        contract="BillboardService.IPublicBillboard">
```

4. At the client side, we need to provide a type that implements the callback interface and supply this type instance when initializing the service proxy, which is done as follows:

```
public partial class MainForm : Form, BillboardProxy.
IPublicBillboardCallback
{
    BillboardProxy.PublicBillboardClient _boardclient = null;

    private void MainForm_Load(object sender, EventArgs e)
    {
        // Subscribe for the Billboard service
```

```
    _boardclient = new
            BillboardProxy.PublicBillboardClient(
            new InstanceContext(this)
            );


    _boardclient.Subscribe();


    btnSubmit.Enabled = true;
}
```

```
// Implement the callback interface
        void BillboardProxy.IPublicBillboardCallback.
            GetAnnouncement(string msg)
    {
        UpdateText(msg);
    }
```

The `MainForm` class implements the callback interface and is assigned to the client proxy (through a constructor) at the loading stage.

5. In the end, the service operation can selectively notify some or all of the clients proactively (refer to the `Announce` operation shown as follows):

```
public void Announce(string msg)
{
    // Enumerate all the client callback channels
    foreach (string key in _receivers.Keys)
    {
        IClientReceiver receiver = _receivers[key];
        receiver.GetAnnouncement(
            string.Format("{0} announced: {1}", sessionId, msg));
    }
}
```

How it works...

The service class is decorated as `InstanceContextMode=InstanceContextMode.Single`, so that all the clients will share the same service instance. Enabling the session makes the service be able to differentiate clients by their `sessionId`. The following screenshot shows the service console, which prints out all new announcements received from the client.

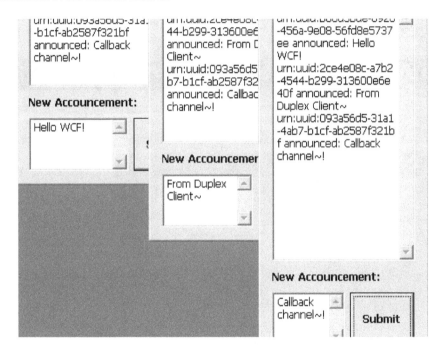

By invoking the Callback channel interface (from each client `OperationContext`), the service proactively pushes the new announcement data to all clients immediately.

At the client side, the callback function simply updates the Forum UI and prints the new announcement in the textbox control.

There's more...

Both the service callback operations are marked as one-way style. This is to make sure that the service operation won't block the client UI thread when directly invoked in the `Button_Click` event (which is also executed in the UI thread).

```
public interface IPublicBillboard
{
    [OperationContract(IsOneWay=true)]
    void Announce(string msg);
```

```
public interface IClientReceiver
{
    [OperationContract(IsOneWay = true)]
    void GetAnnouncement(string msg);
```

If you are interested, you can also use asynchronous service execution to avoid these kinds of thread blocking issues.

See also

▶ *Invoking async operation via ChannelFactory* in *Chapter 5*

▶ *Complete source code for this recipe can be found in the* \Chapter 2\recipe3\ *folder*

Creating a multiple-endpoint service

For traditional distributed communication services, we will open the service over a certain transport-specific endpoint such as HTTP endpoint. If we need to expose it via another different transport layer, we will probably have to add additional code to implement the new endpoint. The WCF programming model separates the service implementation and underlying transport layer so that we can conveniently expose a single service implementation via multiple heterogeneous endpoints (with different a transport layer and binding configuration).

How to do it...

1. First, we make sure our ServiceContract is ready for various endpoint bindings we want to use to expose it. Some bindings may have special requirements on ServiceContract (such as MSMQ-based bindings). The following sample contract is ready for most built-in bindings:

```
[ServiceContract]
public interface ICounterService
{
    [OperationContract]
    void Increment();

    [OperationContract]
    int GetCurrentCount();
}
```

2. For our sample service, we will implement it as a singleton service so as to demonstrate the "multiple endpoints sharing the same service" behavior. The following code is the implementation of the `CounterService`:

```
[ServiceBehavior(InstanceContextMode=InstanceContextMode.Single)]
    public class CounterService : ICounterService
    {
        object _syncobj = new object();
        int _count = 0;

        public void Increment()
        {
            lock (_syncobj)
            {
                _count++;
            }
        }

        public int GetCurrentCount()
        {
            return _count;
        }
    }
```

3. Finally, we need to add the various endpoints and bindings in the service hosting code. In our sample service, we will use three endpoints/bindings to expose the service—BasicHttpBinding, WSHttpBinding, and NetTcpBinding.

```
Uri baseHttp = new Uri("http://localhost:8731/CounterService/");
Uri baseTcp = new Uri("net.Tcp://localhost:9731/CounterService/");

using (ServiceHost host = new ServiceHost(typeof(CounterService),
            baseHttp, baseTcp))
    {
        // Add basicHttpBinding endpoint
        var basicHttp = new
            BasicHttpBinding(BasicHttpSecurityMode.None);
        host.AddServiceEndpoint(typeof(ICounterService),
            basicHttp,"basicHttp");

        // Add wsHttpBinding endpoint
        var wsHttp = new WSHttpBinding(SecurityMode.None, false);
        host.AddServiceEndpoint(typeof(ICounterService), wsHttp,
            "wsHttp");

        // Add netTcpBinding endpoint
        var netTcp = new NetTcpBinding(SecurityMode.None,false);
```

```
host.AddServiceEndpoint(typeof(ICounterService), netTcp,
    "netTcp");

host.Open();
Console.WriteLine("service started .........");
Console.ReadLine();
}
```

How it works...

The previous sample `CounterService` opens three endpoints over HTTP and TCP transport layers. Client applications can use any of the exposed endpoints to consume the service. The sample client uses `ChannelFactory` to construct the client channel to consume the service:

```
string basicHttpAddr =
    "http://localhost:8731/CounterService/basicHttp";
string wsHttpAddr = "http://localhost:8731/CounterService/wsHttp";
string netTcpAddr = "net.Tcp://localhost:9731/CounterService/netTcp";
// For basicHttpBinding
var basicHttp = new BasicHttpBinding(BasicHttpSecurityMode.None);
_basicHttpFactory = new ChannelFactory<ICounterService>(basicHttp,
    basicHttpAddr);
_basicHttpClient = _basicHttpFactory.CreateChannel();
// For wsHttpBinding
var wsHttp = new WSHttpBinding(SecurityMode.None, false);
_wsHttpFactory = new ChannelFactory<ICounterService>(wsHttp,
    wsHttpAddr);
_wsHttpClient = _wsHttpFactory.CreateChannel();
// For netTcpBinding
var netTcp = new NetTcpBinding(SecurityMode.None, false);
_netTcpFactory = new ChannelFactory<ICounterService>(netTcp,
    netTcpAddr);
_netTcpClient = _netTcpFactory.CreateChannel();
```

By invoking an increment operation through all the three endpoints, we can find that they're consuming the same service instance, since the returned count value represents the total service operation calls.

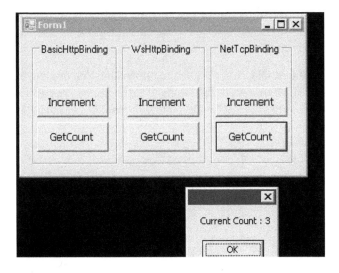

See also

▶ *Complete source code for this recipe can be found in the* `\Chapter 2\recipe4\` *folder*

Implementing a POX HTTP service

WCF services by default use **SOAP** as the message format of service operations, which means each message transferred between the client and service is wrapped in a SOAP envelope that contains one SOAP body and some SoapHeaders. However, sometimes our WCF service will need to work with some legacy **POX** (**Plain Old XML**) clients or our WCF-based client will need to talk to some POX-style service. In such cases, it is necessary to let our WCF client or service generate arbitrary XML messages without strictly obeying the SOAP standard.

How to do it...

We will use a **CustomBinding** to build a POX-enabled WCF service and consume it with a POX-enabled WCF client program. Let's have a look at the complete steps:

1. The first thing to do is to make our `ServiceContract` POX ready. The following code shows a sample operation that is ready for exchanging POX-style messages.

```
[OperationContract(Action="*",ReplyAction="*")]
        Message SayHello(Message reqMsg);
```

Compared with normal service operation, one obvious difference is that we've used the `System.ServiceModel.Channels.Message` class as the only input parameter and return value.

2. For the service endpoint, we will need to apply a custom binding on it. This binding will utilize the HTTP transport layer and set the `messageVersion` as `None`. The following screenshot shows the complete definition of our custom binding:

```
<customBinding>
  <binding name="POXBinding" >
    <textMessageEncoding writeEncoding="utf-8"
                         messageVersion="None" >
    </textMessageEncoding>

    <httpTransport transferMode="Buffered"
                   authenticationScheme="Anonymous"/>
  </binding>
</customBinding>
```

3. After the service endpoint has been configured, we can start the service and consume it with POX-enabled clients. For the service side, we can directly get the XML content from the input `Message` parameter. When returning the result, we also need to construct a `Message` instance and assign it the proper HTTP properties, if necessary. The following code demonstrates a simple message processing scenario:

```
public Message SayHello(Message reqMsg)
{
    // Process request message
    Console.WriteLine(reqMsg.GetBody<XElement>());
    // Construct response message
    HttpResponseMessageProperty properties = new
            HttpResponseMessageProperty() { StatusCode =
            System.Net.HttpStatusCode.OK };
    Message repMsg = Message.CreateMessage(MessageVersion.None,
            string.Empty, new XElement("HelloResponse",
            "Hello POX Client!"));
    repMsg.Properties[HttpResponseMessageProperty.Name] =
            properties;
    return repMsg;
}
```

4. The same code logic applies to the client side if we're using a WCF client to send POX requests to another service. The following code snippet demonstrates sending a POX request with a simple XML element as the entire message body:

```
ChannelFactory<TestClient.IPOXService> factory = new
        ChannelFactory<IPOXService>("POXEndpoint");
TestClient.IPOXService client = factory.CreateChannel();

HttpRequestMessageProperty properties = new
        HttpRequestMessageProperty() { Method = "POST" };
Message reqMsg = Message.CreateMessage(MessageVersion.None,
        string.Empty, new XElement("HelloRequest",
        "Hello POX Service!"));
reqMsg.Properties[HttpRequestMessageProperty.Name] = properties;

Message repMsg = client.SayHello(reqMsg);
Console.WriteLine(repMsg.GetBody<XElement>());
```

How it works...

In the SayHello POX service example we just looked at, there are two key points that enable the service to exchange a POX-style message:

▶ CustomBinding with messageVersion as None

▶ Message type input parameter and return value

By setting messageVersion (of the <textMessageEncoding> binding element) to None, the WCF runtime will no longer force any SOAP format requirement on the exchanging messages.

Also, the System.ServiceModel.Channels.Message type allows us to freely construct arbitrary XML-style messages for service requests and responses.

By capturing the request/response messages on wire, we can confirm that the underlying operation messages are of plain XML format instead of SOAP envelope-based format, as shown in the next screenshot:

```
<!-- Request message of POX service call -->
POST /POXService/ HTTP/1.1
Content-Type: application/xml; charset=utf-8
...

<HelloRequest>Hello POX Service!</HelloRequest>
<!-- Response message of POX service call-->
HTTP/1.1 200 OK
Content-Length: 48
Content-Type: application/xml; charset=utf-8
...

<HelloResponse>Hello POX Client!</HelloResponse>
```

There's more...

This recipe uses a `CustomBinding` to build a POX-enabled service; however, this is not the only way to build POX-style services in WCF. The WCF REST programming model is another good way to build services that can process plain XML messages. And if you're familiar with web application development, you will find the REST programming model much more convenient and familiar.

We will discuss more about the WCF REST programming model in *Chapter 10, RESTful and AJAX-enabled WCF Services*.

See also

- ▶ *Complete source code for this recipe can be found in the* \Chapter 2\recipe5\ *folder*

Defining a CustomBinding without a timestamp header

For WCF bindings that use message-layer security, a timestamp header will be added in the SOAP envelope to ensure the timely delivery of the message so as to prevent a potential message-replaying attach. However, some non-WCF service platforms may not expose this header. When working with this kind of service client or service, we will need to prevent the WCF message engine from generating the timestamp header.

How to do it...

Using WSHttpBinding as an example, we can create a customized binding that derives most of the setting of the built-in WSHttpBinding (but suppresses the timestamp header generation).

The following code snippet demonstrates how to create the CustomBinding and configure the certain binding element to disable timestamp header generation.

```
private static Binding GetCustomHttpBinding()
{
    WSHttpBinding wshttp = new WSHttpBinding();
    var bec = wshttp.CreateBindingElements();

    SecurityBindingElement secbe = bec.Find<SecurityBindingElement>();
    // Not to include Timestamp header
    secbe.IncludeTimestamp = false;
    // Suppress the message relay detection
    secbe.LocalServiceSettings.DetectReplays = false;
    secbe.LocalClientSettings.DetectReplays = false;

    CustomBinding cb = new CustomBinding(bec);
    return cb;
}
```

The code first locates the SecurityBindingElement instance from the default element collection of wsHttpBinding. It then sets the IncludeTimestamp property to false. Also, it is necessary to turn off the DetectReplays property on the LocalServiceSettings and LocalClientSettings members.

Finally, we can apply this CustomBinding to any endpoint that needs to suppress the timestamp header.

How it works...

Since the timestamp header is a security feature that performs a message-replaying check, the WCF programming model exposes this setting through the `SecurityBindingElement` type. However, only setting the `SecurityBindingElement.IncludeTimestamp` to false is not enough, because this only helps remove the timestamp header; the runtime will still perform replay detection on incoming/outgoing messages. Therefore, we also need to turn off the **DetectReplays** property on `LocalServiceSettings` and `LocalClientSettings` collection.

By comparing the underlying SOAP messages, we can find the obvious difference in the SoapHeader section before and after we disable the timestamp header generation. The next screenshot is a SOAP message captured before removing the timestamp header:

```
<s:Envelope xmlns:s="http://schemas.xmlsoap.org/soap/envelope/
  <s:Header>
  ...

    <a:To s:mustUnderstand="1" u:Id="_5">http://localhost:8731
    <o:Security s:mustUnderstand="1" xmlns:o="http://docs.oasi
      <u:Timestamp u:Id="uuid-2090fe67-b1e1-4f8f-a258-012e14cf
        <u:Created>2009-12-07T04:39:10.855Z</u:Created>
        <u:Expires>2009-12-07T04:44:10.855Z</u:Expires>
      </u:Timestamp>
      <c:SecurityContextToken>
```

The following screenshot is for a SOAP message captured after removing the timestamp header:

```
<s:Envelope xmlns:s="http://schemas.xmlsoap.org/soap/envelope/" xmlns:a
  <s:Header>
  ...

    <a:To s:mustUnderstand="1" u:Id="_5">http://localhost:8731/CalcSe
    <o:Security s:mustUnderstand="1" xmlns:o="http://docs.oasis-open.
      <c:SecurityContextToken>
```

See also

> ▶ *Complete source code for this recipe can be found in the* \Chapter 2\recipe6\ *folder*

Suppressing mustUnderstand validation on unknown SoapHeaders

For a WCF service or client proxy, it is common to receive SoapHeaders within the coming request or returned response messages. SoapHeader has a **mustUnderstand** attribute that indicates to the target endpoint (or intermediate message processor) whether the SoapHeader must be processed. The following screenshot shows a typical SOAP message that contains a SoapHeader with the `mustUnderstand` attribute set to 1 (true).

```
<s:Envelope xmlns:s="http://schemas.xmlsoap.org/soap/envelope/">
  <s:Header>
    <MyTestHeader s:mustUnderstand="1"
                  xmlns="urn:wcftest:header">
      some test value.
    </MyTestHeader>
  </s:Header>
...  ...
```

Also for a XML Web Service or WCF service, we can dynamically insert SoapHeaders at runtime or statically apply them at design-time (which will be described via WSDL or service metadata).

By default, a WCF endpoint will perform validation on all the SoapHeaders within incoming messages, and if there are any unknown SoapHeaders (not predefined) which have a `mustUnderstand` attribute as 1 (or **true)**, a validation exception will be raised by the runtime. However, sometimes it is useful to suppress this validation so that the WCF service or client proxy can gracefully handle unknown SoapHeaders that are dynamically added.

Getting ready

If you are not familiar with SoapHeaders and the `mustUnderstand` attribute, or how to set this attribute via the WCF programming model, you can take a look at the following references first:

- SOAP Header Element

  http://www.w3schools.com/soap/soap_header.asp

- SoapHeader.MustUnderstand Property

  http://msdn.microsoft.com/en-us/library/system.web.services.
  protocols.soapheader.mustunderstand.aspx

How to do it...

By injecting `MustUnderstandBehavior` into our WCF endpoint's behavior collection, we can suppress the validation and raising of exceptions on unknown SoapHeaders with `mustUnderstand="1"`. The steps are as follows:

1. First, we need to create a `MustUnderstandBehavior` type instance and set its `ValidateMustUnderstand` property to `false` (which can be done in the `type` constructor).

2. Second, we should locate the service/client endpoint instance on which we want to apply `MustUnderstandBehavior`. For the WCF service, we can use `ServiceHost.Description.Endpoints` collection to find the wanted endpoint. For the client proxy, we can directly use `[ClientProxy].Endpoint` to get the endpoint instance.

3. After we get the endpoint instance, we can simply add the `MustUnderstandBehavior` instance into the endpoint instance's Behaviors collection.

   The following code shows the complete steps for applying `MustUnderstandBehavior` in service hosting code:

```
using (ServiceHost host = new
            ServiceHost(typeof(HeaderTestService)))
{
    // Suppress the MustUnderstand header's validation so that
       exception won't be raised for unknown MustUnderstand headers
    MustUnderstandBehavior mubehavior = new
            MustUnderstandBehavior(false);

    // Find the target endpoint we want
    ServiceEndpoint endpoint =
        host.Description.Endpoints.Find(typeof(IHeaderTestService));

    // Add the MustUnderstandBehavior to our service endpoint's
       Behavior collection
    endpoint.Behaviors.Add(mubehavior);

}
```

How it works...

When you encounter the `ProtocolException` (as shown in the next screenshot), it is probably because the WCF service or client endpoint received an unknown SoapHeader that is marked as `mustUnderstand=true`.

```
Scroll C:\WINDOWS\system32\cmd.exe                                    _ □
Unhandled Exception: System.ServiceModel.ProtocolException: The header 'MyTestHe
ader' from the namespace 'urn:wcftest:header' was not understood by the recipien
t of this message, causing the message to not be processed.  This error typicall
y indicates that the sender of this message has enabled a communication protocol
 that the receiver cannot process.  Please ensure that the configuration of the
client's binding is consistent with the service's binding.
```

After applying `MustUnderstandBehavior` (with `ValidateMustUnderstand` set to `false`), the runtime will ignore validation on any unknown SoapHeaders. But, we can still use code to access them from **OperationContext**, as follows:

```
StringBuilder sb = new StringBuilder();
sb.AppendFormat("{0} headers in message\n",
          OperationContext.Current.IncomingMessageHeaders.Count);
foreach (var header in
          OperationContext.Current.IncomingMessageHeaders)
{
    sb.AppendFormat("HeaderName:{0}, MustUnderstand={1}\n",
            header.Name, header.MustUnderstand);
}
```

There's more...

In this recipe, we demonstrated how to inject the `MustUnderstandBehavior` for a self-hosting scenario. However, in many cases, our WCF service will be hosted on IIS server via `.svc` endpoints. In such cases, we can use a custom `ServiceHostFactory` class to add the behavior injecting code logic. You can have a look at the article *Extending Hosting Using ServiceHostFactory* at `http://msdn.microsoft.com/en-us/library/aa702697.aspx`.

See also

- *Customizing IIS ServiceHost via ServiceHostFactory* in *Chapter 3*
- *Complete source code for this recipe can be found in the* `\Chapter 2\recipe7\` *folder*

Sharing a physical address between multiple endpoints

WCF supports exposing a single service through multiple heterogeneous endpoints. Another great feature is letting multiple endpoints listen over the same physical transport address. For example, you want to host a WCF service that has multiple endpoints exposed. However, you only have a single HTTP URL open for listening. Then you can use this feature to make all those endpoints (as long as they're using the same transport protocol) listen on the same URL.

How to do it...

Our sample service will expose two endpoints (one is IFoo and the other is IBar) and both of them will listen on the same HTTP URL:

1. The first thing we need to do is configure the service endpoints. We will still specify different values for the `address` attribute of the two endpoints. However, we will use a special attribute named `listenUri` to supply the physical address (identical for both endpoints). The following screenshot shows the usage of both attributes:

```
<service>
  <endpoint address="urn:Foo"
            listenUri="http://localhost:8731/FooBarService/Operations"
            binding="wsHttpBinding" bindingConfiguration="simpleWSHttp"
            contract="SharedAddressService.IFoo">
  </endpoint>
  <endpoint address="urn:Bar"
            listenUri="http://localhost:8731/FooBarService/Operations"
            binding="wsHttpBinding" bindingConfiguration="simpleWSHttp"
            contract="SharedAddressService.IBar">
  </endpoint >
```

2. It is also important to configure the client endpoint so that the client proxy or `ChannelFactory` can correctly locate the service endpoint. WCF provides a `ClientViaBehavior` type for specifying the physical address of a client endpoint. You can use the `ChannelFactory.Endpoint.Behaviors` collection to inject the behavior in code, shown as follows:

```
ChannelFactory<SharedAddressService.IFoo> fooFactory = new
        ChannelFactory<SharedAddressService.IFoo>(new
        WSHttpBinding(SecurityMode.None));

SharedAddressService.IFoo foo = fooFactory.CreateChannel(
        new EndpointAddress("urn:Foo"), /* logical address */
```

```
new
Uri("http://localhost:8731/FooBarService/Operations"));
/*physical address*/
        foo.Foo();
```

Alternatively, you can also use the `<clientVia>` element to supply the physical address in a configuration file, as shown in the following screenshot:

```
<behaviors>
  <endpointBehaviors>
    <behavior name="viaBehavior">
      <clientVia viaUri="http://localhost:8731/FooBarService/Operations"/ >
```

How it works...

Generally, we will use the `address` attribute to specify the URL on which the endpoint will listen. However, this `address` is actually a logical address and WCF runtime will use it as a physical address also, if we haven't explicitly provided a physical address. The `listenUri`, on the contrary, represents the physical transport address the service endpoint listens on.

Also, for the endpoints that share the same physical address, they will share the same service **dispatcher** and **channel** stack. Then, how does the WCF runtime differentiate these operation requests when there are multiple endpoints listening on a single physical address? The answer is WCF runtime will try to resolve the request target by the combination of two parts:

- ▶ The Service/Operation **Contract**
- ▶ The logical address specified the via `address` attribute

Therefore, the dispatcher/channel stack can correctly redirect the requests to the corresponding endpoint even if we supply an identical value for both logical and physical address.

There's more...

For more in-depth explanation on **WCF Addressing**, you can have a look at the *WCF Addressing In Depth* MSDN article written by Aaron Skonnard (`http://msdn. microsoft.com/en-us/magazine/cc163412.aspx`).

See also

- ▶ *Creating a multiple-endpoint service*

3
Hosting and Configuration

In this chapter, we will cover:

- ▸ Hosting a service in a console application
- ▸ Hosting a service in Windows Service
- ▸ Hosting a HTTP service with ASP.NET-compatible context
- ▸ Hosting a non-HTTP service in IIS 7
- ▸ Customizing IIS ServiceHost via ServiceHostFactory
- ▸ Specifying a dedicated service instance for a singleton service
- ▸ Hosting a service in WSS 3.0

Introduction

Service hosting and configuration is very important for building WCF services, especially at the service deployment stage. After developers complete the service development, we will need to deploy the service so as to make it available to all the client consumers. In the real world, there are various service deployment scenarios available, which will result in different deployment and configuration requirements on the service configuration or the hosting environment.

As an enhanced service development platform, WCF provides rich, built-in support on service hosting and configuration that can fulfill most of the existing deployment demands and requirements. For example, the most popular IIS hosting approach can provide high availability and stable service for local intranet or public internet-based deployment cases. The Windows service-hosting approach makes WCF service hosting easier to integrate with existing background scheduled tasks, and the self-hosting approach provides the most flexibility and customization points for service deployment in a production environment.

In this chapter, we will look at seven recipes on various WCF hosting and configuration scenarios. The recipes start with four typical hosting cases—self-hosting, Windows service hosting, IIS-based HTTP hosting, and IIS based non-HTTP hosting. This is followed by two customized service-hosting cases—including a custom ServiceHostFactory and a dedicated singleton-instance hosting. The last recipe demonstrates a more advanced WCF service-hosting scenario—Windows SharePoint Service hosting.

Hosting a service in a console application

When creating a simple demo program for .NET framework, we will probably choose a console application. At the same, when talking about WCF service hosting, the console-hosting scenario is the most convenient one, which is especially handy and useful when we want to do some quick demo or testing on some WCF functionality.

How to do it...

1. Create a .NET framework-based Console project through Visual Studio.

   Visual Studio provides various project templates for creating a .NET framework-based application. For our sample console-hosting service here, we will choose the **Console Application** project type from the Visual Studio **New Project** wizard.

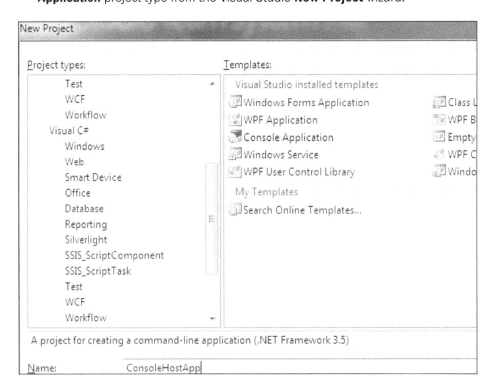

2. Add a new WCF service into the project.

   We can simply accomplish this by using the **Add New Item** function in Visual Studio and choose **WCF Service** as the item type from Visual Studio's **Add New Item** UI.

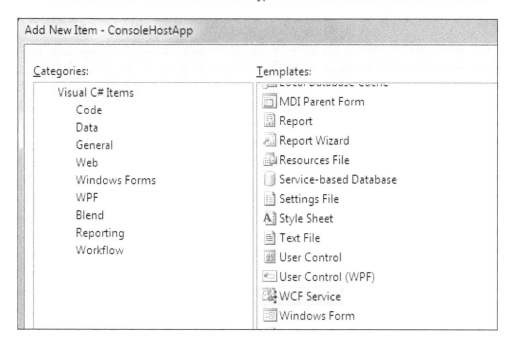

3. Add code into the `Main` function to start up the WCF service. The following code shows the typical `Main` function that starts up a WCF service in a console application:

```
static void Main(string[] args)
{
    using (ServiceHost consoleHost = new
            ServiceHost(typeof(TestService)))
    {
        consoleHost.Open();
        Console.WriteLine("press any key to stop service host...");
        Console.ReadLine();
    }
}
```

How it works...

When you add a new **WCF Service** item in Visual Studio, the IDE actually helps you to finish the following three tasks:

- Creating a `ServiceContract` interface.
- Creating a Service class that implements the `ServiceContract` interface.

   The following code shows the sample `ServiceContract` and implementation class used in this recipe.

```
[ServiceContract]
    public interface ITestService
    {
        [OperationContract]
        void DoWork();
    }
    public class TestService : ITestService
    {
        public void DoWork()
        {
        }
    }
```

- Adding the service endpoint and binding configuration in the `App.config` file.

In addition to the Contract and service type, the IDE will also insert a default configuration setting for the endpoint that can be exposed through the service. The following screenshot shows the sample service configuration section that contains a single endpoint, which uses WSHttpBinding.

```
<service behaviorConfiguration="ConsoleHostApp.TestServiceBehavior"
                name="ConsoleHostApp.TestService">

    <endpoint address="" binding="wsHttpBinding"
            contract="ConsoleHostApp.ITestService">
    </endpoint>
```

With the code and configuration entries as defined previously, we can start our service host by supplying the service type in the constructor of the `ServiceHost` class.

```
using (ServiceHost consoleHost = new
            ServiceHost(typeof(TestService)))
```

What the runtime will do is, it will lookup the configuration file and load the `<service>` entry that has the name identical to the type specified in the constructor, and launch the service and endpoints defined in it.

See also

▶ *Complete source code for this recipe can be found in the* \Chapter 3\recipe1\ *folder*

Hosting a service in Windows Service

Windows Services are widely used on Windows operating systems for hosting applications that will perform some long-run or scheduled tasks in the background. Applications hosted via Windows Service can be running under a specific user account and can choose the startup mode (manually or automatically). As a popular service-application-hosting scenario, it is also quite common to deploy a WCF service as a Windows Service.

How to do it...

In this recipe, we will use a typical .NET-based Windows Service to demonstrate how to host a WCF service in a Windows Service application. Let's go through the detailed steps:

1. Create a Windows Service project.

    The first step is to create a new Windows Service project through the Visual Studio IDE. When creating the project, we simply choose the **Windows Service** project type. The following screenshot shows how we can select the **Windows Service** project type in the Visual Studio **New Project** wizard.

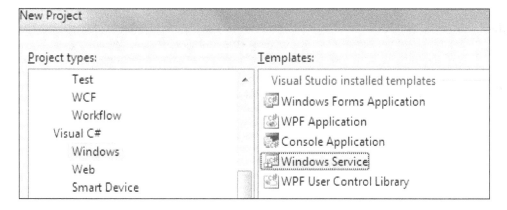

2. Add a new WCF service item.

    As a WCF service hosting application, we certainly need to have a WCF service defined here. The steps for creating a WCF service are the same as what we've discussed in the *Hosting a service in console application* recipe.

3. Add service hosting code into the service startup and shutdown event.

   As for the service-hosting code in the Windows Service, we need to put it in the correct place, since the .NET-based Windows Service type doesn't directly expose the `Main` function. The following code shows how the WCF service startup and shutdown code is defined:

   ```
   public partial class Service1 : ServiceBase
   {
       ServiceHost _svcHost = null;

       protected override void OnStart(string[] args)
       {
           // Start the service host here
           _svcHost = new ServiceHost(typeof(TestService));
           _svcHost.Open();
       }

       protected override void OnStop()
       {
           // Close the service host
           _svcHost.Close();
       }
   }
   ```

4. Add an installer for the Windows Service.

   Now the Windows Service class and WCF service types have been defined. However, we still need to add another component—the installer class for deploying the Windows Service into the Windows Service collection on the target operating system. In the Visual Studio IDE, we can simply add an installer type for the Windows Service by the context menu on the component designer. The following screenshot shows the context menu item for creating the installer class for the Windows Service.

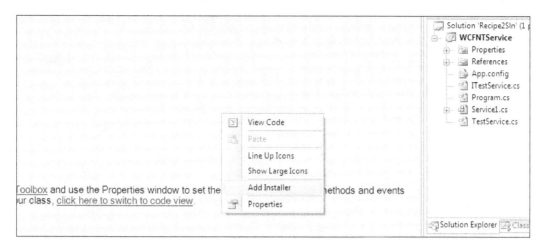

The IDE will help create two helper classes—one is of `ServiceProcessInstaller` type and another of `ServiceInstaller` type. We can specify many deployment parameters for the Windows Service in the **Property** panel of the two classes. The following screenshot shows the properties of the sample `serviceProcessInstaller1` class.

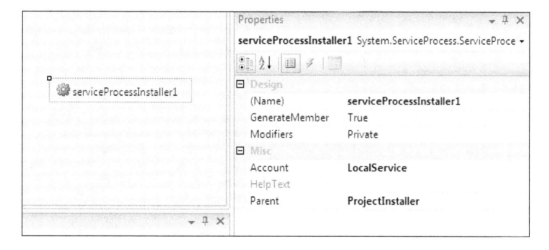

The next screenshot shows the properties of the sample `serviceInstaller1` class.

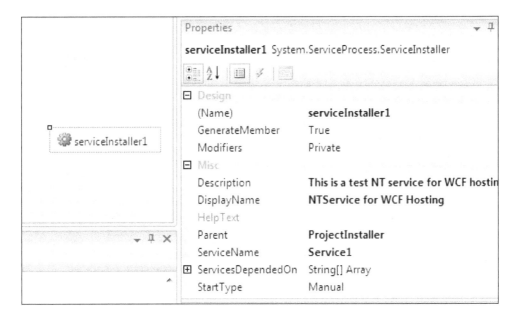

As with the screenshots displayed, Visual Studio will use standard **Properties** windows for displaying and configuring the individual properties of the Windows Service classes.

5. Install the Windows Service through Installutil.exe.

The last step is to install the Windows Service we have created (after building the project) into the operating system. This can be done by using the Installutil.exe tool provided by the .NET framework. You can directly execute the Installutil.exe command within the Visual Studio command-line prompt window or you can choose to launch the tool through its absolute path in the .NET framework folder such as `C:\Windows\Microsoft.NET\Framework\v4.0.30319`.

The following statements show the complete commands for installing and uninstalling a .NET-based Windows Service application via the Installutil. exe tool.

Install the Windows Service:

```
InstallUtil.exe WCFNTService.exe
```

Uninstall the Windows Service:

```
Install Util.exe /u WCFNTService.exe
```

The `WCFNTService.exe` mentioned earlier is the output assembly name of the sample Windows Service project.

How it works...

The `OnStart` event is fired when the Windows Service is starting, while the `OnStop` event is fired when the Windows Service is shutting down. Therefore, they are the best places for us to put the WCF service-hosting code.

Sometimes, we may need to access some remote or protected resource in our Windows Service host program. In such cases, it is important to specify a proper service account, either at development time or in the Windows Service Configuration Manager. The following screenshot shows the service list, which contains the installed sample Windows Service in Windows Service Configuration Manager.

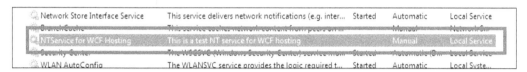

See also

- ▸ *Hosting a service in a console application*
- ▸ *Complete source code for this recipe can be found in the* \Chapter 3\recipe2\ *folder*

Hosting a HTTP service with ASP.NET-compatible context

ASP.NET provides a powerful platform for developing web applications over the .NET framework. An ASP.NET web application is also a natural hosting environment for a WCF service over the web HTTP protocol, which means developers can deploy WCF services with ASP.NET web pages in the same web application side by side without any particular effort.

However, by default, some ASP.NET runtime features or state objects are not available to WCF service code even if they are within the same web application. Those limited features include:

▸ **HttpContext** is always null when accessed from within a WCF service.

▸ Configuration-based **URL Authorization** (via `<authorization>` configuration element) is not available to WCF `.svc` files. These settings are ignored for WCF requests if a service resides in a URL space secured by ASP.NET's URL authorization rules.

▸ Custom **HttpModules** injected into an ASP.NET application to intercept requests at later stages of the pipeline do not intercept WCF requests.

▸ ASP.NET-specific states such as **sessionState** and **Application Cache** are not available to WCF service codes.

Then, how can we make such features accessible to a WCF service again? Well, the WCF-service hosting infrastructure has provided a feature called *ASP.NET Compatibility Mode*, which can help resolve the problem. This feature is by default disabled; we will show you how to enable this feature so that the WCF service continues to enjoy the ASP.NET runtime in this recipe.

How to do it...

1. The first thing we need to do is get an existing ASP.NET web application and then add a new WCF service into the web application. For our sample case, we will use an empty ASP.NET website with two simple ASPX pages as the hosting website. Then, a WCF service named `EchoService.svc` will be added into it so that the two ASPX web pages can run side by side with the `EchoService.svc` service. The following screenshot shows the web application structure in Visual Studio **Solution Explorer**.

The `EchoService` has a very simple `ServiceContract`, which contains a single `Echo` operation to return some data of type String (refer to the following code snippet).

```
[ServiceContract]
public interface IEchoService
{
    [OperationContract]
    string Echo();
}
```

2. Now we have the ASP.NET web pages and WCF service hosting together. However, the WCF service code still cannot access those ASP.NET-specific runtime objects yet. What we need to do is apply ASP.NET Compatibility Mode into the hosting web application and the WCF service deployed in it.

   To enable ASP.NET Compatibility Mode, we can simply set the `aspNetCompatibilityEnabled` attribute to `true` in the `<serviceHostingEnvironment>` setting of the WCF configuration section. The following screenshot shows the configuration fragment with ASP.NET Compatibility Mode enabled.

```
<system.serviceModel>
  <serviceHostingEnvironment
   aspNetCompatibilityEnabled="true"
```

   On the service implementation class of the WCF service, we need to apply the `System.ServiceModel.Activation.AspNetCompatibilityRequirements` attribute and set the `RequirementsMode` property to `AspNetCompatibilityRequirementsMode.Allowed`. This is quite useful, since sometimes we might not want certain WCF services to gain access to those ASP.NET runtime context objects, even if the hosting web application has ASP.NET Compatibility Mode enabled. The following code snippet shows the implementation class of the sample `EchoService`, which has applied the proper `AspNetCompatibilityRequirements` setting:

```
using System.ServiceModel.Activation;

[AspNetCompatibilityRequirements(
    RequirementsMode=AspNetCompatibilityRequirementsMode.Allowed
    )]
public class EchoService : IEchoService
{
...
}
```

3. Having all the services and applications configured appropriately, we can now start enjoying the ASP.NET context objects within the WCF service code. The following code snippet shows the sample `Echo` operation code, which collects several runtime properties from the ASP.NET request context and returns them to the service caller:

```
public class EchoService : IEchoService
{
    public string Echo()
    {
     var approot = HttpContext.Current.Server.MapPath("~/");

     var data = HttpContext.Current.Cache["key1"];

     var url = HttpContext.Current.Request.RawUrl;

     return string.Format("{0}, {1}, {2}", approot, data, url) ;
    }
}
```

By performing a quick test on the WCF service in the WCF Test Client tool, we can get the expected response with all the ASP.NET context properties returned, as shown in the following screenshot:

```
Response
<s:Envelope xmlns:s="http://schemas.xmlsoap.org/soap/envelope/">
  <s:Header />
  <s:Body>
    <EchoResponse xmlns="http://tempuri.org/">
      <EchoResult>C:\workspace\         ASPNETSite\, 5:27:38 PM, /ASPNETSite/EchoService.svc<
    </EchoResponse>
```

How it works...

WCF HTTP services hosted in an ASP.NET web application can be run in two different modes— the default mode and ASP.NET Compatibility Mode.

In the default mode, the ASP.NET runtime intercepts the WCF request in the early stage of the pipeline: BeginRequest (one of the interception points of ASP.NET HttpModule), so most of the ASP.NET Context information is not available to the WCF service code. When ASP.NET Compatibility Mode is enabled on the WCF service, the WCF service runtime hooks up into the ASP.NET HTTP pipeline through both module and handler for the HTTP transport, so those ASP.NET-specific context data become available again.

There's more...

For more detailed information about ASP.NET Compatibility Mode for WCF service hosting, you can refer to the following article from Wenlong Dong's Blog:

▸ *ASP.NET Compatibility Mode*

  `http://blogs.msdn.com/b/wenlong/archive/2006/01/23/516041.aspx`

See also

▸ *Using the WCF Test Client tool to test a service* in *Chapter 12*

▸ *Complete source code for this recipe can be found in the* `\Chapter 3\recipe3\` *folder*

Hosting a non-HTTP service in IIS 7

Since Windows 2003 Server, IIS is increasingly playing a more important role in the Windows Server operating system (for deploying server applications that will need to expose HTTP-based endpoints for client consumers). And IIS host is also a popular deployment scenario for a WCF service application. However, starting from IIS 7, the new process activation model (**Windows Activation Service**) provides non-HTTP support also, which makes deploying non-HTTP endpoint-based WCF services also possible.

How to do it...

1. Install WCF non-HTTP activation components on the host machine.

   Though IIS 7 supports hosting non-HTTP-based WCF service endpoints, we need to make sure the **WCF Non-HTTP Activation Components** are correctly installed on the hosting server. The following MSDN reference provides detailed steps on installing the WCF Non-Http Activation Components:

   ❑ *How to: Install and Configure WCF Activation Components* (`http://msdn.microsoft.com/en-us/library/ms731053.aspx`)

2. Configure the hosting IIS site and application virtual directory to enable non-HTTP binding support.

   After installing the activation components, we need to enable a certain type of binding in a particular IIS site and application virtual directory, in which our WCF service will deploy. In our sample WCF service, we will use NetTcpBinding. Therefore, we will add a `net.Tcp` binding into the IIS default site. This can be done through the **Edit Bindings...** wizard in IIS7's manager tool. The next screenshot shows how we can launch the **Edit Bindings...** configuration wizard against a particular IIS site in the manager tool.

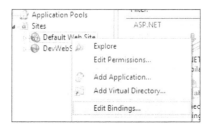

   Also, we need to enable the binding protocol at individual virtual directory level (refer to the following screenshot). This will give developers and administrators more flexible granularity of control over multiple applications deployed in the same IIS site.

3. Create a WCF service in the web application.

   Like hosting a normal HTTP-based WCF service in a web application, we need to add a `.svc` file and configure it to use a certain WCF service type (see the following directive).

```
<%@ ServiceHost Language="C#" Debug="true" Service="ServiceLib.
CalcService,ServiceLib, Version=1.0.0.0, Culture=neutral, PublicKe
yToken=3d43fe2725af75c2"    %>
```

   However, the most important thing here is to make our WCF service use the correct non-HTTP binding and address. In the sample service here, our `CalcService` service will use NetTcpBinding and the endpoint address will use the TCP port (8099) we added in step 2. The following screenshot shows the detailed endpoint configuration.

```
<services>
  <service name="ServiceLib.CalcService"
           behaviorConfiguration="ServiceBehavior" >
    <endpoint
      address="net.tcp://localhost:8099/TestWebApp/Service.svc"
      binding="netTcpBinding"
      contract="ServiceLib.ICalcService"
               />
    <endpoint
      address="net.tcp://localhost:8099/TestWebApp/Service.svc/mextcp"
      binding="mexTcpBinding"
      contract="IMetadataExchange "/>
```

How it works...

In the previous sample service, we add a MexTcpBinding-based endpoint in addition to the main service endpoint. This MexTcpBinding endpoint is used for a client application to acquire the metadata of the service. If you use the Visual Studio Add ServiceReference command to generate the proxy, you can directly type the metadata address in the metadata browser's address bar.

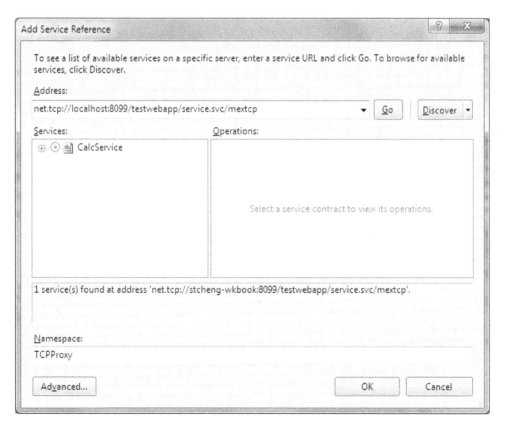

See also

▸ *Complete source code for this recipe can be found in the* \Chapter 3\recipe4\ *folder*

Customizing IIS ServiceHost via ServiceHostFactory

When hosting in an IIS server, the WCF service and endpoints configuration are, by default, loaded from the Web.config file. So, developers do not need to explicitly create and initiate the ServiceHost like we do in a self-hosting scenario. Sometimes, however, we still need to customize the service or endpoints through code. This recipe will use a custom metadata configuration case to demonstrate how to programmatically adjust service behaviors in an IIS-hosting scenario.

How to do it...

Here we will go through the steps of applying a customized ServiceMetadataBehavior into an IIS-hosted WCF service:

1. Create the WCF service in the hosting web application.

   We can simply create a new WCF service by adding a new WCF Service item in the hosting web application. The resulting WCF service is represented by a .svc file and an optional code-behind file (the CalcService.svc and CalcService.svc.cs files shown in the following screenshot).

   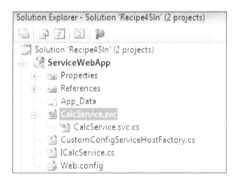

2. Define a custom ServiceHostFactory class for customizing the metadata configuration.

   As what we want to do is customize the metadata configuration, we should override the CreateServiceHost method and inject our custom code logic there. The following code snippet shows a sample implementation of the custom ServiceHostFactory.

```csharp
public class CustomConfigServiceHostFactory : ServiceHostFactory
{
    protected override System.ServiceModel.ServiceHost
      CreateServiceHost(Type serviceType, Uri[] baseAddresses)
    {
        ServiceHost host = base.CreateServiceHost(serviceType,
                baseAddresses);

        // Configure service behaviors here
        ServiceMetadataBehavior smb =
    host.Description.Behaviors.Find<ServiceMetadataBehavior>();
        if (smb == null)
        {
            smb = new ServiceMetadataBehavior();
            host.Description.Behaviors.Add(smb);
        }
        smb.HttpGetEnabled = true;
        smb.HttpGetUrl = new
            Uri("http://localhost:10394/CalcService.svc/wsdl");

        return host;
    }
}
```

As we can see, the `CreateServiceHost` method locates the `ServiceMetadataBehavior` from the `ServiceHost` instance (created automatically by the web application runtime) and adjusts the metadata properties.

3. Apply the custom `ServiceHostFactory` to the target service.

   In order to apply our custom `ServiceHostFactory`, we can use the `Factory` attribute on the `@ServiceHost` directive in the `.svc` file as shown in the following code snippet:

```
<%@ ServiceHost Language="C#" Debug="true" Service="ServiceWebApp.
CalcService" CodeBehind="CalcService.svc.cs"
Factory="CustomConfigServiceHostFactory" %>
```

How it works...

Though we do not explicitly create the `ServiceHost` instance, when the first client request reaches the IIS server, the WCF Service Activation module will help load the `ServiceHostFactory` specified in the `.svc` file. This Activation module is added in the `machine.config` file when installing the .NET 3.0 framework, as shown in the following configuration fragment.

```
<httpModules>
  ...
  <add name="ServiceModel"
       type="System.ServiceModel.Activation.HttpModule,
       System.ServiceModel,
       Version=3.0.0.0,
       Culture=neutral,
       PublicKeyToken=b77a5c561934e089"/>
```

So, this activation model provides the opportunity for developers to inject their own code logic into the `ServiceHost` by supplying a custom `ServiceHostFactory` type. Also, if you do not explicitly specify the ServiceHostFactory, the runtime will use a default factory to create the `ServiceHost`.

See also

► *Hosting a non-HTTP service in IIS 7*

► *Complete source code for this recipe can be found in the* `\Chapter 3\recipe5\` *folder*

Specifying a dedicated service instance for a singleton service

Normally, when hosting a WCF service, we only need to specify the service type in the `ServiceHost` and the runtime will help create the service instance internally, according to the `InstanceContextMode` we apply on the service class. This makes hosting a WCF service quite simple and convenient; the service developers do not need to know when and how the runtime creates the service instance. However, in some cases, it is useful and necessary to let the developer control when and how the service instance is created.

Getting ready

Singleton is one of the popular design patterns. This pattern can help design a class that will expose one and only one instance of the class over the entire lifecycle of the class or application context. This is very useful in cases where we want to restrict the number of instances of a given class or component.

How to do it...

In this recipe, we will use a sample `Voting service` to demonstrate how to supply a dedicated service instance for a WCF service hosting in **singleton** mode. The hosting environment can manipulate and communicate with the service instance directly throughout the hosting lifetime.

1. Define the `ServiceContract` and implement the service with special properties.

   The sample voting service contains a single operation `Vote`. This is used by the client to submit a vote request for a certain item. The following code shows the complete `ServiceContract` and implementation of the VotingService:

```
[ServiceContract()]
 public interface IVotingService
 {
     [OperationContract]
     void Vote(string name);
 }

   [ServiceBehavior(InstanceContextMode=InstanceContextMode.
Single)]
 public class VotingService : IVotingService
 {
     private object _syncobj = new object();
     private Dictionary<string, int> _votelist = new
         Dictionary<string, int>();

     public void Vote(string name)
     {
       lock (_syncobj)
       {
         if (!_votelist.ContainsKey(name)) _votelist.Add(name, 0);

         _votelist[name] = _votelist[name] + 1;
       }
     }
 }
```

```
public KeyValuePair<string, int>[] GetVoteList()
{
    return _votelist.ToArray<KeyValuePair<string, int>>();
}

}
```

Note that in the implementation class (type `VotingService`), we add an additional member function called `GetVoteList`. This function is not a WCF service operation and is used for the service hosting program to query the current voting status list.

2. Create the service instance and supply it to the ServiceHost.

The next step, also the most important step, is to tell the WCF ServiceHost to use the service instance created by our code. For the sample VotingService, we simply create the service instance and assign it to the ServiceHost in the constructor as shown in the following code:

```
ServiceHost host = null;
try
{
    _serviceInstance = new VotingService();
    host = new ServiceHost(_serviceInstance);
    host.Open();

    string input = "";
    while (input != "exit")
    {
        // Print voting list
        Console.WriteLine("name:  voting count");
        foreach (var pair in _serviceInstance.GetVoteList())
        {
            Console.WriteLine("{0}:  {1}", pair.Key, pair.Value);
        }
        Thread.Sleep(1000 * 3);
        input = Console.ReadLine();
    }
}
finally
{
    host.Close();
}
```

Similar to using a service type name, the constructor here (which takes an instance object) will also correctly load the service configuration from the `App.config` file.

How it works...

WCF allows developers to control how the service instance objects are created, and the relation between service instance and client channel through the `ServiceContractAttribute.InstanceContext` property. The following table shows every possible `InstanceContextMode` along with its description.

InstanceContextMode	Description
PerSession	A new `InstanceContext` object is created for each session.
PerCall	A new `InstanceContext` object is created prior to, and recycled subsequent to, each call. If the channel does not create a session, this value behaves as if it were `PerCall`.
Single	Only one `InstanceContext` object is used for all incoming calls and is not recycled subsequent to the calls. If a service object does not exist, one is created. Note that for singleton lifetime behavior (for example, if the host application calls the ServiceHost constructor and passes an object to use as the service), the service class must set `InstanceContextMode` to `InstanceContextMode.Single`, or an exception is thrown when the service host is opened.

For our sample service here, we use the Singleton mode so as to make our WCF service expose a single service instance object to process client requests. However, only applying the `InstanceContextMode.Singleton` is not enough, since we also need to control the creation of the service instance object. Therefore, we also add code to manually create the service instance object and supply it into the ServiceHost via the constructor.

By supplying a dedicated service instance object, we can conveniently communicate with the service instance in the hosting code. For example, in the above sample voting service, the console service host can query the voting count at any time by accessing the public methods for properties on the service instance type.

There's more...

For more information about the Singleton design pattern, you can refer to the following page:

▸ *Singleton pattern*

    http://en.wikipedia.org/wiki/Singleton_pattern

See also

- ▸ *Hosting a singleton instance service* in *Chapter 8*
- ▸ *Complete source code for this recipe can be found in the* \Chapter 3\recipe6\ *folder*

Hosting a service in WSS 3.0

ASP.NET ASMX Web Service is naturally supported in WSS 3.0, and developers can also write their own Web Services and deploy them into WSS 3.0 servers and sites. With the WCF coming in .NET Framework 3.0, people are also interested in how to deploy their custom WCF service into WSS 3.0 sites.

How to do it...

1. Creating the WCF service.

    The sample service here is quite straightforward and contains a service operation that will return the current WSS site's URL (see the GetCurrentWebUrl function shown as follows):

```
[ServiceContract]
    public interface ISimpleWSSService
    {
        [OperationContract]
        void DoWork();

        [OperationContract]
        string GetCurrentWebUrl();
}
```

    Our sample service will use BasicHttpBinding without any requirement for authentication. The service configuration of the sample service is shown in the following screenshot.

```
<configuration>
  <system.serviceModel>
    <serviceHostingEnvironment aspNetCompatibilityEnabled="true" />
    <behaviors>
      <serviceBehaviors>
        <behavior name="WSSSVCLib.SimpleWSSServiceBehavior">
          <serviceMetadata httpGetEnabled="true" />
          <serviceDebug includeExceptionDetailInFaults="true" />
        </behavior>
      </serviceBehaviors>
    </behaviors>
    <services>
      <service behaviorConfiguration="WSSSVCLib.SimpleWSSServiceBehavior"
          name="WSSSVCLib.SimpleWSSService">
        <endpoint address=""
                binding="basicHttpBinding"
                contract="WSSSVCLib.ISimpleWSSService">
        </endpoint>
      </service>
    </services>
```

In the service configuration section, we have enabled
`aspNetCompatibilityEnabled` so that our service code can access the object
model of the ASP.NET/WSS hosting environment.

2. Create a `VirtualPathProvider` for intercepting SVC endpoint requests in WSS.

   The next step is very important; we need to add a custom `VirtualPathProvider`
   for the WSS web application to correctly forward the SVC endpoint requests. The
   following code shows a very simple `VirtualPathProvider` implementation that
   will do the job:

```
public class SVCVirtualPathProvider : VirtualPathProvider
{

    public override bool FileExists(string virtualPath)
    {
        // Patches requests to WCF services: That is a virtual
        path ending with ".svc"
        string patchedVirtualPath = virtualPath;
        if (virtualPath.StartsWith("~", StringComparison.Ordinal)
        && virtualPath.EndsWith(".svc",
        StringComparison.InvariantCultureIgnoreCase))
        {
            patchedVirtualPath = virtualPath.Remove(0, 1);
        }
```

```
        return Previous.FileExists(patchedVirtualPath);
    }
}
```

The `FileExits` function is the only one where we need to add customized code; our implementation simply checks whether the request is coming for a `.svc` extension. If it is an SVC request, remove the ~ char from the URL and continue the execution. In addition, we need to create a custom HttpModule that is responsible for registering the custom `VirtualPathProvider` into the WSS runtime. The following code shows this HttpModule used in our sample service:

```
public class SVCVirtualPathProviderModule : IHttpModule
{
    static bool _inited = false;
    static object _syncobj = new object();
    ...

    public void Init(HttpApplication context)
    {
        if (!_inited)
        {
            lock (_syncobj)
            {
                if (!_inited)
                {
                    SVCVirtualPathProvider svcVPP = new
                        SVCVirtualPathProvider();
                    HostingEnvironment.RegisterVirtualPath
                                        Provider(svcVPP);

                    _inited = true;
                }
            }
        }
    }
}
```

3. Deploying the WCF SVC endpoint into a WSS web application.

   For our sample service, we will deploy it into the WSS **LAYOUTS** folder. We will create a sub directory so as to make the structure look more clear. The complete path of the directory in which we deploy our WCF service is `C:\Program Files\Common Files\Microsoft Shared\web server extensions\12\TEMPLATE\LAYOUTS\MyCustomApp`.

   There are two things that we need to add into the deploying directory—one is the `.svc` service file, and the other is the `web.config` file that contains the service configuration entries.

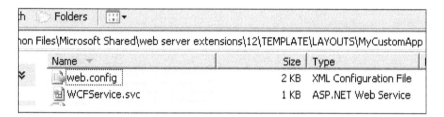

   Another thing we need to do here is to install the service assembly (including the `VirtualPathProvider` components) into the system **GAC (Global Assembly Cache)** so that the WSS hosting runtime can correctly locate them. The assembly name is also referenced in the `.svc` service file, as shown in the following code:

```
<%@ ServiceHost Service="WSSSVCLib.SimpleWSSService, WSSSVCLib,
Version=1.0.0.0, Culture=neutral, PublicKeyToken=d5ae877ce0946ee3"
%>
```

4. Configuring the WSS web application to enable WCF endpoints.

   After deploying our WCF service into the target WSS application folder, we still need to apply some further changes so as to make the WSS environment WCF-enabled. These preparations include:

   ❑ Enabling anonymous access on the virtual directory that contains our WCF SVC service files. We can enable anonymous access for our specific `MyCustomApp` directory through the IIS management console.

❑ Registering the custom `VirtualPathProvider` in the WSS web application. As we use a custom HttpModule to register the custom `VirtualPathProvider`, we need to add our custom HttpModule into the WSS web application's `web.config` file. The following screenshot shows the sample `web.config` section that registers our HttpModule.

```
<httpModules>
  <clear />
  ... ...
  <!-- our virualPathProvider registering module -->
  <add name="svcVPP"
       type="WSSSVCLib.SVCVirtualPathProviderModule,
       WSSSVCLib, Version=1.0.0.0, Culture=neutral, PublicKeyToken
```

How it works...

In our WSS service hosting sample, we created a custom `VirtualPathProvider` for intercepting the `.svc` requests coming into the WSS web application. This is necessary, since the WSS 3.0 runtime will raise a path-processing exception if we do not manually intercept the request and alter the original path. The following screenshot shows the error page if we deployed a WCF service in a WSS 3.0 web application without configuring a custom `VirtualPathProvider`.

Go back to site

Error

virtualPath   at System.ServiceModel.AsyncResult.End[TAsyncResult](IAsyncResult result)
   at System.ServiceModel.Activation.HostedHttpRequestAsyncResult.End(IAsyncResult result)
   at System.ServiceModel.Activation.HostedHttpRequestAsyncResult.ExecuteSynchronous(HttpApplication context, Boolean flowContext)
   at System.ServiceModel.Activation.HttpHandler.ProcessRequest(HttpContext context)
   at System.Web.HttpApplication.CallHandlerExecutionStep.System.Web.HttpApplication.IExecutionStep.Execute()
   at System.Web.HttpApplication.ExecuteStep(IExecutionStep step, Boolean& completedSynchronously)

Troubleshoot issues with Windows SharePoint Services.

After the WCF service is correctly deployed in the WSS web application, we can use a web browser to visit the default metadata page like a normal SVC service.

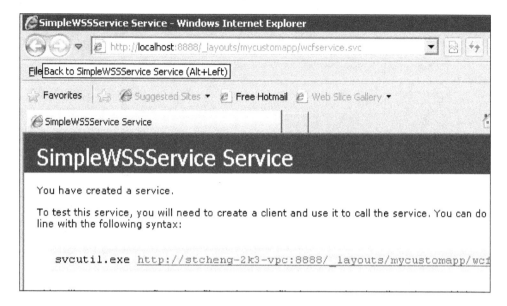

See also

> ▸ *Hosting a singleton instance service* in *Chapter 8*

> ▸ *Complete source code for this recipe can be found in the* \Chapter 3\recipe7\ *folder*

4

Service Discovery and Proxy Generation

In this chapter, we will cover:

- ▸ Creating a typed service client
- ▸ Choosing a specific type for representing a collection parameter
- ▸ Reusing types between service and client
- ▸ Customizing an auto-generated service proxy class in Visual Studio
- ▸ Building an ad-hoc auto-discoverable service
- ▸ Using managed `ServiceDiscovery`
- ▸ Generating a service proxy in code
- ▸ Customizing auto-generated service metadata

Introduction

As a unified communication platform, WCF can be consumed by various kinds of client applications. And the most common means to consume a WCF service is using a .NET Framework-based client proxy class. There are also different ways to create such kinds of client proxy types using Visual Studio IDE or the .NET Framework SDK utility.

Also, WCF proxy generation relies highly on the service metadata.

Service metadata contains a machine-readable description of the service. Service metadata includes descriptions of the service endpoints, bindings, contracts, operations, and messages. You can use service metadata for a variety of purposes, including automatically generating a client for consuming the service, implementing the service description, and dynamically updating the binding for a client. Metadata can be exposed to a client through many different ways, including using a HTTP-based static metadata endpoint, using dynamic metadata discovery, using custom metadata generation, and so on.

In this chapter, we will go through eight recipes focusing on WCF client proxy generation and metadata publishing and discovery. The first four recipes demonstrate the typical service proxy generation scenarios and how to apply some special configuration options on the generated service proxy components. The fifth, *Building an ad-hoc auto-discoverable service*, and sixth, *Using managed ServiceDiscovery*, recipes show the new auto-discovery feature of WCF 4.0, including ad-hoc auto-discoverable services and managed auto-discoverable service development. The last two recipes focus on the customization scenarios of WCF service metadata and client proxy generation.

Creating a typed service client

WCF services can be consumed by a client through various means. If our client application is also built upon .NET Framework 3.x or above, the most common and convenient way of consuming the WCF service is by using a typed service proxy class. This recipe will show you how to create a typed service proxy through WCF service metadata.

How to do it...

We will go through the typed service proxy generation steps via a simple WCF service that is hosted at the address `http://localhost:29671/service1.svc`.

Following are the detailed steps:

1. Get the WSDL metadata of the targeting service.

    For our sample service, we can directly get the service metadata at the SVC endpoint file (from the previous address).

2. Locate the service metadata in the Visual Studio **Add Service Reference** dialog.

    The next step is to create the WCF service proxy components for the client project in Visual Studio. We can simply do it through the **Add Service Reference** command in the project context menu item, in the **Solution Explorer** pane.

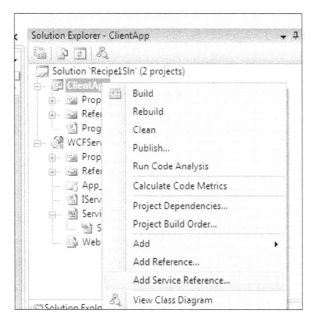

Selecting **Add Service Reference** will launch a dialog where one can control the configuration options on how the WCF service proxy gets generated.

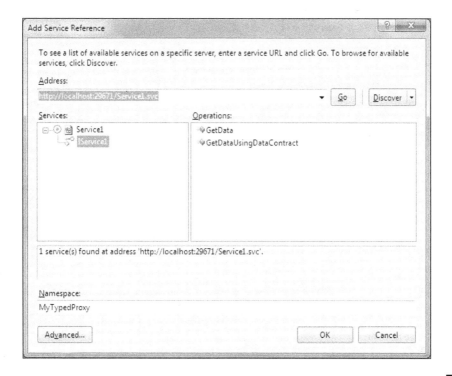

As shown in the dialog window, after we type in the metadata location and submit it, the panels under the **Address** bar will show the **Services** and **Operations** detected from the metadata retrieved. Click on the **OK** button so that the IDE will help generate the necessary types for the WCF service proxy.

3. Create the proxy class and review the generated components.

After the IDE generates the proxy types, we can review them in the Visual Studio **Class View** as shown in the following screenshot.

The main class in the proxy components is the ServiceClient type (highlighted in the previous screenshot). If we look into the detailed code of this class, we will find that it is derived from the System.ServiceModel.ClientBase<T> type and has implemented all the service operations of the service. The following code snippet shows the entire Service1Client class used in our sample project:

```
[System.Diagnostics.DebuggerStepThroughAttribute()]
    [System.CodeDom.Compiler.GeneratedCodeAttribute(
        "System.ServiceModel", "3.0.0.0")]
    public partial class Service1Client :
System.ServiceModel.ClientBase<ClientApp.MyTypedProxy.IService1>,
ClientApp.MyTypedProxy.IService1 {

        public Service1Client() {
        }

        public Service1Client(string endpointConfigurationName) :
                base(endpointConfigurationName) {
        }

        public Service1Client(string endpointConfigurationName,
                string remoteAddress) :
                base(endpointConfigurationName, remoteAddress) {
        }
```

```
public Service1Client(string endpointConfigurationName,
        System.ServiceModel.EndpointAddress remoteAddress) :
        base(endpointConfigurationName, remoteAddress) {
}

public Service1Client(System.ServiceModel.Channels.Binding
binding, System.ServiceModel.EndpointAddress
remoteAddress) : base(binding, remoteAddress) {
}

public string GetData(int value) {
    return base.Channel.GetData(value);
}

public ClientApp.MyTypedProxy.CompositeType
GetDataUsingDataContract(ClientApp.MyTypedProxy.CompositeType
composite) {
    return
        base.Channel.GetDataUsingDataContract(composite);
}
}
```

How it works...

For our sample WCF service, we used Visual Studio **Add Service Reference** to generate the typed client proxy components. In addition to Visual Studio UI, we can also use the Svcutil.exe tool to create a typed WCF service proxy on the command line. The following command shows the simplest syntax for creating a WCF typed service proxy from a given metadata location:

```
Svcutil.exe http://localhost:29671/service1.svc
```

See also

 ▸   *Complete source code for this recipe can be found in the* \Chapter 4\recipe1\ *folder.*

Choosing a specific type for representing a collection parameter

For any data object transferred from the WCF service to the client, WCF runtime will serialize it from a .NET object into raw XML or binary format at the server side and deserialize it into an object of the mapping type at the client side.

We will usually use an array or collection-like type as parameter or return value type in a service operation. When calling such operations, the client-side proxy will need to define the corresponding types that will match the parameters or return values. WCF service proxy generation provides a flexible option that lets the developer choose the preferred collection type that will be used to match the array/collection objects in the service operation.

How to do it...

Here we will demonstrate how to specify the collection parameter type when generating the service proxy in Visual Studio. The detailed steps are as follows:

1. Launch the Visual Studio **Add Service Reference** wizard and open the **Advanced** option panel.

   When using the **Add Service Reference** wizard, we can click on the **Advanced** button to launch the advanced configuration panel, which contains those additional settings that control service proxy generation.

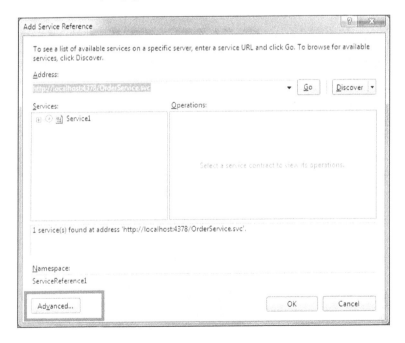

2. Choose the expected type from the given **Collection type** drop-down list.

   We can choose the collection types from a combo box that contains all the available types. Available **Collection types** include `Array`, `ArrayList`, `Generic.List`, `Generic.LinkedList`, and so on. The following screenshot shows the **Collection type** selection drop-down list.

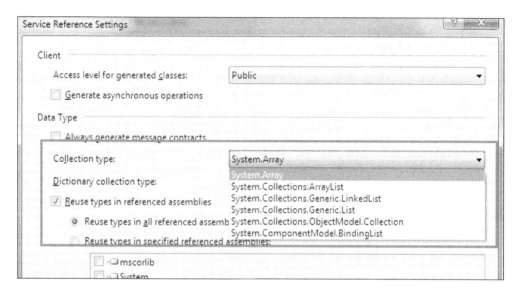

How it works...

After specifying a custom collection type, the **Add Service Reference** wizard will generate the proxy class that uses the selected type to represent any collection-based parameters or return values in service operations. For example, suppose the target service has the following `ServiceContract`:

```
[ServiceContract]
public interface IOrderService
{
    [OperationContract]
    Order[] GetOrders();
}
```

And if we select `System.Collections.Generic.LinkedList<T>` as the collection type, the generated client proxy class will contain the following style operation signature:

```
public partial class OrderServiceClient : System.ServiceModel.
ClientBase<TestClient.TestProxy.IOrderService>, TestClient.TestProxy.
IOrderService {
```

```
        public System.Collections.Generic.LinkedList<TestClient.
        TestProxy.Order> GetOrders() {
            return base.Channel.GetOrders();
        }
    }
```

As we can see, the return value of the `GetOrders` operation is of the `LinkedList<T>` type.

There's more...

As mentioned in the *Create a typed service client* recipe, we can use Svcutil.exe to generate a service proxy in addition to the Visual Studio **Add Service Reference** wizard. When using Svcutil.exe for proxy generation, we can still specify the collection type for array-like parameters through the `/collectionType` option. For example:

```
Svcutil.exe /collectionType:System.Collections.Generic.LinkedList~1
http://localhost:4378/OrderService.svc
```

See also

▶ *Creating a typed service client*

▶ *Complete source code for this recipe can be found in the* `\Chapter 4\recipe2\` *folder*

Reusing types between service and client

Usually, we will use some custom types in our WCF service operations as parameters or return values. When generating a WCF client proxy through the Visual Studio **Add Service Reference** context menu item, it will help to generate some skeleton types (that have the same serialization format with the custom types used in the server-side service) at the client-side instead of directly using the server-side types. However, sometimes we will need to reuse the existing types used at the server side instead of using the auto-generated skeleton types.

How to do it...

1. Centralize all the types that we need to reuse, in a separate class library/assembly.

    The first thing we need to do is gather all those custom types (used in our WCF service operation) in one or several class library assemblies. This can help separate them from other service definition-related code and make them more convenient to be reused. For our sample WCF service, we will use a single assembly with the custom type defined as follows:

    ```
    namespace ClassLib
    {
    ```

```
[DataContract]
public class SearchResult
{
    [DataMember]
    public int Count { get; set; }
    [DataMember]
    public string[] Items { get; set; }
}
}
```

The WCF service application project will reference this assembly and use the `ClassLib.SearchResult` type in the service operation as shown in the following code:

```
[ServiceContract]
  public interface IService1
  {
      [OperationContract]
      ClassLib.SearchResult Search(string criteria);
  }
```

2. Reference the class library/assembly (which contains those custom types that we need to reuse) in the client application.

   To make the custom types available to the client application that needs to consume the WCF service, we need to reference the assembly first, which can be done via **Add Reference** in the Visual Studio **Solution Explorer** pane.

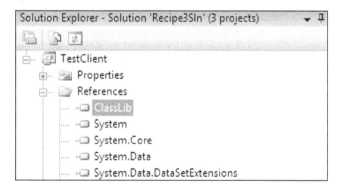

   In the previous screenshot, the `ClassLib` assembly is the shared class library, contains the custom types that need to be shared between the WCF service and client projects.

3. Specify the assembly for looking up reusable types when generating the WCF service proxy in Visual Studio.

The last thing we need to do is to specify the assembly in which we should probe for reusable types when using the **Service Reference Settings** dialog to generate the WCF service proxy in Visual Studio, as shown in the following screenshot:

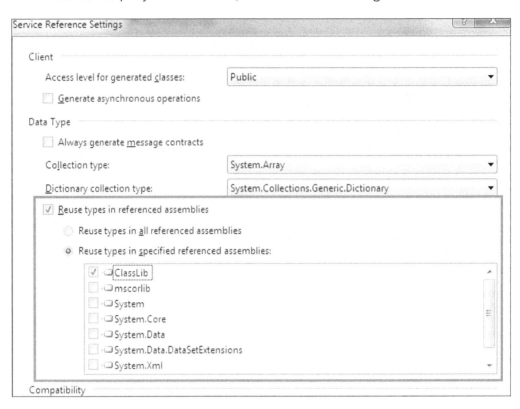

As the previous screenshot shows, the advance options in Visual Studio's **Add Service Reference** UI has provided a **Reuse types in referenced assemblies** option that can let developers choose the assembly for probing reusable types (between the server-side service and the client proxy).

After the service proxy is generated, we can open the main proxy class code to verify that the types defined in the centralized assembly have been used in the auto-generated service proxy (as shown in the following code).

```
public partial class Service1Client : System.ServiceModel.
ClientBase<TestClient.TestProxy.IService1>, TestClient.TestProxy.
IService1 {

        public ClassLib.SearchResult Search(string criteria) {
            return base.Channel.Search(criteria);
        }
    }
```

How it works...

The .NET Framework/Visual Studio tools for generating WCF service proxy let developers specify some optional assemblies, in which the tool will probe for types that can be reused between the WCF service and auto-generated client proxy components. The type probing is based on the WCF service operation's method signature (such as parameter type and return value type or other types marked as knowable types).

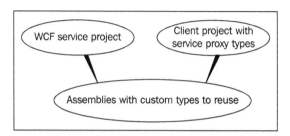

Also, such kinds of assemblies being probed must be referenced by both client and service projects as shown in the previous figure.

By using the type reusing functionality, developers can avoid generating redundant and duplicated skeleton types in client projects that will consume WCF service projects using custom types.

See also

- ▶ *Creating a typed service client*
- ▶ *Complete source code for this recipe can be found in the* \Chapter 4\recipe3\ *folder*

Customizing an auto-generated service proxy class in Visual Studio

The Visual Studio **Add Service Reference** dialog can help in generating a WCF client proxy component through service metadata. However, sometimes we will need to do some customization or adjustment on the generated proxy classes, such as add some custom methods, manipulate some of the method signature, or add additional member properties in the proxy class. In this recipe, we will cover the way to manually modify the auto-generated WCF service proxy class in a Visual Studio project.

How to do it...

In this recipe, we will look at the steps to customize an auto-generated WCF service proxy in Visual Studio by adding custom code.

1. Generate the WCF service proxy class through the **Add Service Reference** dialog.

    This is quite straightforward and we can just refer to the steps mentioned in the *Creating a typed service client* recipe. After generating the service proxy and expanding the service reference node in Visual Studio, it will show you the view shown in the following screenshot:

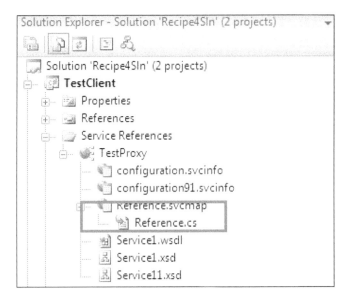

    Also, this time we will need to inspect the main class of the service proxy in the `Reference.cs` file, which contains all the service proxy codes by default. The following code snippet shows the main class definition in our sample WCF service proxy:

```
public partial class Service1Client :
    System.ServiceModel.ClientBase<TestClient.TestProxy.IService1>,
    TestClient.TestProxy.IService1 {


    ......... . .

    public System.Xml.Linq.XElement GetData(int value) {
        return base.Channel.GetData(value);
    }
}
```

As the code indicates, the service proxy contains a service operation, which will take an integer and return an `XElement` instance that contains the data.

2. Get the main proxy class and create a partial class file to extend the main proxy class.

   The next step is to add our customization code, which will extend the auto-generated service proxy class. To do this, we need to add a partial class file into the project and define a partial class with a name identical to the auto-generated main service proxy class shown previously. The following code fragment shows the partial class definition in our sample client project:

```
public partial class Service1Client
{
    public int GetIntData(int value)
    {
        XElement xelm = GetData(value);

        return int.Parse(xelm.Value);
    }
    ...
}
```

3. Now that the default generated service proxy class has been extended via our partial class definition, we can use the custom member functions (defined in the partial class) on the proxy instance. As the following code snippet shows, the code for invoking the service operations through a service proxy instance remains the same as before:

```
var client = new TestProxy.Service1Client();

Console.WriteLine(client.GetIntData(33));
```

How it works...

Here we used a partial class file to extend the WCF auto-generated service proxy type. The partial class `Service1Client` is identical to the auto-generated service proxy type and has a custom method called `GetIntData`. The `GetIntData` method will call the auto-generated `GetData` service operation and do some post-processing on the return value before returning it to the caller. We can also add other custom methods or properties into the partial class so as to further extend the auto-generated proxy class. When using the main proxy class to consume the WCF service, we can call any of our custom-defined members instead of the auto-generated operations so as to include our custom code logic seamlessly in the client-side code.

The advantage of this approach is that our custom code will be combined with the auto-generated proxy code and compiled together, which makes the proxy caller able to use our extended proxy members (properties or functions) seamlessly. Another highlight is that by using a partial class file, the custom code to extend the proxy class will not be discarded when you update the WCF proxy via the **Update Service Reference** context menu item in Visual Studio.

See also

> ▸ *Creating a typed service client*

> ▸ *Complete source code for this recipe can be found in the \Chapter 4\recipe4\ folder*

Building an ad-hoc auto-discoverable service

In some service hosting environments, the endpoint address of each hosted service is dynamic or frequently changing; or some services will constantly change their base address after every service or server restarts. In such cases, it is quite important to let the service client be able to dynamically discover the service location. Fortunately, WCF 4 provides a new feature called **service discovery**, which can properly address this issue. The discovery feature enables services to be discoverable at runtime in an interoperable way using the WS-Discovery protocol. WCF services can announce their availability to the network using a multicast message or to a discovery proxy server. Client applications can search the network or a discovery proxy server to find services that meet a set of criteria. In this recipe, we will cover how to build a simple and powerful ad-hoc auto-discoverable service through the service discovery feature.

Getting ready

▶ WS-Discovery is an OASIS specification that defines a SOAP-based protocol for dynamically discovering the location of service endpoints at runtime. The service discovery feature in WCF 4 is based on this specification. More information on this specification is available at Web Services Dynamic Discovery (WS-Discovery):

```
http://docs.oasis-open.org/ws-dd/ns/discovery/2009/01
```

How to do it...

Our sample service will use the WCF 4 built-in discovery endpoint to demonstrate the steps for creating a WCF service with ad-hoc discoverable ability:

1. Enable the auto-discovery feature on the WCF service.

   The first thing to do is make the WCF service application auto-discovery ready. For ad-hoc auto-discoverable services, we can simply add an udpDiscoveryEndpoint into the service's endpoint collection. The following screenshot shows the complete service configuration with discovery endpoint and corresponding behaviors defined.

```
<system.serviceModel>
  <behaviors>
    <serviceBehaviors>
      <behavior>
        ...
        <serviceDiscovery />
      </behavior>
    </serviceBehaviors>
  </behaviors>
  <services>
    <service name="AutoDiscoverableService.CalcService">
      <endpoint address=""
                binding="wsHttpBinding"
                contract="AutoDiscoverableService.ICalcService">
      </endpoint>
      ...
      <!-- udp discovery endpoint -->
      <endpoint name="udpDiscoveryEndpoint"
                kind="udpDiscoveryEndpoint"/>
      ...
    </service>
  </services>
</system.serviceModel>
```

2. Add dynamic service-discovering code in the client application.

For an auto-discovery-enabled WCF service, we can still use the **Add Service Reference** context menu item or Svcutil.exe to generate the client proxy components. However, instead of using a static endpoint address, we can use the `DiscoveryClient` class to locate the service endpoint address programmatically. The following code demonstrates how to dynamically find an auto-discoverable service and assign the dynamic `EndpointAddress` to client a proxy:

```
private static void CallService()
{
    // Dynamically detect the service endpoint address
    DiscoveryClient discoveryClient = new
            DiscoveryClient("udpDiscoveryEndpoint");
    // Specify which endpoint we want to discover
    FindCriteria criteria = new FindCriteria(typeof(ICalcService));

    FindResponse response = discoveryClient.Find(criteria);
    // Retrieve the detected endpoint address in FindResponse
    EndpointAddress address = response.Endpoints[0].Address;
    Console.WriteLine("target service is at {0}", address );
    // Assign the discovered address to service proxy dynamically
    CalcProxy.CalcServiceClient client = new
            CalcProxy.CalcServiceClient();
    client.Endpoint.Address = address;
    // Call service operation on proxy...
}
```

As the `CallService` function shows, the client application can use a `DiscoveryClient` type to search for a certain WCF service and the search criteria can be a certain `ServiceContract` type. Also, like the service-side, the client application also needs to configure the `udpDiscoveryEndpoint` entry.

```
<client>
  ...
  <endpoint name="udpDiscoveryEndpoint" kind="udpDiscoveryEndpoint"/>
</client>
</system.serviceModel>
```

How it works...

The ad-hoc auto-discovery feature in WCF 4.0 relies on a built-in discovery endpoint like `udpDiscoveryEndpoint`. As used in the sample service, by applying `udpDiscoveryEndpoint` in the service, the runtime will start a UDP server for listening to any discovery requests from client applications.

In the sample service's configuration file, the `<serviceDiscovery/>` element within the default service behavior enables the auto-discovery feature at service level. And the `udpDiscoveryEndpoint` within the endpoint collection represents the built-in Discovery endpoint which will serve the discovery requests from a client application that is looking for the hosting service.

Also, the discovery communication between client and service conforms to the WS-Discovery specification.

See also

▸ *Configuring Default Endpoints* in *Chapter 2*

▸ *Complete source code for this recipe can be found in the* `\Chapter 4\recipe5\` *folder*

Using managed ServiceDiscovery

The ad-hoc auto-discoverable service recipe demonstrates using the built-in discovery endpoint for automatic service publishing, which is simple and convenient. However, sometimes we may need a more advanced service-discovering functionality for our WCF service. For example, we may need to make the auto-discovery feature go across different subnets in the local network or we may need to perform some filtering against all the discoverable services. Fortunately, WCF provides interfaces for us to build a custom discovery proxy for service announcement and service probing.

In this recipe, we will show you how to create a custom service-discovery proxy through the WCF built-in discovery extension types.

How to do it...

1. Create a custom `DiscoveryProxy` type.

   The first thing to do is create a custom type derived from the `DiscoveryProxy` class. This class is the main component for processing WCF service publishing and service-probing requests. It is also required that the custom `DiscoveryProxy` class be defined as a singleton service, so that there is a single entry point for all the service announcement and probing requests.

In our sample `DiscoveryProxy` class, we use a `Dictionary` object to hold the information of all available services online. The following code snippet demonstrates the custom `DiscoveryProxy` class definition and those core functions for maintaining the service list:

```
[ServiceBehavior(InstanceContextMode = InstanceContextMode.Single,
            ConcurrencyMode = ConcurrencyMode.Multiple)]
    public class DemoDiscoveryProxy : DiscoveryProxy
    {
        // For thread synchronizing
        private object _syncObj = new object();
        // List of online services that are available
        private Dictionary<EndpointAddress,
                EndpointDiscoveryMetadata> _liveServices;

        public DemoDiscoveryProxy()
        {
            _liveServices = new Dictionary<EndpointAddress,
                    EndpointDiscoveryMetadata>();
        }
        // Helper methods for maintain live service list
        void AddService(EndpointDiscoveryMetadata discMetadata)
        {
            lock (this._syncObj)
            {
                this._liveServices[discMetadata.Address] =
                        discMetadata;
            }

            Console.WriteLine("service online--{0}",
                    discMetadata.Address);
        }

        void RemoveService(EndpointDiscoveryMetadata discMetadata)
        {
            if (discMetadata != null)
            {
                lock (this._syncObj)
                {
                    this._liveServices.Remove(discMetadata.Address);
                }

                Console.WriteLine("service offline--{0}",
                        discMetadata.Address);
            }
```

```
   }

   void FindService(FindRequestContext ctx)
   {
      Console.WriteLine("FindService request for {0}",
               ctx.Criteria.ContractTypeNames[0]);
      lock (this._syncObj)
      {
         foreach (EndpointDiscoveryMetadata discMetadata in
                  this._liveServices.Values)
         {
            if (ctx.Criteria.IsMatch(discMetadata))
            {
               ctx.AddMatchingEndpoint(discMetadata);
            }
         }
      }
   }

   EndpointDiscoveryMetadata ResolveService(ResolveCriteria
         criteria)
   {
      Console.WriteLine("ResolveService request for {0}",
               criteria.Address);
      lock (this._syncObj)
      {
         foreach (EndpointDiscoveryMetadata discMetadata in
                  this._liveServices.Values)
         {
            if (criteria.Address == discMetadata.Address)
            {
               return discMetadata;
            }
         }
      }

      return null;     // Not found
   }
}
```

The WCF discovery framework implements all the operations on the `DiscoveryProxy` type in an asynchronous manner. The following code snippet shows the implementation of service probing and announcement operations:

```
protected override IAsyncResult OnBeginFind(FindRequestContext
        ctx, AsyncCallback callback, object state)
{
   this.FindService(ctx);
   return new DummyAsyncResult(callback, state);
}

protected override void OnEndFind(IAsyncResult result)
{
   DummyAsyncResult ar = (DummyAsyncResult)result;
   ar.DoComplete();
}

protected override IAsyncResult
           OnBeginOnlineAnnouncement(DiscoveryMessageSequence
           messageSequence, EndpointDiscoveryMetadata
           endpointDiscoveryMetadata, AsyncCallback callback,
           object state)
{
   this.AddService(endpointDiscoveryMetadata);
   return new DummyAsyncResult(callback, state);
}

protected override void OnEndOnlineAnnouncement(IAsyncResult
        result)
{
   DummyAsyncResult ar = (DummyAsyncResult)result;
   ar.DoComplete();
}

protected override IAsyncResult
        OnBeginOfflineAnnouncement(DiscoveryMessageSequence
        messageSequence, EndpointDiscoveryMetadata
        endpointDiscoveryMetadata, AsyncCallback callback,
        object state)
{
   this.RemoveService(endpointDiscoveryMetadata);
   return new DummyAsyncResult(callback, state);
}

protected override void OnEndOfflineAnnouncement(IAsyncResult
        result)
```

```
    {
        DummyAsyncResult ar = (DummyAsyncResult)result;
        ar.DoComplete();
    }
```

2. Launch the custom `DiscoveryProxy` type in a host application.

   The next step is to set up the custom `DiscoveryProxy` in a host application, just like a standard WCF service. Here we use a console application to host the custom `DiscoveryProxy` through the following `StartDiscoveryProxy` function:

```
static void StartDiscoveryProxy()
{
    Uri probeUri = new Uri("net.tcp://localhost:8011/Probe");
    Uri announceUri = new
            Uri("net.tcp://localhost:8022/Announcement");

    using (ServiceHost host = new ServiceHost(new
            DemoDiscoveryProxy()))
    {
        // Add DiscoveryEndpoint to receive Probe and Resolve
                messages
        DiscoveryEndpoint discoveryEndpoint =
                new DiscoveryEndpoint(new NetTcpBinding(), new
                EndpointAddress(probeUri));
        discoveryEndpoint.IsSystemEndpoint = false;

        // Add AnnouncementEndpoint to receive Hello and Bye
                announcement messages
        AnnouncementEndpoint announcementEndpoint =
                new AnnouncementEndpoint(new NetTcpBinding(), new
                EndpointAddress(announceUri));

        host.AddServiceEndpoint(discoveryEndpoint);
        host.AddServiceEndpoint(announcementEndpoint);

        host.Open();
...
    }
}
```

3. Make WCF service applications use the custom `DiscoveryProxy`.

   Having the custom `DemoDiscoveryProxy` running, we can let our WCF services use this discovery proxy for announcement registration. This can be done through a simple change in the `<serviceDiscovery>` behavior setting in the target service's service behavior configuration setting. The following screenshot shows the configuration fragment of a sample service that uses the custom `DemoDiscoveryProxy` as the new announcement center:

```xml
<serviceBehaviors>
    <behavior>
      <serviceDiscovery>
        <announcementEndpoints>
          <endpoint address="net.tcp://localhost:8022/Announcement"
                    binding="netTcpBinding"
                    kind="announcementEndpoint" />

        </announcementEndpoints>
      </serviceDiscovery>
```

4. Probe for the service from the custom `DiscoveryProxy` in client applications.

   At the client side, we will now change the service-probing code to use the new `DemoDiscoveryProxy` for locating the WCF service, too. The following code shows the sample client application that uses the new probing endpoint for searching the service.

```csharp
var probeUri = new Uri("net.tcp://localhost:8011/Probe");
var discoveryEndpoint =
        new DiscoveryEndpoint(new NetTcpBinding(), new
        EndpointAddress(probeUri));

var discoveryClient = new DiscoveryClient(discoveryEndpoint);
```

How it works...

The `DemoDiscoveryProxy`, uses a `Dictionary` object to maintain a list of all the WCF services currently online (registered at this `DiscoveryProxy` instance). Whenever it receives an announcement request from the WCF service, it will determine whether to add the service into the dictionary or remove it, based on the request type.

Since all the service-announcement and probing interfaces are of asynchronous pattern, to simplify the implementation, we create a dummy `IAsyncResult` class that always marks itself as *Completed* at the construction time, so that the announcement and find operations in `DemoDiscoveryProxy` still work in synchronous manner. Here is the complete definition of the `DummyAsyncResult` class:

```csharp
public class DummyAsyncResult : IAsyncResult
{
   private object _syncObj = new object();
   private AsyncCallback _callback = null;
   private object _state;
   private ManualResetEvent _event = new ManualResetEvent(true);
   private bool _isCompleted = false;
   private bool _completedSync = false;

   public DummyAsyncResult(AsyncCallback callback, object state)
   {
      _callback = callback;
      _state = state;

      // Always set to completed state
      lock (_syncObj)
      {
         _completedSync = true;
         _isCompleted = true;
         if (_event != null) _event.Set();
      }
   }

   // For storing additional data on Find Requests
   public EndpointDiscoveryMetadata DiscoveryData { get; set; }
   // Helper method for clear the IAsyncResult object
   public void DoComplete()
   {
      lock(_syncObj)
      {
         _isCompleted = true;
         _completedSync = true;
      }
   }

   #region IAsyncResult Members
   public object AsyncState
   {
      get { return _state; }
   }

   public System.Threading.WaitHandle AsyncWaitHandle
   {
      get {
         if (_event == null)
         {
            lock (_syncObj)
```

```
            {
                if (_event == null) _event = new
                     ManualResetEvent(_isCompleted);
            }
        }
        return _event;
    }
}
public bool CompletedSynchronously
{
    get { return _completedSync; }
}
public bool IsCompleted
{
    get { return _isCompleted; }
}
#endregion
}
```

See also

► *Building an ad-hoc auto-discoverable service*

► *Complete source code for this recipe can be found in the* \Chapter 4\recipe6\ *folder*

Generating a service proxy in code

In most cases, we will create the WCF service proxy types via Visual Studio's **Add Service Reference** option or the Svcutil.exe tool in the .NET SDK. Both of them actually import the metadata from the WCF service and generate proxy types from it. In addition to these kinds of static proxy generation approaches, WCF also provides powerful a interface for programmatically creating service proxy types.

How to do it...

To generate the client proxy types in code, we need to reference the necessary assemblies and import the proper namespaces. Following are the namespaces that contain those key types for generating the service proxy dynamically:

```
using System.ServiceModel;
using System.ServiceModel.Description;
using System.CodeDom;
using System.CodeDom.Compiler;
```

In our sample client application, we will programmatically generate the WCF service proxy through the following steps:

1. Locate and import the service metadata.

   WCF provides the `MetadataExchangeClient` class that can help import service metadata from a given metadata endpoint programmatically.

2. Extract the target `ServiceContract` type for which we want to generate a client proxy.

   It is possible that the service metadata contains multiple endpoints and ServiceContracts. We need to find the expected one for which we want to generate the client proxy.

3. Generate source code of the service proxy from the extracted ServiceContract type and metadata.

   After the metadata is imported correctly and has identified the correct ServiceContract, we can use the .NET **CodeDom** API to generate source code of the service proxy type. In our sample client, we will save the source code into a C# code file.

4. Compile the source code into a binary assembly.

   To make the service types executable, we need a further step to compile the proxy code into a .NET assembly. The CodeDom API is also capable of dynamic source code compilation.

   The `GenerateServiceProxy` function in the following code snippet demonstrates all the previously mentioned steps:

```
static Assembly  GenerateServiceProxy()
{
    // Import service metadata
    string wsdlUrl = "http://localhost:35167/Service1.svc?wsdl";

    MetadataExchangeClient metadataClient = new
                MetadataExchangeClient(new Uri(wsdlUrl),
                MetadataExchangeClientMode.HttpGet);
    WsdlImporter importer = new
                WsdlImporter(metadataClient.GetMetadata());
    Collection<ContractDescription> allContracts =
                importer.ImportAllContracts();

    // Extract the ServiceContract types from metadata
    CodeCompileUnit unit = new CodeCompileUnit();
    ServiceContractGenerator generator = new
                ServiceContractGenerator(unit);
    generator.GenerateServiceContractType(allContracts[0]);
```

```csharp
// Generate source code of the WCF service proxy
CodeDomProvider provider =
            CodeDomProvider.CreateProvider("C#");

CodeGeneratorOptions options = new CodeGeneratorOptions() {
            BracingStyle = "C" };
StreamWriter sw = new
            StreamWriter("DynamicServiceProxy.cs",false,
            Encoding.UTF8);
provider.GenerateCodeFromCompileUnit( unit, sw, options);
sw.Close();

// Compile the source code into .NET assembly
CompilerParameters comParameters = new CompilerParameters()
{
    GenerateExecutable = false,
    OutputAssembly = "DynamicServiceProxy.dll"
};
comParameters.ReferencedAssemblies.Add(
  @"C:\WINDOWS\Microsoft.NET\Framework\v2.0.50727\System.dll");
comParameters.ReferencedAssemblies.Add(
 @"C:\Program Files\Reference
 Assemblies\Microsoft\Framework\v3.0\System.ServiceModel.dll");


var results = provider.CompileAssemblyFromFile(comParameters,
            "DynamicServiceProxy.cs");

if (results.Errors.Count > 0)
{
    foreach (CompilerError err in results.Errors)
    Console.WriteLine(err.ErrorText);
}
else Console.WriteLine("Service proxy has been successfully
            generated!");

return results.CompiledAssembly;


}
```

How it works...

There are two components that play a big role in the process of dynamic proxy generation. The first is the `MetadataExchangeClient` type, which exposes the programming interface for importing WCF service metadata in a .NET-based application.

Another key component is the .NET CodeDom API, which provides the programming interface for source code generation and dynamic code compilation. Also, by using the .NET reflection APIs together, we can directly load the dynamically-generated proxy types in code without hardcoding the code logic statically at design time.

There's more...

For more information on MetadataExchangeClient, you can refer to the following MSDN document:

▶   How to: Use MetadataExchangeClient to Retrieve Metadata

    `http://msdn.microsoft.com/en-us/library/ms729834.aspx`

For more information on CodeDom API, you can refer to the following article:

▶   How *to programmatically compile code using C# compiler*

    `http://support.microsoft.com/kb/304655`

See also

▶   *Complete source code for this recipe can be found in the* `\Chapter 4\recipe7\` *folder*

Customizing auto-generated service metadata

WCF provides metadata endpoints that can help to automatically publish WSDL metadata for the hosted service. And this auto-generated WSDL metadata can be easily customized through the `IWsdlExportExtension` interface so as to fit some special requirements in our service development.

How to do it...

In this recipe, we will use a web-hosted WCF service (with a metadata endpoint enabled) as an example to demonstrate how to customize the auto-generated WSDL metadata.

1. Create a class that implements both the `IWsdlExportExtension` and `IEndpointBehavior` interfaces.

    The first thing to do is create a custom type that implements the `IWsdlExportExtension` and `IEndpointBehavior` interfaces. The `IWsdlExportExtension` interface provides extension points for injecting custom code logic in the WSDL metadata generation, while the `IEndpointBehavior` interface will make the custom extension type be able to inject into the target service endpoint's behavior collection. In our sample service, we will use the `IWsdlExportExtension` to add some custom XML schema into the WSDL document (see the following code snippet):

    ```
    public class WSDLExporterExtension : IWsdlExportExtension,
                IEndpointBehavior
    {
        public void ExportContract(WsdlExporter exporter,
                WsdlContractConversionContext context)
        { }
        public void ExportEndpoint(WsdlExporter exporter,
                WsdlEndpointConversionContext context)
        {
            WEBSVC.ServiceDescription sd =
                    exporter.GeneratedWsdlDocuments[0];

            FileStream fs = File.OpenRead(@"d:\schemas\mytypes.xsd");
            XmlSchema schema = XmlSchema.Read(fs,null);
            fs.Close();

            sd.Types.Schemas.Add(schema);
        }
        // Other members
    }
    ```

2. Create a custom ServiceHost and ServiceHostFactory to inject our WSDL extension component.

    After creating the custom `WsdlExportExtension` component, we need to apply it into the WCF ServiceHost. If you're using a self-hosting scenario, it is quite straightforward to add the `WsdlExportExtension` object into the `Behaviors` collection of the target endpoint. For our sample service, since we use a web hosting scenario with a `.svc` file as the activation point, the ServiceHost instance is not directly exposed.

To inject our extension component, we need to create a custom ServiceHost and ServiceHostFactory. The following code shows the custom ServiceHost and ServiceHostFactory implementation in our sample case:

```
public class WSDLServiceHost : ServiceHost
{
    public WSDLServiceHost() { }

    protected override void ApplyConfiguration()
    {
        base.ApplyConfiguration();

        AddExtensions();
    }

    private void AddExtensions()
    {
        foreach (ServiceEndpoint endpoint in
                this.Description.Endpoints)
        {
            endpoint.Behaviors.Add(new WSDLExporterExtension());
        }

    }
}

public class WSDLServiceHostFactory : ServiceHostFactory
{

    protected override ServiceHost CreateServiceHost(Type
                serviceType, Uri[] baseAddresses)
    {
        return new WSDLServiceHost(serviceType, baseAddresses);
    }
}
```

3. Apply the custom ServiceHostFactory into the .svc files.

   Finally, we need to change the ServiceHostFactory type of those .svc service files to the custom types we have defined, as follows:

```
<%@ ServiceHost ... Factory="TestService.WSDLServiceHostFactory"
%>
```

How it works...

When we request the metadata page of our WCF service, the runtime will go through all the endpoints on the service and generate the WSDL document for them. And during the metadata generation process of each endpoint, any `IWsdlExportExtension` components registered at the endpoint will be invoked and the custom code logic in each extension class is applied into the metadata.

In the sample `WSDLExporterExtension` class, the `ExportEndpoint` function provides the `WsdlExporter` object from which we can enumerate all the `ServiceDescription` document instances generated by the metadata runtime and customize them. And in the previous `WSDLServiceHost` type, it manually enumerates all the registered service endpoints and injects our custom `WsdlExportExtension` instance into the `Behavior` collection of those endpoints. The `WSDLServiceHostFactory` class will return our custom `WSDLServiceHost` object when the runtime demands a WCF **ServiceHost** instance.

For our sample service, after applying the `WsdlExportExtension`, the output WSDL document will include the additional XML Schema added by our custom code as shown in the following screenshot:

```
- <wsdl:types>
  - <xsd:schema targetNamespace="http://tempuri.org/Imports">
      <xsd:import schemaLocation="http://localhost:36754/Service1.svc?xsd
      <xsd:import schemaLocation="http://localhost:36754/Service1.svc?xsd
      <xsd:import schemaLocation="http://localhost:36754/Service1.svc?xsd
    </xsd:schema>
  - <xs:schema elementFormDefault="qualified" targetNamespace="http://tempi
      xmlns:mstns="http://tempuri.org/mytypes.xsd" xmlns="http://tempuri
    - <xs:element name="UserObject">
      - <xs:complexType>
        - <xs:sequence>
            <xs:element name="FirstName" type="xs:string" />
            <xs:element name="LastName" type="xs:string" />
          </xs:sequence>
        </xs:complexType>
      </xs:element>
    </xs:schema>
  </wsdl:types>
```

See also

▶ *Complete source code for this recipe can be found in the* `\Chapter 4\recipe8\` *folder*

5
Channel and Messaging

In this chapter, we will cover:

- ▶ Using `ChannelFactory` to consume a WCF service
- ▶ Invoking async operation via `ChannelFactory`
- ▶ Creating a service via `ChannelListener`
- ▶ Getting the IP address of a client consumer of a WCF service
- ▶ Adding a dynamic SoapHeader into a message

Introduction

When developing WCF services, we look at `ServiceContract`, endpoint, and binding configurations, which are very important in the service-oriented design view. However, under the service-oriented design view, there are many raw components that construct the WCF client and service. All these raw components provide a **Channel model** that allows developers to develop WCF services at a very low level. Instead of service operations and method parameters, we will work with raw **Message** objects directly at the Channel Model programming layer. Though the Channel Model programming adds more complexity, it does give much more flexibility and a clearer overview of how the WCF runtime works under the hood.

In this chapter, we will go through the common use cases at the WCF Channel and Message layers. The first and second recipes demonstrate how to use `ChannelFactory` and the Channel object model to consume a WCF service. The third recipe shows how to build a raw WCF service through the `ChannelListener` component. The last two recipes cover the usage of an underlying Message context of WCF service operation calls and shows how developers can add custom data into the raw Message layer of WCF service communication.

Using ChannelFactory to consume a WCF service

When consuming a WCF service, it is common to generate a strong-typed client proxy class (either through Visual Studio's **Add Service Reference** context menu item or .NET SDK's Svcutil.exe tool) for invoking service operation. However, there are many cases in which we will need to get rid of this kind of auto-generated service proxy class. For example, we may need to directly reuse the existing types (including the `ServiceContract` type and custom data types) used in the service definition, or we might just need a lightweight component to invoke a service operation. For such scenarios, we can use the `ChannelFactory` class to directly communicate with the target WCF service endpoint.

How to do it...

Here are the steps for using `ChannelFactory` to invoke a WCF service operation.

1. Define or import the `ServiceContract` types.

   The first thing we should do is to make sure that the client application has the `ServiceContract` type that is identical to the one used in the server-side WCF service. For our sample service, we will use a test `ServiceContract` as shown in the following code snippet:

   ```
   [ServiceContract]
   public interface IService1
   {
       [OperationContract]
       string GetData(int value);
   }
   ```

   There is a single service operation `GetData` in the `ServiceContract`.

2. Build the `ChannelFactory` and a Channel against the target service endpoint.

   Given the `ServiceContract` type (and any referenced types if necessary), we can start building the `ChannelFactory` and Channels for consuming the WCF service. Typically, we will need to supply the binding and endpoint address of the target WCF service we want to consume. For our test client application, we will build the binding and endpoint address in code without loading them from the application configuration file (`App.config`). The following code shows how to build the `ChannelFactory` and Channel, along with invoking the service operation through the generated channel:

   ```
   static void CallService()
   {
       string svc_url = "http://localhost:44424/Service1.svc";
   ```

```
BasicHttpBinding binding = new BasicHttpBinding();

ChannelFactory<IService1> cf = new
        ChannelFactory<IService1>(binding, svc_url);
IService1 svc_channel = cf.CreateChannel();

Console.WriteLine("Data:{0}", svc_channel.GetData(1));
}
```

As the `CallService` function demonstrates, we can supply binding and an endpoint address through the `ChannelFactory<T>` constructor. The `T` generic parameter indicates the `ServiceContract` of the target service endpoint. By calling the `CreateChannel` method on the `ChannelFactory` object, we can get the `Channel` object on which we can invoke the service operations, defined in the `ServiceContract`.

How it works...

In WCF, there are well-designed message processing stacks at both server and client sides. At the client side, creating channels is the responsibility of `ChannelFactory` and is used for sending messages. These channels are responsible for getting the message from the layer above, performing whatever processing is necessary, and then sending the message to the layer below. The following figure illustrates this process.

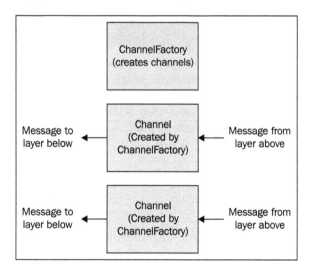

Though the `CreateChannel` method returns an instance of the `ServiceContract` type, we can explicitly convert it to an `IClientChannel` object and manipulate it. For example, we can get the underlying channel and close it as shown in the following code snippet:

```
IService1 svc_channel = cf.CreateChannel();
IClientChannel cc = svc_channel as IClientChannel;
cc.Close();
```

There's more...

For more information about the WCF Channel and `ChannelFactory` programming, you can refer to the following MSDN document:

- Client: Channel Factories and Channels

  `http://msdn.microsoft.com/en-us/library/ms789050.aspx`

See also

- *Creating a typed service client* in *Chapter 4*
- *Complete source code for this recipe can be found in the* `\Chapter 5\recipe1\` *folder*

Invoking async operation via ChannelFactory

WCF supports asynchronous service operation invoking at the client side, which doesn't require the WCF service to be designed as asynchronous. When we use Visual Studio's **Add Service Reference** or .NET SDK's Svcutil.exe to generate the client proxy types, we can choose to generate asynchronous methods on the client proxy class (for each service operation). Then, how do we add asynchronous invoking support for a `ChannelFactory`-based WCF client?

How to do it...

1. Add *async* style operation definition into the `ServiceContract` type (in the service client).

   As described in *Use ChannelFactory to consume a WCF service* recipe, we need to import the `ServiceContract` definition into our client application that needs to invoke the service operation via `ChannelFactory`. And to make the `ChannelFactory`-based WCF client be able to invoke service operation asynchronously, the most important thing is adding the asynchronous pattern **OperationContract** into the `ServiceContract` type. The following code demonstrates the sample `ServiceContract` in the client application that supports service invoking via both synchronous and asynchronous style.

```
//serviceContract type at client-side
[ServiceContract]
   public interface ICalcService
   {
       [OperationContract]
       int Add(int lv, int rv);

       [OperationContract(AsyncPattern = true)]
       IAsyncResult BeginAdd(int lv, int rv, AsyncCallback
                   callback, object state);
       int EndAdd(IAsyncResult ar);
   }
```

As the `ICalcService` contract type shows, there are two special members in addition to the normal `Add` operation. They are `BeginAdd` and `EndAdd`, which conform to the .NET **Asynchronous Programming Pattern** (**APP**).

2. Invoke service operations through the *async* style operation methods.

   After we have defined the asynchronous invoking-enabled `ServiceContract` type, we can simply use `ChannelFactory` and Channel to invoke the service operation in async mode, which is almost the same as what we do for synchronous invoking. The following `CallServiceAsync` function shows a complete example of invoking a service operation synchronously:

```
static void CallServiceAsync()
{
    string svc_url = "http://localhost:64671/CalcService.svc";

    BasicHttpBinding binding = new BasicHttpBinding();

    ChannelFactory<ICalcService> cf = new
                ChannelFactory<ICalcService>(binding, svc_url);
    ICalcService calc = cf.CreateChannel();

    calc.BeginAdd(
                1, 2,
                delegate(IAsyncResult ar)
                {
                    int result = calc.EndAdd(ar);
                    Console.WriteLine("result is {0}", result);
                } ,
                null);

    cf.Close();
}
```

How it works...

The asynchronous service invoked here is completely implemented at the client side. The WCF service side has no sense of whether the client application is using sync or async mode to call itself. Also, from the `ServiceContract` type in client we can find that the asynchronous operation signature completely conforms to the .NET asynchronous method pattern.

There's more...

For more information on .NET Asynchronous Programming Pattern, you can refer to the following MSDN document:

- Asynchronous Programming Overview

  `http://msdn.microsoft.com/en-us/library/ms228963.aspx`

See also

- *Using ChannelFactory to consume a WCF service*
- *Complete source code for this recipe can be found in the* `\Chapter 5\recipe2\` *folder*

Creating a service via ChannelListener

`ChannelFactory` provides a raw programming interface for building a WCF client. Likewise, there are also corresponding components at the Channel level for building a WCF service. Though the Channel level-based service might not look as comprehensible and convenient as those built via `ServiceContract` and `ServiceHost`, it is no less powerful than the former. It is quite simple and straightforward and clearly shows how the WCF service and endpoint actually work under the hood (at Channel level).

How to do it...

In this recipe, we will use a simple HTTP service that receives and returns text data to demonstrate how we can use a `ChannelListener` to build a raw WCF service:

1. The first step is to construct a `ChannelListener` instance with binding and endpoint address information supplied. In our sample service, we will use a `BasicHttpBinding` with all the default binding configuration settings. Also, `ChannelListener<T>` is a generic type, which will expect a generic template type that represents the Channel type used in this service. Our sample `ChannelListener` uses the most popular `IReplyChannel` as the Channel type.

2. After the `ChannelListener` is constructed with proper configuration, we can open it and start listening for requests from client applications. Just like standard TCP socket programming, we can use `AcceptChannel` or `BeginAcceptChannel` to acquire a client-side request channel in either synchronous or asynchronous style. Our sample service will use an asynchronous pattern for handling client-side requests.

The following code snippet shows the complete application code of the sample `ChannelListener` service:

```
class Program
{
    static IChannelListener<IReplyChannel> listener;
    static Binding binding;

    static void Main(string[] args)
    {
        binding = new BasicHttpBinding();
        listener = binding.BuildChannelListener<IReplyChannel>(
                     new Uri("http://localhost:8080/ChannelSVC"),
                     new BindingParameterCollection());

        listener.Open();

        Thread th = new Thread(new ThreadStart(RunChannelService));
        th.Start();

        string cmd = "";
        while (cmd.ToUpper().Trim() != "QUIT")
        {
            Console.WriteLine("Press QUIT to exit....");
            cmd = Console.ReadLine();
        }

        th.Abort();
        listener.Close();
    }

    static void RunChannelService()
    {
        // Start waiting for client request
        listener.BeginAcceptChannel(
                 new AsyncCallback(RequestCallback),
                 ""
                 );
    }
}
```

```
// Callback function for handling client request
static void RequestCallback(IAsyncResult ar)
{
    IReplyChannel channel = listener.EndAcceptChannel(ar);
    channel.Open();

    RequestContext request = channel.ReceiveRequest();

    Message message = request.RequestMessage;
    Console.WriteLine("Message received");

    string requestData = message.GetBody<string>();
    Console.WriteLine("Message body: {0}", requestData);

    Message replymessage = Message.CreateMessage(
    binding.MessageVersion,
    "http://localhost:8080/ChannelSVC", requestData);
    request.Reply(replymessage);

    message.Close();
    request.Close();
    channel.Close();

    // Waiting for next request
    listener.BeginAcceptChannel(
            new AsyncCallback(RequestCallback),
            ""
            );

}
}
```

How it works...

As the sample service shows, we create a `ChannelListener` instance, which acts as a connection point for accepting service requests from the client side. When processing service requests, each request is associated with a certain Channel coupled with the `ChannelListener` at the initializing stage. Our sample service uses `IReplyChannel`, which is often used with `IRequestChannel` (at the client side) like most WCF service operations (with input parameter and return value) use. In addition to `IRequestChannel`/ `IReplyChannel`, there are also other supported built-in Channel shapes, such as `IInputChannel`/`IOutputChannel`, `IDuplexChannel`, and so on.

There's more...

More information about Channel shapes can be found in the following references:

▸ Choosing a Message Exchange Pattern

  `http://msdn.microsoft.com/en-us/library/aa751829.aspx`

▸ Windows Communication Foundation Channel Shapes

  `http://blogs.msdn.com/drnick/archive/2006/03/07/544724.aspx`

See also

▸ *Complete source code for this recipe can be found in the* `\Chapter 5\recipe3\` *folder*

Getting the IP address of a client consumer of a WCF service

When developing those network hosting services (over HTTP or TCP), it is useful to get the IP address of the client-side callers/consumers so as to perform some counting or analysis work. Started from .NET Framework 3.5, WCF also provides built-in interfaces for service developers to conveniently get the IP address of client consumers of certain WCF services/endpoints. We can get the IP address of a client consumer as long as the underlying transport protocol is HTTP or TCP based (such as WSHttpBinding, NetTcpBinding, BasicHttpBinding, and so on).

How to do it...

1. Get a reference to the message properties from `OperationContext`.

    The IP address information is embedded in the message properties transferred from client to server. We can use the `OperationContext.Current` property to access those message properties in the service operation code. The following code snippet shows how to obtain the reference to message properties within service operation code:

    ```
    // Get all the message properties from current operation
    context
    MessageProperties msgProps =
                OperationContext.Current.IncomingMessageProperties;
    ......
    ```

2. Extract the IP address from the `RemoteEndpointMessageProperty` entry.

The IP address information is stored in a specific message property item, which is of the `RemoteEndpointMessageProperty` type. The next remaining code shows how we can extract the `RemoteEndpointMessageProperty` instance from the message property collection and get the IP and port information:

```
// Find the RemoteEndpointMessageProperty
RemoteEndpointMessageProperty remProp =
                (RemoteEndpointMessageProperty)msgProps[
                RemoteEndpointMessageProperty.Name];
Console.WriteLine("Client Address:{0}, Port:{1}", remProp.Address,
                remProp.Port);
```

How it works...

Our helper function uses the `OperationContext` class to access the `RemoteEndpointMessageProperty` object, which contains the IP address of the client consumer. Actually, WCF uses `OperationContext` to carry data and properties during the service operation call context. For example, if the service endpoint is using an HTTP-based endpoint, we can use `OperationContext` to get the HTTP message headers from the underlying message properties.

See also

▶ *Complete source code for this recipe can be found in the* `\Chapter 5\recipe4\` *folder*

Adding a dynamic SoapHeader into a message

When designing a WCF `ServiceContract`, we can add custom **SoapHeaders** into the WCF service operation through the `ServiceContract` member statically. In addition to this, we can also programmatically create a custom SoapHeader and add it into a WCF request dynamically.

How to do it...

1. Create a custom SoapHeader instance.

The first thing to do here is to generate an instance of the SoapHeader we want to add into the request message. WCF provides a built-in generic type called `MessageHeader<T>` for creating custom SoapHeaders containing different kinds of inner data properties. The following code snippet shows how we can generate a custom SoapHeader that contains some string data through the `MessageHeader<T>` type:

```
MessageHeader<string> user = new MessageHeader<string>(Environme
nt.UserName);

MessageHeader userheader = user.GetUntypedHeader("ClientUser",
                "urn:test:calcservice");
```

2. Inject a custom SoapHeader object through `OperationContext`.

   Like getting a client IP address, we will also use the `OperationContextScope` and `OperationContext` for injecting our custom SoapHeader into the request message. However, instead of using the `OutgoingMessageProperties` collection, we will use the `OutgoingMessageHeaders` collection to add the custom SoapHeaders. The following code snippet shows the complete steps for adding an untyped SoapHeader into a WCF client request:

```
var client = new TestProxy.CalcServiceClient();
var user = GetCustomHeader();

using (OperationContextScope scope = new
                        OperationContextScope(client.InnerChannel))
{
    OperationContext.Current.OutgoingMessageHeaders.Add
    (
    Userheader
    );

    Console.WriteLine("3+5={0}",client.Add(3, 5));
}
```

How it works...

In WCF, a SoapHeader is represented by the `MessageHeader` type. To simplify the SoapHeader generation and manipulation process, WCF also provides a generic type `MessageHeader<T>` so that developers can use the generic type to construct untyped SoapHeaders with the particular data type we want to embed in the SOAP header content. Also, we can define a custom header type derived from the `MessageHeader` class instead of using the untyped MessageHeader-based SoapHeader.

In the server-side code, we can also conveniently extract the particular SoapHeader from the incoming `OperationContext`. The following code shows how we can read the custom SoapHeader we added in the earlier sample client code:

```
public class CalcService : ICalcService
{
    public int Add(int lv, int rv)
```

```
    {
        string user =
    OperationContext.Current.IncomingMessageHeaders.GetHeader<string>(
    "ClientUser", "urn:test:calcservice");

        Console.WriteLine("Client User is {0}", user);
        return lv + rv;
    }
}
```

See also

▶   *Complete source code for this recipe can be found in the* \Chapter 5\recipe5\
    folder.

6
Dealing with Data in Service

In this chapter, we will cover:

- ▶ Binding a WPF element with data from a WCF service
- ▶ Returning `ReadOnlyCollection` data
- ▶ Using raw XML as an operation parameter
- ▶ Returning a DataTable/DataSet in a service operation
- ▶ Transferring binary data with MTOM encoding
- ▶ Specifying `ServiceKnownType` information in a programmatic way
- ▶ Using XmlSerializer for custom data serialization

Introduction

Data transfer is always a hot topic in distributed communication. WCF supports transferring various kinds of data such as database records, custom data objects, XML document, and even raw binary data.

In this chapter, we will go through different kinds of data transferring cases in WCF service development. The recipes will start with a simple data binding scenario with WPF and WCF returned data. We will then use four recipes to demonstrate how we can exchange various kinds of data in a WCF service operation. And the last two recipes will cover the features related to WCF data serialization.

Binding a WPF element with data from a WCF service

WPF (**Windows Presentation Foundation**) is the new UI presentation technology provided since .NET 3.0, and released together with WCF. For client applications that use a WPF-based front UI and consume WCF for data retrieving, it is quite common to display data objects retrieved from a WCF service to a WPF front UI.

In this recipe, we will use a simple WPF window application to demonstrate how to bind WCF service data to WPF UI elements.

How to do it...

1. Create an XAML-based WPF Window application.

    First, we need to create a WPF client application with an XAML-based window as the main user interface. The following screenshot shows the main window of the WPF application.

    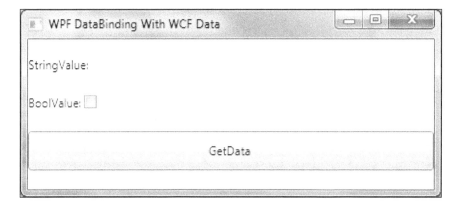

    For this sample case, we will put all the window UI definition within the XAML file so as to make the code focus on data binding functionality. The following screenshot shows the complete XAML template of the main window. The XAML file contains the definition of three main UI elements—one `TextBlock` for displaying a String value, one `CheckBox` for displaying a Boolean value, and a `Button` for performing data binding operations.

```
□ Design    ↑↓    ⊡ XAML
⊟ <Window x:Class="WPFClient.Window1"
     xmlns="http://schemas.microsoft.com/winfx/2006/xaml/presentation"
     xmlns:x="http://schemas.microsoft.com/winfx/2006/xaml"
     Title="WPF DataBinding With WCF Data" Height="176" Width="300">

        <StackPanel x:Name="spForm" Orientation="Vertical" Height="115">
        <StackPanel Orientation="Horizontal" Height="38">
            <TextBlock Text="StringValue: "></TextBlock>
            <TextBlock x:Name="tbStringValue" Text="{Binding Path=StringValue}"></TextBl
        </StackPanel>
        <StackPanel Orientation="Horizontal" Height="38">
            <TextBlock Text="BoolValue: "></TextBlock>
            <CheckBox x:Name="cbBooleanValue" IsChecked="{Binding Path=BoolValue}"></Ch
        </StackPanel>
        <Button x:Name="btnGetData" Content="GetData" Click="btnGetData_Click" Height="3
        </StackPanel>

 <!-- </Window> -->
```

As the previous screenshot shows, all the three key UI elements are organized by
StackPanel so that they can be displayed vertically on the entire window. Also, the
tbStringValue and cbBooleanValue elements have both been associated with
a data binding expression so that they will populate the corresponding property from
the DataContext object in their container UI element.

2. Bind service-returned data to the WPF UI elements.

   After defining the XAML template, we need to add data binding code so that the
   data objects retrieved from the WCF service can be bound to the UI elements. Our
   sample application will use a button click event to perform the data binding task.
   The following code snippet shows the entire code for retrieving WCF data and binding
   them to WPF UI elements:

```
private void btnGetData_Click(object sender, RoutedEventArgs e)
{
    TestProxy.Service1Client client = new
                TestProxy.Service1Client();

    TestProxy.CompositeType ct = client.GetDataUsingDataContract(
                new TestProxy.CompositeType()
                { BoolValue = true, StringValue = "TestString" }
                );

    spForm.DataContext = ct;
}
```

As the btnGetData_Click handler shows, the WCF service operation returns a
composite data object, which contains a string property and a boolean property. And
this composite object is bound to the spForm UI element through the DataContext
property.

How it works...

As the button click event handler in the previous section shows, we can assign WCF service-returned data objects to the `DataContext` property of any existing WPF UI elements so that the data objects become visible (for data binding) to any other sub UI elements nested in the container element. And WPF uses the following data binding expression to locate the exact data member for populating values on the UI element.

```
{Binding Path= [Property Name]}
```

There's more...

For more information about WPF UI data binding, you can have a look at the WPF data binding reference in the MSDN library.

> ▸ *Data Binding (WPF)*
>
>   `http://msdn.microsoft.com/en-us/library/ms750612.aspx`

See also

> ▸ *Complete source code for this recipe can be found in the* `\Chapter 6\recipe1\` *folder*

Returning ReadOnlyCollection data

It is quite common to return a collection of data objects in a WCF service operation. However, sometimes we need to return a list of objects that are stored in the `ReadOnlyCollection<T>` type instance. This cannot be done directly, since `ReadOnlyCollection<T>` is not supported by the WCF `DataContractSerializer`. To make a WCF service operation return an `ReadOnlyCollection<T>` collection, we need to perform some customization on the `OperationContract`.

How to do it...

To return `ReadOnlyCollection<T>` collection instances, we need to modify our WCF service operation's `OperationContract`—the return type should be changed to use a base/generic Collection type other than `ReadOnlyCollection<T>`. For example, in our sample service, we use `ICollection<T>` as the return value type in the service operation that will return instance of `ReadOnlyCollection<T>`:

```
[OperationContract]
        ICollection<CompositeType> GetDataCollection();
    public ICollection<CompositeType> GetDataCollection()
```

```
{
    var objs = new CompositeType[]{
        new CompositeType{ BoolValue=true, StringValue="CT1"},
        new CompositeType{ BoolValue=true, StringValue="CT2"},
        new CompositeType{ BoolValue=true, StringValue="CT3"}
    };
    ReadOnlyCollection<CompositeType> roCol = new
                      ReadOnlyCollection<CompositeType>(objs);


    return roCol;
}
```

As shown in the `GetDataCollection` operation, we have defined the return value type as a `ICollection<T>` base type. So, we can directly return an instance of `ReadOnlyCollection<T>` without explicitly performing type converting.

How it works...

Data objects transferred (as parameters or return value) will be serialized from a .NET object into message content at the sender side, and deserialized back to objects on the other side. By default, WCF uses `DataContractSerializer` and the serialization focuses on type/class contract format instead of business/application logic (such as `ReadOnly`, singleton access, and so on). Therefore, we can sometimes return complex type instances as the type of their base class/interface and reconstruct them into their original type at the receiving side. This can help reduce the complexity of types that will be transferred over WCF communication.

The following code snippet shows the client code, which will accept the generic `ICollection<T>`-based return value and convert it back to `ReadOnlyCollection<T>`;

```
private static void CallService()
{
    DataSVC.Service1Client client = new DataSVC.Service1Client();

    ReadOnlyCollection<DataSVC.CompositeType> roCol = new
                      ReadOnlyCollection<DataSVC.CompositeType>(
                      client.GetDataCollection()
                      );
    foreach (DataSVC.CompositeType ct in roCol)
    {
        Console.WriteLine("String:{0}, Bool:{1}", ct.StringValue,
                  ct.BoolValue);
    }
}
```

▸ *Complete source code for this recipe can be found in the* \Chapter 6\recipe2\ *folder*

Using raw XML as an operation parameter

WCF service operation calls are transferred as SOAP messages (of XML format) over the transport layer. These kinds of SOAP XML messages are automatically generated via the WCF message/data serialization system. In addition to this, we can also explicitly return custom data of **raw XML** format.

How to do it...

To return raw XML format data, the simplest way is using a .NET built-in XML data type, such as System.Xml types or LINQ to XML types. In our sample service, we use the XElement type of LINQ to XML to return some custom XML data in service operation.

The following code shows the ServiceContract of the sample service:

```
[ServiceContract]
public interface IService1
{
    [OperationContract]
    XElement GetXmlData();
}
```

In the implementation code of the service operation, we directly construct an XElement instance and return it to the client (see the Service1 class shown as follows):

```
public class Service1 : IService1
{
    public XElement GetXmlData()
    {
        var xml = XElement.Parse(

                @"<root>
                    <items>
                        <item id='001'>item 1</item>
                        <item id='002'>item 2</item>
                    </items>
                </root>"
            );

        return xml;
    }
}
```

How it works...

For data parameters or return values of .NET XML types, the WCF runtime will directly embed them as XML format inside the entire SOAP request/response message. This is done without performing XML encoding/escaping (like what it did for normal string parameters). The following screenshot shows the response SOAP message of our sample service operation, which returns an XElement instance.

```
<s:Envelope xmlns:s="http://schemas.xmlsoap.org/soap/envelope/">
  <s:Body>
    <GetXmlDataResponse xmlns="http://tempuri.org/">
      <GetXmlDataResult>
        <root xmlns="">
          <items>
            <item id="001">item 1</item>
            <item id="002">item 2</item>
          </items>
        </root>
      </GetXmlDataResult>
    </GetXmlDataResponse>
  </s:Body>
</s:Envelope>
```

There's more...

When trying to transfer raw XML data in a WCF service operation, sometimes people will directly use a String parameter to hold the XML document/element content. This is not recommended, since a String parameter in a WCF service operation will be encoded by the runtime so as to avoid including XML syntax tags (which will potentially break the SOAP XML envelope). Therefore, if we try to send raw XML through a String type parameter, the XML is actually in escaped format instead of real XML format in the underlying SOAP message.

See also

▶ *Complete source code for this recipe can be found in the*\Chapter 6\recipe3\ *folder*

Returning a DataTable/DataSet in a service operation

A very frequently asked question in a WCF Data transfer service is how to return a **DataTable/DataSet** in a WCF service operation. The DataTable class is a member of the System.Data namespace within the .NET framework class library. You can create and use a DataTable independently or as a member of a DataSet, and DataTable objects can also be used in conjunction with other .NET framework objects.

There are various possible solutions for DataTable or DataSet transferring in a WCF service; we will go through the most common ones in this recipe.

Getting ready

In our sample service, we will demonstrate several means to return data from a DataTable to client consumers. The sample DataTable consists of three simple columns, as shown in the following screenshot.

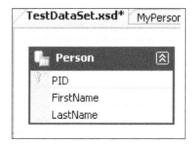

How to do it...

Let's go through three commonly used methods for returning data from ADO.NET DataTable/DataSet objects

> ► Directly return a DataTable within a DataSet container.
>
>   If both the WCF service and client sides are built upon .NET Framework 3.x or 4.0, then there are no interoperability issues between them. We can directly use a DataSet as service operation argument or return type, and return our DataTable through a DataSet instance as the container. The following code snippet shows the operation that returns a DataTable through a container DataSet instance:
>
>   ```
>   // OperationContract definition
>   [OperationContract]
>   DataSet GetDataTable();();
>   ```

```
// Operation implementation
public DataSet GetDataTable()
{
    DataTable dt = GetTestDataTable();

    DataSet ds = new DataSet();
    ds.Tables.Add(dt);

    return ds;
}
```

At the client side, we can directly access the returned DataTable from the `DataSet.` `Tables` collection.

▶ Convert a DataTable to a custom data object collection.

For a WCF data transfer service, it is recommended that we return data objects that are only focused on the data members we need to send, instead of any other function/code logic. Types like DataTable contain many non-data-specific features that are not quite efficient for being transferred in WCF service SOAP messages. Therefore, in many cases we can define custom types to represent DataTable rows and return an Array/List of such custom type instances instead. The `GetDataTableAsCustomCollection` operation in the following code snippet demonstrates how to do this:

```
// Return DataTable as custom data collection
  [OperationContract]
List<MyPerson> GetDataTableAsCustomCollection();
public List<MyPerson> GetDataTableAsCustomCollection()
{
    DataTable dt = GetTestDataTable();

    var persons = from row in dt.AsEnumerable()
                        select new MyPerson {
                            PID = (int)row["PID"],
                            FirstName = (string)row["FirstName"],
                            LastName = (string)row["LastName"] };

    return persons.ToList<MyPerson>();
}
```

▶ Return a DataTable as an XML document.

In the third recipe in this chapter, we have discussed how to return raw XML content in a WCF service operation. Since a .NET DataTable is fully compatible and convertible to XML format, we can convert the DataTable instance into an XML document and return it as raw XML data. The following `GetDataTableAsXML` operation demonstrates how to return the `PersonTable` as an `XElement` instance:

```
// OperationContract definition for operation that
//returns a DataTable as raw XML content
  [OperationContract]
XElement GetDataTableAsXML();

// Implementation of the GetDataTableAsXML //OperationContract
public System.Xml.Linq.XElement GetDataTableAsXML()
{
    DataTable dt = GetTestDataTable();

    StringWriter strwtr = new StringWriter();
    dt.WriteXml(strwtr);

    return XElement.Parse(strwtr.ToString());
}
```

Also, since XML is naturally interoperable, we can easily make our DataTable data accessible to other non-.NET client applications through the XML format.

See also

▶ *Using raw XML as an operation parameter*

▶ *Complete source code for this recipe can be found in the*`\Chapter 6\recipe4\` *folder*

Transferring binary data with MTOM encoding

For Web Services/WCF services that use SOAP XML as the natural message format, binary data in service operations will be transferred as the Base64-encoded string over the transport layer. This is not quite efficient for binary data transfer, as the encoded Base64 string will increase the data size compared to raw binary bytes. Fortunately, WCF supports the MTOM message encoding that can help transfer binary data as their raw bytes within a standard SOAP envelope.

In this recipe, we will use a sample service to demonstrate the steps necessary for applying MTOM message encoding for WCF service endpoints.

Getting ready

Most of the HTTP-based WCF built-in bindings support the MTOM encoding format. A detailed list is provided in the MSDN WCF Binding description at:

▶ System-Provided Bindings

http://msdn.microsoft.com/en-us/library/ms730879.aspx

How to do it...

1. Make ServiceContract MTOM ready.

    The first thing to do is to define a ServiceContract type, which is compatible with MTOM encoding. For ServiceContract or OperationContract, and the types used as parameters or return values, we need to make sure that they conform to the following two points:

    ❑ The method that is sending MTOM content can only receive or return classes that have the [MessageContract] attribute, not [DataContract], or *primitive* types.

    ❑ All the byte array properties must have a [MessageBodyMember] attribute, not [DataMember] nor [MessageHeader], and all the other properties must have a [MessageHeader] attribute.

    The following code snippet shows the sample OperationContract and the MessageContract type used as the return value of the operation:

    ```
    [OperationContract]
    DataMessage GetMixedData();


    [MessageContract(WrapperName="DataMessage", WrapperNamespace="urn:
    WCFTest:MTOM")]
    public class DataMessage
    {
        [MessageHeader]
        public string TextContent { get; set; }

        [MessageBodyMember]
        public byte[] ImageData { get; set; }
    }
    ```

    As we can see, the DataMessage type contains both a string member and a binary data member. Only the ImageData, which is of byte[] type, is marked with MessageBodyMemberAttribute.

2. Apply MTOM encoding on the target service endpoint through binding configuration.

In addition to defining an MTOM-ready Contract type, we also need to set the `messageEncoding` of our WCF service endpoint's binding to MTOM, as shown in the following screenshot:

```xml
    <service behaviorConfiguration="MTOMService.MTOMServiceBehavior"
      name="MTOMService.MTOMService">
      <endpoint address="" binding="wsHttpBinding" bindingConfiguration="MTOMBinding"
                contract="MTOMService.IMTOMService">
      </endpoint>
      |
    </service>
  </services>

  <bindings>
    <wsHttpBinding>
      <binding name="MTOMBinding" messageEncoding="Mtom" >
        <security mode="None"></security>
      </binding>
    </wsHttpBinding>
  </bindings>
  </system.serviceModel>
</configuration>
```

See also

▸ *Complete source code for this recipe can be found in the* `\Chapter 6\recipe5\` *folder*

Specifying ServiceKnownType information in a programmatic way

WCF provides the `ServiceKnownType` feature for developers to declare all the custom types (which are not directly used as service operation parameters or return types) that will be sent as part of a WCF request/response object graph. However, the default declaration requires a developer to specify the `ServiceKnownType` statically in the source code. For example, the `IService1` `ServiceContract` in the following code snippet shows a sample `ServiceContract` that specifies a custom type `Circle` as an additional known type:

```csharp
[ServiceContract]
[ServiceKnownType(typeof(Circle))]
public interface IService1
{
    [OperationContract]
    ShapeBase GetShape(string name);

}
```

In some cases, we will need to specify multiple ServiceKnownType for our WCF service and those types may be changeable. Thus, it would be useful to provide such types of ServiceKnownType in a programmatic way so that developers or service administrators can conveniently configure the ServiceKnownType without the need to recompile the service code.

How to do it...

In order to specify ServiceKnownType programmatically, we need to use the constructor overload of the ServiceKnownTypeAttribute class, which can let us specify a custom type and method name for supplying multiple ServiceKnownType.

The custom type needs to define a static method that accepts a parameter of the ICustomAttributeProvider interface and returns an instance of List<Type> type. The List<Type> instance represents the object in which we are able to store all the ServiceKnownType we want to apply on our WCF service. The following code snippet shows a sample ServiceContract IService1, which loads several ServiceKnownType from the KnownTypeHelper.GetKnownTypes method.

```
[ServiceContract]
[ServiceKnownType("GetKnownTypes", typeof(KnownTypeHelper))]
public interface IService1
{
}

public class KnownTypeHelper
{
    public static IEnumerable<Type> GetKnownTypes(System.Reflection.
ICustomAttributeProvider provider)
    {
        string strTypes =
                ConfigurationManager.AppSettings["KnownTypeList"];
        var lstTypes =
                (
                from strType in strTypes.Split(';')
                select Type.GetType(strType)
                ).ToList();
        return lstTypes;
    }
}
```

The `KnownTypeHelper.GetKnownTypes` method simply looks up the `KnownTypeList` item in the `App.config` file and parses out all the `ServiceKnownType` from the item content. Whenever developers or service hosts want to change the `ServiceKnownType`, they can simply modify the `appSettings` entries (as shown in the following screenshot) without recompiling the `ServiceContract` code.

```
<appSettings>
  <add key="KnownTypeList" value="TestService.Circle;TestService.Rectangle"/>
</appSettings>
  <connectionStrings/>
```

How it works...

By supplying `ServiceKnownType` on the WCF `ServiceContract`, the auto-generated WCF service metadata will include those `ServiceKnownType` in the XML schema published by the metadata. In our sample `ServiceContract` mentioned in the previous section, the auto-generated WSDL document will include a schema that contains the XML complex type definition of the `Circle` and `Rectangle` classes (shown in the next screenshot). Thus, whenever the WCF service consumers generate WCF client proxy types from the metadata, those `ServiceKnownType` will also be detected and have corresponding types generated together with the service proxy classes.

```xml
<?xml version="1.0" encoding="utf-8" ?>
<xs:schema elementFormDefault="qualified" targetNamespace="http://sche
    xmlns:xs="http://www.w3.org/2001/XMLSchema" xmlns:tns="http://s
 <xs:complexType name="Circle">
  <xs:complexContent mixed="false">
   <xs:extension base="tns:ShapeBase">
    <xs:sequence>
      <xs:element minOccurs="0" name="Radius" type="xs:int" />
    </xs:sequence>
   </xs:extension>
  </xs:complexContent>
 </xs:complexType>
 <xs:element name="Circle" nillable="true" type="tns:Circle" />
 <xs:complexType name="ShapeBase">
  <xs:sequence>
    <xs:element minOccurs="0" name="Name" nillable="true" type="xs:stri
  </xs:sequence>
 </xs:complexType>
 <xs:element name="ShapeBase" nillable="true" type="tns:ShapeBase" />
 <xs:complexType name="Rectangle">
  <xs:complexContent mixed="false">
   <xs:extension base="tns:ShapeBase">
    <xs:sequence>
      <xs:element minOccurs="0" name="Length" type="xs:int" />
      <xs:element minOccurs="0" name="Width" type="xs:int" />
    </xs:sequence>
   </xs:extension>
  </xs:complexContent>
 </xs:complexType>
 <xs:element name="Rectangle" nillable="true" type="tns:Rectangle" />
</xs:schema>
```

See also

▶ *Complete source code for this recipe can be found in the* `\Chapter 6\recipe6\` *folder*

Using XmlSerializer for custom data serialization

When transferring custom data objects in a WCF service operation (as parameters or return values), the runtime will serialize the objects into XML elements, which are embedded in the underlying SOAP XML message. By default, WCF runtime uses the `DataContractSerializer` for serializing the .NET objects into XML or binary content. And the `DataContractSerializer` does have many advantages for `DataContract` serialization as compared to the traditional XmlSerializer used in ASMX Web Service. However, sometimes we will prefer using the XmlSerializer for data object serialization in a WCF service. For example, when talking to some non-.NET platform, like a Java-based service or client, using XmlSerializer will help us to gain more control over the serialization/deserialization between a .NET object and XML content. This is to produce a compatible `DataContract` between service and client more conveniently.

In this recipe, we will use a sample WCF service that returns a custom data object, to demonstrate how to switch the WCF runtime to use XmlSerializer.

How to do it...

1. Switch the `DataContract` type to use XML serialization formatting attributes.

   First, we need to decorate our custom `DataContract` types (which will be transferred as parameters in the WCF service operation) with certain XML serialization attributes
   (see the `SimpleData` type in the following code snippet):

```
[DataContract(Namespace = "urn:WCFTest:DataContract",
  Name = "SimpleData_DataContract")]
[XmlRoot(Namespace = "urn:WCFTest:XML",
  ElementName = "SimpleData_XML")]
public class SimpleData
{
    [DataMember(Name = "ID_DataContract")]
    [XmlElement(ElementName = "ID_XML")]
    public int ID { get; set; }

    [DataMember(Name = "Subject_DataContract")]
    [XmlElement(ElementName = "Subject_XML")]
    public string Subject { get; set; }
```

```
    [DataMember(Name = "Enabled_DataContract")]
    [XmlElement(ElementName = "Enabled_XML")]
    public bool Enabled { get; set; }
}
```

To get a better view of the effect when a WCF service can easily switch between different serializers, we will also apply `DataContractSerializer`-specific attributes on the `SimpleData` type.

2. Apply the `XmlSerializerFormat` attribute on the target `ServiceContract` type.

    After defining an XML serialization ready type, we can apply it in our service operation and, more importantly, add the `XmlSerializerFormatAttribute` on the `ServiceContract` type. This is to inform the WCF runtime to use XmlSerializer instead of the default DataContractSerializer (see the following `IService1` sample `ServiceContract`).

```
[ServiceContract]
 [XmlSerializerFormat]
public interface IService1
{
    [OperationContract]
    SimpleData GetData();
}
```

How it works...

As our sample service code shows, we have applied both `DataContractSerializer` and XmlSerializer formatting attributes on the custom type. This means that the `SimpleData` type is ready for both `DataContractSerializer` and XmlSerializer. When using the `DataContractSerializer` (default), the WCF runtime will generate the SOAP XML message as shown in the following screenshot. The `DataContractSerializer` generated message contains the corresponding XML element of `SimpleData` type, which conforms to the settings in the `DataContract` serialization attributes.

```
<s:Envelope xmlns:s="http://schemas.xmlsoap.org/soap/envelope/">
  <s:Body>
    <GetDataResponse xmlns="http://tempuri.org/">
      <GetDataResult xmlns:a="urn:WCFTest:DataContract" xmlns:i="h
        <a:Enabled_DataContract>true</a:Enabled_DataContract>
        <a:ID_DataContract>1</a:ID_DataContract>
        <a:Subject_DataContract>Test Data Object</a:Subject_DataCo
      </GetDataResult>
    </GetDataResponse>
  </s:Body>
</s:Envelope>
```

After applying the `XmlSerializerFormatAttribute` on the `ServiceContract`, the WCF runtime will serialize the `SimpleData` object following the XML serialization settings. The XmlSerializer-generated SOAP message is shown in the following screenshot :

```
<s:Envelope xmlns:s="http://schemas.xmlsoap.org/soap/envelope/">
  <s:Body xmlns:xsi="http://www.w3.org/2001/XMLSchema-instance" xmlns:xsd="
    <GetDataResponse xmlns="http://tempuri.org/">
      <GetDataResult>
        <ID_XML xmlns="urn:WCFTest:XML">1</ID_XML>
        <Subject_XML xmlns="urn:WCFTest:XML">Test Data Object</Subject_XML>
        <Enabled_XML xmlns="urn:WCFTest:XML">true</Enabled_XML>
      </GetDataResult>
    </GetDataResponse>
  </s:Body>
</s:Envelope>
```

See also

▸ *Complete source code for this recipe can be found in the* `\Chapter 6\recipe7\` *folder*

7
Security

In this chapter, we will cover:

- ▸ Setting up ad hoc Windows authentication over plain HTTP
- ▸ Getting an authenticated client identity in a service operation
- ▸ Using username authentication with an ASP.NET membership provider
- ▸ Sending a clear text username token over unsecured HTTP transport
- ▸ Using transport and message security at the same time
- ▸ Authorizing through declarative role-based access control
- ▸ Impersonating with a client caller identity
- ▸ Adding multiple tokens in a service request (`supportingToken`)
- ▸ Supplying dedicated credentials for firewall or proxy authentication
- ▸ Securing a dynamic SoapHeader

Introduction

Security is a big topic in distributed communication applications. When the client consumers call a service operation through an intranet or the Internet, it is necessary to consider how we will secure the communication between the two sides, or how we can make sure that we are talking to the correct service or the correct client consumers.

WCF provides a lot of built-in features for developers to address all these kinds of problems in service application development. The most commonly used WCF security features include authentication, authorization, and message protection (signing and encrypting).

In this chapter, we will use 10 recipes to demonstrate some useful security scenarios in WCF service development. The first five recipes will focus on various authentication use cases, including Windows authentication, username authentication, and so on. These are followed by two recipes that introduce some role-based authorization and identity impersonation cases. In addition, there are also some special topics in the last three recipes—the multiple token recipe shows how to use the `SupportingToken` feature, the supplying dedicated credentials recipe shows how we can resolve WCF client authentication across an intermediate web proxy, and the securing dynamic SoapHeader recipe extends the *Adding a dynamic SoapHeader into a message* recipe in *Chapter 5*.

Setting up ad hoc Windows authentication over plain HTTP

WCF supports various authentication types and Windows authentication is a common authentication method used in existing distributed communication components on the Windows platform. A very common use case is to enable Windows authentication at transport layer without an additional secure connection like SSL (just like what the traditional ASMX Web Service uses).

In this recipe, we will demonstrate how to apply Windows authentication for a WCF service endpoint using plain HTTP as the transport protocol, without additional security.

How to do it...

1. Make the service endpoint use `BasicHttpBinding`.

    The first thing to do is choose `BasicHttpBinding` as the binding type of our WCF service endpoint. Also, in the binding configuration, we need to specify the security mode as `TransportCredentialOnly` and `clientCredentialType` as `Windows`. The following screenshot shows the `app.config` section of our sample service endpoint.

    ```xml
    <services>
      <service name="WCFServiceApp.Service1" >
        <endpoint name="simpleHttpEndpoint" address=""
                  binding="basicHttpBinding" bindingConfiguration="AdhocWindowsHttpBinding"
                  contract="WCFServiceApp.IService1" ></endpoint>
      </service>
    </services>

    <bindings>
      <basicHttpBinding>
        <binding name="AdhocWindowsHttpBinding">
          <security mode="TransportCredentialOnly">
            <transport clientCredentialType="Windows" ></transport>
          </security>
        </binding>
      </basicHttpBinding>
    </bindings>
    </system.serviceModel>
    ```

2. Adjust the Windows authentication settings in IIS server.

    For a WCF service, if we use IIS as the hosting environment, we also need to apply proper configuration on the application virtual directory in which we will deploy the service endpoints. For our ad hoc Windows authentication service, it is necessary to turn on the Windows authentication and disable anonymous access on the IIS virtual directory so that the Windows authentication on the WCF endpoint can work correctly. All these configurations can be done through the IIS virtual directory settings in the management console. The following screenshot shows the configuration manager UI of IIS 7.

How it works...

After the service endpoint has been properly configured as ad hoc Windows authentication mode, the client consumer can use the generated proxy class or `ChannelFactory` to invoke the target service operations. Also, either the service proxy or `ChannelFactory` provides the `ClientCredential` property for the caller to supply their Windows credentials (see the following code snippet):

```
static void CallService()
{
    TestProxy.Service1Client client = new TestProxy.Service1Client();

    client.ClientCredentials.Windows.ClientCredential =
    System.Net.CredentialCache.DefaultNetworkCredentials;

    Console.WriteLine( client.GetData(11));
}
```

▶ *Complete source code for this recipe can be found in the* `\Chapter 7\recipe1\` *folder*

Getting an authenticated client identity in a service operation

WCF provides various built-in authentication methods either at the transport layer or at the message layer. The client consumer can use a WCF service proxy or `ChannelFactory` to supply certain client credentials to the service. The following MSDN reference lists all the built-in credential types supported by WCF:

▶ Selecting a Credential Type

`http://msdn.microsoft.com/en-us/library/ms733836.aspx`

After the service request passes authentication, a valid identity will be associated with each service-operation execution context and the service operation code can retrieve the identity information within the operation context.

This recipe will show you how to programmatically retrieve the client authenticated identity information in service operation code.

How to do it...

WCF runtime provides an `OperationContext` object associated with each request processing so that the developers can access some operation/request context-specific data from it. For example, we can access and manipulate SOAP headers or other underlying transport protocol properties through `OperationContext`. For operation authentication, the authenticated identity is also accessible through `OperationContext`, and the minor difference is that we need to get the identity by a `ServiceSecurityContext` member of the `OperationContext` object. The `ServiceSecurityContext` type contains several member properties, which represent security information transferred from the client side.

Name	Description
Anonymous	Returns an instance of the `ServiceSecurityContext` class that contains an empty collection of claims, identities, and other context data usually used to represent an anonymous party.
AuthorizationContext	Gets the authorization information for an instance of this class. The `AuthorizationContext` contains a collection of `ClaimSet` that the application can interrogate, and retrieve the information of the party.

Name	Description
AuthorizationPolicies	Gets the collection of policies associated with an instance of this class.
Current	Gets the current `ServiceSecurityContext`.
IsAnonymous	Gets a value that indicates whether the current client has provided credentials to the service.
PrimaryIdentity	Gets the primary identity associated with the current setting.
WindowsIdentity	Gets the Windows identity of the current setting.

The `WindowsIdentity` and `PrimaryIdentity` properties are the corresponding members which contain the authentication identity information of the client service caller. We can inspect the identity details such as identity name or authentication type from the two properties. The following screenshot shows the code for obtaining main authentication identity information from the `PrimaryIdentity` property.

```
// Retrieve client identity information for any kind of authentication type
public string GenericIdentityOperation()
{
    return string.Format(
        "Client Identity: {0}, Auth Type:{1}",
        ServiceSecurityContext.Current.PrimaryIdentity.Name,
        ServiceSecurityContext.Current.PrimaryIdentity.AuthenticationType
        );
}
```

Likewise, we can use the `Windows Identity` property to get the Windows security identity associated with the current operation call (as shown in the following screenshot):

```
// Retrieve windows identity of the authenticated client caller
public string WindowsIdentityOperation()
{
    return string.Format(
        "Windows Identity: {0}",
        ServiceSecurityContext.Current.WindowsIdentity.Name
        );
}
```

See also

▸ *Complete source code for this recipe can be found in the* `\Chapter 7\recipe2\` *folder*

Using username authentication with an ASP. NET membership provider

WCF supports username authentication, which requires the service caller to supply a username/password token for validation. By default, if we simply turn on username authentication at the message layer, the WCF service runtime will use the Windows SAM database to validate the username/password credentials. However, we can also use our custom database or account storage to perform the validation, and if you are familiar with ASP.NET web application development, you will find it quite convenient to directly use the ASP. NET membership database for WCF username authentication.

In this recipe, we will show you how to enable username authentication against the ASP.NET membership database for a WCF service. And we will use a web application for hosting our sample WCF service which uses the ASP.NET membership database for username token validation.

How to do it...

1. Enable an ASP.NET membership provider and user accounts.

    The first thing to do is enable an ASP.NET membership provider in our web application. The following screenshot shows the complete membership provider configuration fragment, which includes the provider and connectionString section. The membership provider will reference the connectionString through the `connectionStringName` attribute. For our sample service, we use the default SQL Express database file as the account database. Also, our user-defined membership provider needs to be set as `defaultProvider` so that the ASP.NET and WCF application will use it automatically (see the `defaultProvider` attribute in the next screenshot).

```
<system.web>
  <compilation debug="true" targetFramework="4.0" />

  <membership defaultProvider="MyMembershipProvider" >
    <providers>
      <clear />
      <add
        name="MyMembershipProvider"
        type="System.Web.Security.SqlMembershipProvider"
        connectionStringName="MyASPNETMembershipDB"
        applicationName="MembershipAndRoleProviderSample"
        enablePasswordRetrieval="false"
        enablePasswordReset="false"
        requiresQuestionAndAnswer="false"
        requiresUniqueEmail="false"
        passwordFormat="Hashed" />
    </providers>
  </membership>
```

After enabling the proper membership provider, we need to add some user accounts for testing. In our sample service, we use the ASP.NET web application `Global.asax` component to initialize some test accounts; the initialize code will add a predefined account named `user1` (see the `Global` class in the following screenshot).

```
public class Global : System.Web.HttpApplication
{
    protected void Application_Start(object sender, EventArgs e)
    {
        if (null == Membership.GetUser("user1"))
            Membership.CreateUser("user1", "user1@password");
    }
```

2. Configure our WCF service to use a membership provider for username authentication.

   Our sample service will use `wsHttpBinding` along with a username authentication type as shown in the following screenshot:

```
<bindings>
  <wsHttpBinding>
    <binding>
      <security mode="Message">
        <message clientCredentialType="UserName"/>
      </security>
    </binding>
  </wsHttpBinding>
```

Although we have registered our custom membership provider and added test user accounts, WCF username authentication will not automatically choose ASP.NET membership as the repository for validating the username account. To make the WCF service username authentication validation associated with our predefined membership provider, we need to manipulate the `serviceBehavior` of the WCF service. The following screenshot shows the serviceBehavior fragment that makes our WCF service use the membership provider for username authentication validation.

```
<serviceBehaviors>
  <behavior>
    <!-- enable membership provider for authentication-->
    <serviceCredentials>
      <serviceCertificate storeLocation="LocalMachine" storeName="My"
                           x509FindType="FindByThumbprint"
                           findValue="E4C6FF05123EDAE4368A39588714562BD4FCDEF8"/

      <userNameAuthentication
        userNamePasswordValidationMode="MembershipProvider"
        membershipProviderName="MyMembershipProvider"
        />
    </serviceCredentials>
```

As we can see, the `userNameAuthentication` element has two attributes defined. The `userNamePasswordValidationMode` controls what we use for username validation; here it is set to `MembershipProvider`. And the `membershipProviderName` further identifies which membership provider is selected as the one that will be called by the WCF username validation code.

How it works...

With the membership provider and WCF service correctly configured, any requests from the client (with a username token attached in the message) will be validated through the membership provider. For our sample service, the client caller should provide the correct account credentials, which are stored in the membership provider database at the service side (see the following code snippet):

```
private static void CallService()
{
    TestProxy.Service1Client client = new TestProxy.Service1Client();

    client.ClientCredentials.UserName.UserName = "user1";
    client.ClientCredentials.UserName.Password = "user1@password";

    Console.WriteLine(client.GetData(11));
}
```

See also

▶ *Complete source code for this recipe can be found in the* `\Chapter 7\recipe3\` *folder*

Sending a clear text username token over unsecured HTTP transport

For a WCF service endpoint that uses the username authentication type, it requires, by default, the service endpoint to secure the service channel through either message-layer or transport-layer security. In other words, we need to either use the HTTPS transport protocol or message-layer signing and encryption to make the service endpoint able to transfer a username token. However, for some very special cases, we might need to send clear text username/password credentials (for username authentication) over an unsecured HTTP channel. Though this is not supported out of the box, there still exists some workarounds that can help us achieve this. Yaron Naveh has created `ClearUsernameBinding`, which successfully achieves this goal. Here we will demonstrate how to apply this `ClearUsernameBinding` in our own WCF HTTP service.

Getting ready

The full source code of `ClearUsernameBinding` and samples can be found at the following location:

 ▶ Introducing WCF ClearUsernameBinding

   `http://webservices20.blogspot.com/2008/11/introducing-wcf-clearusernamebinding.html`

How to do it...

Now, let's go through the detailed steps about how we can apply `ClearUsernameBinding` in our service.

1. Register `ClearUsernameBinding`.

   To use the `ClearUsernameBinding`, we need to first add a reference to the `ClearUsernameBinding.dll` assembly in the projects that will host the WCF service and run the WCF client. WCF provides various extension points that allow developers to extend the existing bindings or binding elements. The next screenshot shows the configuration fragment that registers `ClearUsernameBinding` in the `app.config` file.

```
<extensions>
  <bindingExtensions>
    <add name="clearUsernameBinding"
         type="WebServices20.BindingExtenions.ClearUsernameCollectionElement, Clear
  </bindingExtensions>
</extensions>


/system.serviceModel>
```

2. Configure the service endpoint to use `ClearUsernameBinding`.

   The next step is to make our WCF service endpoint use `ClearUsernameBinding`. Since we have already defined the `ClearUsernameBinding` extension, what we need to do is to just change the `binding` attribute of the service endpoint to `clearUsernameBinding`.

```
<services>
    <service name="HttpServiceApp.HelloWorld">
        <endpoint address=""
                binding="clearUsernameBinding"
                bindingConfiguration="myClearUsernameBinding"
                contract="HttpServiceApp.IHelloWorld">
        <identity>
            <dns value="localhost" />
        </identity>
        </endpoint>
```

3. Use a custom `UsernamePasswordValidator` for testing.

    By default, WCF will validate a username token against the Windows account system. To override this in our sample service, we create a test `UsernamePasswordValidator` that will allow any account from the client to pass validation. The custom `UsernamePasswordValidator` can be enabled through the `<userNameAuthentication>` element in the `<serviceCredentials>` setting, as shown in the following screenshot.

```
<serviceCredentials>
  <userNameAuthentication
    userNamePasswordValidationMode="Custom"
    customUserNamePasswordValidatorType="HttpServiceApp.TestUsernamePasswordValidator,
                    />
</serviceCredentials>
```

Since this custom `UsernamePasswordValidator` is for testing purposes, we will not put any real validation code logic in it. The code snippet in the following screenshot shows the implementation code of our test username password validator, which simply returns so as to pass the validation.

```
public class TestUsernamePasswordValidator : UserNamePasswordValidator
{
    public override void Validate(string userName, string password)
    {
        // Do nothing
    }
}
```

How it works...

To consume the WCF service that uses `ClearUsernameBinding`, we can use a programmatically generated `ChannelFactory` instance, as shown in the following code snippet:

```
private static void CallService()
{
    ClearUsernameBinding binding = new ClearUsernameBinding();
    binding.SetMessageVersion(MessageVersion.Soap11);

    ChannelFactory<HttpServiceApp.IHelloWorld> factory =
                new ChannelFactory<HttpServiceApp.IHelloWorld>(
                        binding,
                        "http://ipv4.fiddler:8732/HelloWorld/"
                        );
    factory.Credentials.UserName.UserName = "WCFUser";
    factory.Credentials.UserName.Password = "Password";
```

```
    HttpServiceApp.IHelloWorld helloproxy = factory.CreateChannel();

    helloproxy.Hello();
}
```

As the service endpoint is using a plain HTTP transport channel (without SSL) and no message security, we can use network trace tools like Fiddler to capture the SOAP message that contains the username token in clear text format (shown in the next screenshot).

```
<s:Envelope xmlns:s="http://www.w3.org/2003/05/soap-envelope" xml
  <s:Header>
    <o:Security s:mustUnderstand="1" xmlns:o="http://docs.oasis-o
      <u:Timestamp u:Id="_0">...</u:Timestamp>
      <o:UsernameToken u:Id="uuid-42d63cd4-6767-48c8-a652-a87c026
        <o:Username>WCFUser</o:Username>
        <o:Password>Password01!</o:Password>
      </o:UsernameToken>
    </o:Security>
  </s:Header>
  <s:Body>
    <Hello xmlns="http://tempuri.org/"/>
  </s:Body>
```

See also

► *Using username authentication with an ASP.NET membership provider*

► *Complete source code for this recipe can be found in the* `\Chapter 7\recipe4\` *folder*

Using transport and message security at the same time

WCF supports both transport- and message-layer security. By using transport-layer security, the SOAP message of our WCF service operation is completely unsecured, and the transport protocol (such as HTTPS, TCP) helps to secure the data transferred over them. By using message-layer security, the SOAP message itself is secured and the WCF runtime needs to perform the message-secure processing. Generally, we suggest that to developers that using either of the transport- or message-layer security is enough and this is also what the built-in system bindings allow us to do. However, it is still necessary to apply secure protection at both layers in some cases, especially when talking to some non-WCF service platforms. This recipe will use a simple HTTP-based WCF service to demonstrate how to apply secure protection at both transport and message layer.

How to do it...

Since built-in system bindings only support enabling security at one layer (either the transport or the message layer), what we can do to enable security at both layers is to leverage the custom binding. Here we will use a sample service over HTTP transport to demonstrate the scenario. The security settings we use at both layers are as follows:

- ▸ Transport layer: HTTPS/SSL channel
- ▸ Message layer: Username authentication secured by certificate

We use the `app.config` file to define the custom binding stack. The following screenshot shows the custom binding with all the necessary binding elements defined.

```
<bindings>
    <customBinding>
        <binding name="usernameWithTransportAndMessageBinding">
            <textMessageEncoding/>
            <security authenticationMode="UserNameForCertificate" />
            <httpsTransport  />
        </binding>
```

As we can see, the `<httpsTransport>` binding element represents the HTTPS-based transport channel and the `<security>` element represents the secure channel at the message layer.

When consuming this service, the client caller needs to take care of both the HTTPS channel at the transport layer and the X.509 certificate-based username authentication at the message layer.

How it works...

By turning on the WCF message-logging feature, we can get the underlying message at the message layer. The SOAP message at the service layer is secured via the username authentication token and X.509 certificate. The following screenshot shows the raw SOAP message captured at the WCF service layer.

```
MessageLogTraceRecord>
 <s:Envelope xmlns:s="http://www.w3.org/2003/05/soap-envelope" xmlns:a="ht
   <s:Header>
     <a:Action s:mustUnderstand="1" u:Id="_4">http://tempuri.org/ICalcService
     <a:MessageID u:Id="_5">urn:uuid:ba04be8d-587f-4922-9806-239d8f72e6d
     <a:ReplyTo u:Id="_6">
       <a:Address>http://www.w3.org/2005/08/addressing/anonymous</a:A
     </a:ReplyTo>
     <a:To s:mustUnderstand="1" u:Id="_7">https://stch179369:7033/CalcServi
     <o:Security s:mustUnderstand="1" xmlns:o="http://docs.oasis-open.org/wss
       <u:Timestamp u:Id="uuid-e054c09e-eb48-446d-9518-80229fb0d1cc-2">
         <u:Created>2010-04-17T11:14:53.809Z</u:Created>
         <u:Expires>2010-04-17T11:19:53.809Z</u:Expires>
       </u:Timestamp>
       <e:EncryptedKey Id="uuid-e054c09e-eb48-446d-9518-80229fb0d1cc-1"
         <e:EncryptionMethod Algorithm="http://www.w3.org/2001/04/xmlenc#
```

At the transport layer, the message is further signed and encrypted by the SSL/TLS channel. The next screenshot shows the transport message information captured in Fiddler.

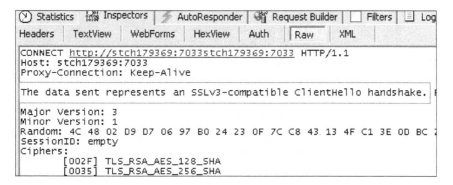

See also

▶ *Defining a CustomBinding without a timestamp header* in *Chapter 2*

▶ *Complete source code for this recipe can be found in the* \Chapter 7\recipe5\ *folder*

Authorizing through declarative role-based access control

Role-based authorization is a commonly used access control approach in .NET-based applications. Developers can either use code (programmatically) or apply attributes (declaratively) so as to define particular access control rules on .NET code based on the current security identity principal. For WCF service operations, it also naturally supports role-based authorization and access control, and it is quite straightforward to add declarative style role-based access control over service operations without writing any code.

How to do it...

Here we will go through the steps for applying declarative style role-based access control for WCF service operations.

1. Choose a proper authentication type for the service.

    The first step is choosing a client authentication type for our service operations. We can choose any kind of authentication type as long as it will populate a valid security principal/identity in the server-side service operation context.

Let's use `UserName` authentication as shown in the following screenshot:

```
<bindings>
  <wsHttpBinding>
    <binding name="usernameBinding" >
      <security mode="Message">
        <message clientCredentialType="UserName"/>
      </security>
    </binding>
```

2. Define access control rules for service operations.

   After selecting the proper authentication type, we need to define the access control rules on our service operation. To do this, we can directly leverage `System.Security.Permissions.PrincipalPermissionAttribute`. The following code snippet shows the sample service operation that uses `PrincipalPermissionAttribute` to demand a certain security identity/role requirement from the client caller.

```
public class RoleBasedService : IRoleBasedService
{
    [PrincipalPermission(SecurityAction.Demand,
                     Name="servername\\WCFAdmin")]
    public void DoWork()
    {
        // Requires WCFAdmin account to do the work
    }
}
```

   As the code shows, only a caller with a WCFAdmin account can correctly access this operation. There are also many other properties on `PrincipalPermissionAttribute` that can help further configuration access control settings (refer to the following table).

Name	Description
Action	Gets or sets a security action (inherited from `SecurityAttribute`).
Authenticated	Gets or sets a value indicating whether the current principal has been authenticated by the underlying role-based security provider.
Name	Gets or sets the name of the identity associated with the current principal.
Role	Gets or sets membership in a specified security role.
TypeId	When implemented in a derived class, gets a unique identifier for this attribute (inherited from the attribute).
Unrestricted	Gets or sets a value indicating whether full (unrestricted) permission to the resource protected by the attribute is declared (inherited from `SecurityAttribute`).

3. Supply correct credentials according to access requirements in the client application.

   At the client side, the caller just needs to supply the correct username token, which has the proper permission to access the operation being called (see the following code snippet).

```
TestProxy.RoleBasedServiceClient client = new
                    TestProxy.RoleBasedServiceClient();

client.ClientCredentials.UserName.UserName =
                    "machineName\\WCFAdmin";
client.ClientCredentials.UserName.Password = "Password";

client.DoWork();
```

How it works...

When the client caller sends a particular security token (such as the username token) to the service, the service will validate the token and assign a generated security identity into the current service operation context. Then, the role-based access control rules will perform code-access authorization based on the security identity in the current service operation context. We can also get this identity in code, as we've discussed in the *Getting an authenticated client identity in a service operation* recipe.

If the current security identity doesn't meet the declared role-based access requirement, the service will throw out an exception, which results in a `SecurityAccessDeniedException` (shown in the following screenshot).

```
C:\Windows\system32\cmd.exe                                    _ □
Unhandled Exception: System.ServiceModel.Security.SecurityAccessDeniedException
  Access is denied.

Server stack trace:
    at System.ServiceModel.Channels.ServiceChannel.ThrowIfFaultUnderstood(Messag
```

See also

- ▶ *Getting an authenticated client identity in a service operation*
- ▶ *Complete source code for this recipe can be found in the* `\Chapter 7\recipe6\` folder

Impersonating with a client caller identity

When using Windows authentication for either the transport layer or the message layer, the client authenticated user identity will be associated with the corresponding service operation context as a `WindowsIdentity` instance. The service operation can check the name and roles of the identity, and in some cases we can also make the service operation code execute under the client authenticated user identity, which is commonly called identity impersonation. This recipe will demonstrate how we can perform client identity impersonation in a WCF service operation that uses a Windows authentication type.

Getting ready

Impersonation is quite common in distributed applications or component services (like ASP. NET, COM+, Web Service, and so on). You can get more information about impersonation in the following MSDN reference:

▶   How To: Use Impersonation and Delegation in ASP.NET 2.0

   `http://msdn.microsoft.com/en-us/library/ms998351.aspx`

How to do it...

In WCF, we can use either a declarative or imperative style to enable impersonation.

1.   Declarative style.

   When using declarative style impersonation, we can use `System.ServiceModel.OperationBehaviorAttribute` to configure the impersonation setting for each operation. For example:

   ```
   [OperationBehavior(Impersonation=ImpersonationOption.Required)]
   Void MyOperation(…)
   ```

   The following table shows all the available impersonation options we can apply through `OperationBehaviorAttribute`.

Name	Description
NotAllowed	Impersonation is not performed. If `ImpersonateCallerForAllOperations` is equal to `true`, a validation exception occurs at service startup time.
Allowed	Impersonation is performed if credentials are available and `ImpersonateCallerForAllOperations` is equal to `true`.
Required	Impersonation is required.

2. Imperative style.

When using imperative style impersonation, we need to programmatically get the `WindowsIdentity` instance associated with the current service operation context and call the impersonate method on it (see the following code snippet):

```
using(ServiceSecurityContext.Current.WindowsIdentity.
Impersonate())
{
                // Access resources here....

}
```

In addition, no matter whether we impersonate the client identity declaratively or imperatively, we need to make sure that the client service invoker has allowed impersonation on the authenticated token. To allow impersonation, we need to set the `AllowedImpersonationLevel` to `Impersonation` or above:

```
var client = new TestProxy.Service1Client();
client.ClientCredentials.Windows.AllowedImpersonationLevel =
                TokenImpersonationLevel.Impersonation;
```

Here is the complete code of our sample WCF service, which contains three operations for demonstrating client identity impersonation:

```
public class Service1 : IService1
{
    public string GetData(int value)
    {
        return WindowsIdentity.GetCurrent().Name;
    }

    [OperationBehavior(Impersonation=
                    ImpersonationOption.Required)]
    public string GetDataWithImpersonation(int value)
    {
        return WindowsIdentity.GetCurrent().Name;
    }

    public string GetDataWithImpersonationInCode(int value)
    {
        using
      (ServiceSecurityContext.Current.WindowsIdentity.Impersonate())
        {
            return WindowsIdentity.GetCurrent().Name;
        }
    }
}
```

The `GetData` operation does not perform impersonation at all; the `GetDataWithImpersonation` uses declarative style impersonation and the `GetDataWithImpersonationInCode` uses imperative style impersonation. Each of them will return the current Windows security account of the thread context.

How it works...

By invoking all the three operations from the client, we can get the result values that indicate the impersonation status at server side. The following screenshot shows the service operation execution results in the client console window.

```
C:\Windows\system32\cmd.exe
Operation without impersonation:STCH179369\Administrator
Operation with impersonation:STCH179369\WCFUser
Operation with impersonation in code:STCH179369\WCFUser
Press any key to continue . . . _
```

`GetData` returns the Administrator account because it is not using impersonation, while the other two operations will return the impersonated account (sent by the client caller through a Windows authentication token).

There's more...

In cases where you need to turn on impersonation for all operations of the WCF service, you can consider using the `impersonateCallerForAllOperations` option of the `serviceAuthorization` behavior. The following screenshot shows how we can apply it through the entries in the `app.config` file.

```xml
<behaviors>
    <serviceBehaviors>
        <behavior name="impersonateBehavior" >
            <serviceAuthorization impersonateCallerForAllOperations="true" />
        </behavior>
```

See also

▶ *Complete source code for this recipe can be found in* the `\Chapter 7\recipe7\` *folder*

Adding multiple tokens in a service request (supportingToken)

Generally, a given WCF service with security configured will only demand a single security authentication token (the primary identity) from the client consumer so as to ensure the client caller identification. However, sometimes it is useful to ask the client to supply multiple security tokens so as to acquire more information for server-side authentication or business-logic-specific validation. For such scenarios, WCF provides the `supportingToken`, which can help developers in designing services that can demand and accept multiple security tokens from the server client.

In this recipe, we will use the sample service, which demands both username and X.509 certificate tokens to demonstrate how we can use the `supportingToken` feature to achieve the multi-token requirement.

How to do it...

Here we will go through the three steps to make a WCF service use multiple security tokens in client service communication.

1. Define a custom binding that allows multiple security tokens.

    To make a WCF service support multiple security tokens, we need to define a custom binding that will demand both a primary security token and additional tokens. Our sample service will use a username authentication token as the primary token. Therefore, the custom binding will adopt the `UsernameForCertificate` binding element.

    As we want to add an additional X.509 certificate token, we will need to add an `X509SecurityTokenParameters` instance into the security binding element. The following code snippet shows the complete code logic for creating the custom binding that demands both a username and X.509 certificate token from the client.

    ```
    private static Binding CreateMultiTokenBinding()
    {
        var httpTransport = new HttpTransportBindingElement();

        var messageSecurity = SecurityBindingElement.
        CreateUserNameForCertificateBindingElement();

        // Create supporting token parameters(for x509 certificate
        token type)
    ```

```
var clientX509SupportingTokenParameters =
                new X509SecurityTokenParameters();

// Specify that the supporting token is passed in the message
send by the client to the service.
clientX509SupportingTokenParameters.InclusionMode =
                SecurityTokenInclusionMode.AlwaysToRecipient;
clientX509SupportingTokenParameters.RequireDerivedKeys = false;

// Declare the requirement of an additional X.509 certificate
token
messageSecurity.EndpointSupportingTokenParameters.Endorsing.Add
(clientX509SupportingTokenParameters);

TextMessageEncodingBindingElement textEncoding =
                new TextMessageEncodingBindingElement();

return new CustomBinding(
                    textEncoding,
                    messageSecurity,
                    httpTransport
                    );
}
```

2. Attach multiple security tokens in the service proxy.

    At the client side, the service invoker needs to supply both security tokens through the client credentials collection. For our sample service, the client consumer application will set both the username token and the X.509 certificate token through the `ChannelFactory.Credentials` property (see the following code snippet).

```
private static void CallService()
{
    var multiTokenBinding = CreateMultiTokenBinding();

    ChannelFactory<IHelloService> factory =
                new ChannelFactory<IHelloService>(
                multiTokenBinding, svcAddress);

    // Set the two client authentication tokens required by service
    //      Set primary username token first
    factory.Credentials.UserName.UserName =
                @"[ServerName]\WCFUser";
```

```
factory.Credentials.UserName.Password = "Password01!";

//       Set the additional x509 certificate token
factory.Credentials.ClientCertificate.SetCertificate(
                StoreLocation.LocalMachine,
                StoreName.My,
                X509FindType.FindByThumbprint,
                "eefb5ee92d20963fb420bdd1808703ebc5589e9f");


// Create the channel and call the service operation
. . . . . .
}
```

3. Inspect the security tokens in the service operation code.

    If the service operation call passes the server-side validation, we can use the `OperationContext.SupportingTokens` collection to query all the existing security token information supplied by the client. The `DisplayTokenInfo` function is used in our sample service for displaying the username and X.509 certificate tokens sent by the client proxy:

```
private void DisplayTokenInfo()
{
    var tokens = OperationContext.Current.SupportingTokens;

    Console.WriteLine("supportingToken count: {0}", tokens.Count);

    foreach (var token in tokens)
    {
        if (token.SecurityToken is UserNameSecurityToken)
          Console.WriteLine("Username Token: {0}",
              ((UserNameSecurityToken)token.SecurityToken).UserName);

        if (token.SecurityToken is X509SecurityToken)
          Console.WriteLine("x509 Certificate Token: {0}",
          ((X509SecurityToken)token.SecurityToken).Certificate.Subject);
    }
}
```

How it works...

Our sample WCF service defines the X.509 certificate `supportingToken` as an endorsing token (by adding it into the endorsing token collection). Actually, the WS-SecurityPolicy specification defines four ways to attach a `supportingToken` to the message. The following table shows the four supported ways and their description:

Purpose	Description
Signed	The supporting token is included in the security header and is signed by the message signature.
Endorsing	An endorsing token signs the message signature.
Signed and Endorsing	Signed, endorsing tokens sign the entire `ds:Signature` element produced from the message signature and are themselves signed by that message signature; that is, both tokens (the token used for the message signature and the signed endorsing token) sign each other.
Signed and Encrypting	Signed, encrypted supporting tokens are signed supporting tokens that are also encrypted when they appear in the wsse:SecurityHeader.

A `supportingToken` can be attached at both the endpoint and operation level. The endpoint level supports adding the token for all operations of an endpoint. That is, the credentials that the supporting token represents can be used whenever any endpoint operations are invoked.

The sample service uses a custom binding that requires the X.509 certificate token to be provided. However, this is not necessary, as WCF also supports an optional `supportingToken`. As indicated by the name, the optional `supportingToken` is used if it is present. But the authentication will not fail if it is not present.

By combining the `supportingToken` level and optional criteria, we can define a `supportingToken` in the following four collections of the custom security binding element:

- `EndpointSupportingTokenParameters`
- `OperationSupportingTokenParameters`
- `OptionalEndpointSupportingTokenParameters`
- `OptionalOperationSupportingTokenParameters`

There's more...

Adding supportingTokens requires the service to adopt custom binding that demands the primary security token and optional additional tokens. However, this may result in a non-standard service security policy within the service metadata exposed to client consumers. Therefore, we need to take care when trying to use `supportingToken` in our WCF service, especially when the service is possibly consumed by client applications based on non-.NET or WCF-specific platforms.

See also

▸ *Defining a CustomBinding without a timestamp header* in *Chapter 2*

▸ *Complete source code for this recipe can be found in* the`\Chapter 7\recipe8\` folder

Supplying dedicated credentials for firewall or proxy authentication

For WCF services over the HTTP transport protocol, it is possible that the server machine and client callers are located in different network environments and the client might need to pass some intermediate firewall or proxy to reach the server endpoint. If the proxy or firewall requires client authentication, the WCF client consumer also needs to supply credentials for the firewall or proxy server in addition to the authentication of the WCF service endpoint itself. If you're familiar with .NET HttpWebRequest programming, you will find it quite straightforward to handle this kind of web proxy authentication, since HttpWebRequest type provides a `Proxy` property (of `System.Net.WebProxy` type) that lets developers assign proxy information, including the authentication credentials (see the following code snippet):

```
HttpWebRequest req =
(HttpWebRequest)WebRequest.Create("http://www.msn.com");

req.Proxy.Credentials = new System.Net.NetworkCredential("username",
"password");
```

However, the WCF client proxy class or ChannelFactory has not supplied such a property for us to configure dedicated web proxy authentication information. The default proxy authentication will use the same credentials as the service endpoint authentication. This results in problems if we need to supply different credentials for WCF service authentication and the intermediate firewall proxy authentication. Fortunately, we can still resolve the problem through the existing `System.Net` programming interfaces.

Getting ready

For basic information about web proxy detection and configuration with Windows and the .NET framework platform, you can refer to the following MSDN article:

▸ Take the Burden Off Users with Automatic Configuration in .NET

   `http://msdn.microsoft.com/en-us/magazine/cc300743.aspx`

To supply dedicated credentials for firewall/proxy authentication in the WCF client, we need to leverage the `WebRequest.DefaultWebProxy` property. The WCF runtime will acquire a proxy setting from the `WebRequest.DefaultWebProxy` property if the `<system.net>` and WCF `<binding>` remains with `useDefaultproxy` as `true` (the default value).

Thus, our WCF service client can simply construct a new `WebProxy` instance and replace the existing one (or only modify the credentials of the default `WebProxy` instance without completely constructing a new `WebProxy` instance).

The following sample code demonstrates how we can construct a new `WebProxy` with authentication credentials supplied and assign it as the new default proxy used by the underlying HTTP network communication:

```
//first customize the default proxy
WebProxy wproxy = new WebProxy("new proxy",true);
wproxy.Credentials = CredentialCache.DefaultNetworkCredentials;

//or you can construct your own credentials via System.Net.
NetworkCredential

WebRequest.DefaultWebProxy = wproxy;

//do WCF calls....
WCFSVC.ServiceClient client = new WCFSVC.ServiceClient();
```

Securing a dynamic SoapHeader

As described in the *Adding a dynamic SoapHeader into a message* recipe in *Chapter 5*, WCF supports dynamically adding SoapHeaders into request/response messages without defining them statically in `ServiceContract` or `OperationContract`. This works fine for those scenarios where the dynamic SoapHeader doesn't need to be secured (either signing or encrypting), since the programmatically-injected SoapHeader is transferred as unsecured in the `<headers>` section of a SOAP envelope. Then, how do we secure the dynamically added SoapHeader?

In this recipe, we will demonstrate how to secure a SoapHeader that is added into the WCF request message, programmatically.

How to do it...

To secure a dynamically added SoapHeader, we need to hook into the underlying security binding configuration of the WCF service endpoint. WCF provides a `ChannelProtectionRequirements` type, which contains the message security definition (such as the digital signature and encryption) on a different part of a SOAP message. By default, WCF will help add security requirements for the SOAP body and those built-in security SoapHeaders if we have applied bindings that secure request/response messages automatically. For a dynamically added SoapHeader, we need to manually apply the security requirements. Let's take a look at the detailed steps to do it:

1. Define a custom behavior that adds protection requirements for dynamic SoapHeaders.

    For our dynamically added SoapHeader, we need to manually add a security protection definition for it. To add this definition, we can create a custom `ContractBehavior` or `EndpointBehavior` to achieve this. In our sample service, we will use a custom `ContractBehavior` to inject the protection requirement for our dynamic SoapHeader. Here is the complete code of the custom `ContractBehavior`:

```
public class SecureHeaderContractBehavior : IContractBehavior
{
    string action;
    string header;
    string ns;

    public SecureHeaderContractBehavior(string header, string ns,
                      string action)
    {
        this.header = header;
        this.ns = ns;
        this.action = action;
    }

    #region IContractBehavior Members

    public void AddBindingParameters(ContractDescription
    contractDescription, ServiceEndpoint endpoint,
    System.ServiceModel.Channels.BindingParameterCollection
                      bindingParameters)
    {
        ChannelProtectionRequirements requirements =
        bindingParameters.Find<ChannelProtectionRequirements>();
```

```
XmlQualifiedName headerName = new XmlQualifiedName(header,
                      ns);
requirements.IncomingSignatureParts.ChannelParts.
HeaderTypes.Add(headerName);

// Uncomment following statement to enable encryption on the
header
//requirements.IncomingEncryptionParts.ChannelParts.
HeaderTypes.Add(headerName );
}
```

. . .

```
    #endregion
}
```

As the `SecureHeaderContractBehavior.AddBindingParameters` member function demonstrates, we first locate the `ChannelProtectionRequirements` instance from the binding parameters collection. We then add the `XmlQualifiedName` name of our dynamic SoapHeader into the `IncomingSignatureParts` collection, which contains all the security definitions of SOAP message parts that need to be digitally signed. In addition to `IncomingSignatureParts`, we can also use the `IncomingEncryptionParts` collection to specify SOAP message parts that need to be both signed and encrypted.

2. Apply the custom behavior to our WCF service endpoint.

   After creating the custom ContractBehavior for injecting security protection requirements, we need to apply it to our WCF client proxy. This can be done at the proxy construction stage. The following code snippet shows the sample client code, which shows how we can inject the custom ContractBehavior:

```
static void CallService()
{
    TestProxy.CalcServiceClient calc =
                new TestProxy.CalcServiceClient();

    var cb = new SecureHeaderContractBehavior("hostHeader",
                "urn:wcf:test", "Host");
    calc.Endpoint.Contract.Behaviors.Add(cb);

    using (OperationContextScope scope =
                new OperationContextScope(calc.InnerChannel))
    {
        // Construct the dynamic soap header
```

```
MessageHeader<string> hostHeader = new
                  MessageHeader<string>()
{
    Content = Dns.GetHostName(),
    Actor = "Host",
    MustUnderstand = false
};


var header = hostHeader.GetUntypedHeader(
                  "hostHeader", urn:wcf:test");


// Add the header into
OperationContext.Current.OutgoingMessageHeaders.Add(header);


    }
}
```

As the `CallService` function shows, we directly locate the `Contract` instance from the Endpoint member of the WCF proxy instance and add the custom ContractBehavior instance (`SecureHeaderContractBehavior`) into its `Behaviors` collection. Also, it is worth noticing that we have supplied the Namespace, LocalName, and Action to both the ContractBehavior and the dynamic SoapHeader; they need to be identical, since that's how the runtime associates the security protection requirement and the target SOAP message part (body or header) that needs to be secured.

How it works...

By using WCF message logging, we can capture the underlying SOAP messages sent by the WCF client proxy. Here is the SOAP message captured before we apply `SecureHeaderContractBehavior` (shown in the following screenshot).

```
nvelope xmlns:s="http://www.w3.org/2003/05/soap-envelope" xml
s:Header>
 <a:Action s:mustUnderstand="1" u:Id="_2">http://tempuri.org/ICalc
 <hostHeader s:role="Host" xmlns="urn:wcf:test">                </hostH
 <a:MessageID u:Id="_3">urn:uuid:e3e0521b-2f63-482d-a527-a4c0
 <a:ReplyTo u:Id="_4">
    <a:Address>http://www.w3.org/2005/08/addressing/anonymo
 </a:ReplyTo>
 <a:To s:mustUnderstand="1" u:Id="_5">http://localhost:8732/CalcS
 <o:Security s:mustUnderstand="1" xmlns:o="http://docs.oasis-open.
```

As we can see, the `hostHeader` SoapHeader is not signed, since we haven't applied the custom behavior into the ServiceContract.

Now, let's take a look at the SOAP message captured after we have applied the custom behavior (which injects the protection requirements for the `hostHeader` SoapHeader). You can get the SOAP message fragment in the next screenshot.

```
Envelope xmlns:s="http://www.w3.org/2003/05/soap-envelope" xmlns:a="htt
s:Header>
  <a:Action s:mustUnderstand="1" u:Id="_2">http://tempuri.org/ICalcService/
  <hostHeader s:role="Host" u:Id="_3" xmlns="urn:wcf:test">?    ???  </host
  <a:MessageID u:Id="_4">urn:uuid:2e1720c7-2ec8-4056-b005-aae8ee080cb
  <a:ReplyTo u:Id="_5">
    <a:Address>http://www.w3.org/2005/08/addressing/anonymous</a:Ac
  </a:ReplyTo>
  <a:To s:mustUnderstand="1" u:Id="_6">http://localhost:8732/CalcService/<
  <o:Security s:mustUnderstand="1" xmlns:o="http://docs.oasis-open.org/wss/
```

As the SOAP fragment shows, after applying `SecureHeaderContractBehavior`, the `hostHeader` SoapHeader (added dynamically) has been digitally signed and contains a unique ID in its header tag.

See also

▸ *Adding a dynamic SoapHeader into a message* in *Chapter 5*

▸ *Altering an operation message via MessageInspector* in *Chapter 9*

▸ *Complete source code for this recipe can be found in the* `\Chapter 7\recipe10\` *folder*

8
Concurrency

In this chapter, we will cover:

- ▶ Hosting a singleton instance service
- ▶ Invoking a WCF service without blocking the front UI
- ▶ Using throttling to control service concurrency
- ▶ Ensuring termination of a client session
- ▶ Tuning WCF concurrency performance via Visual Studio testing tools

Introduction

Concurrency behavior reflects the performance characteristics of services such as throughput and scalability. WCF provides many built-in features for developers to control the concurrency of our services built upon it.

This chapter covers some typical and useful cases of WCF concurrency management, including service instancing mode control, concurrent service invoking within GUI client application, and service session management.

Hosting a singleton instance service

Singleton is a very popular design pattern used in application development. And for WCF services, sometimes it is useful to build a singleton-style service that will only use one instance object to serve all the operation calls from the client. This recipe will show you how to make a WCF service in singleton style.

How to do it...

In order to make a WCF service create a single instance of the Service type, we can apply `InstanceContextMode` through `ServiceBehaviorAttribute` on the service implementation type of our service. The following code snippet shows the sample service class, which has `ServiceBehaviorAttribute` applied and the `InstanceContextMode` property set to `Single`.

```
[ServiceBehavior(InstanceContextMode=InstanceContextMode.Single)]
public class TimeService : ITimeService
{
    public TimeService()
    {
        Console.WriteLine("A new instance of TimeService is constructed
                          at {0}", DateTime.Now);
    }

    public DateTime GetCurrentTime()
    {
        return DateTime.Now;
    }
}
```

Also, the `InstanceContextMode` supports two other possible values that can control the instance activation of our service class (refer to the following table).

Name	Description
PerSession	A new `InstanceContext` object is created for each session.
PerCall	A new `InstanceContext` object is created prior to, and recycled subsequent to, each call. If the channel does not create a session, this value behaves as if it were `PerCall`.
Single	Only one `InstanceContext` object is used for all incoming calls and is not recycled subsequent to the calls. If a service object does not exist, one is created.
	Note:
	For singleton lifetime behavior (for example, if the host application calls the `ServiceHost` constructor and passes an object to use as the service), the service class must set `InstanceContextMode` to `InstanceContextMode.Single`, or an exception is thrown when the service host is opened.

How it works...

By applying `InstanceContextMode` as `Single` to the service type, the WCF runtime will make sure that only one `Single` of the service type will be activated when running the target service. The following screenshot shows the service host screen, which indicates that the WCF runtime creates one and the only one instance at the service startup time:

```
C:\Windows\system32\cmd.exe
A new instance of TimeService is constructed at 7/22/2010 4:5
service started at http://localhost:8732/TimeService/
```

See also

▸ *Complete source code for this recipe can be found in the* `\Chapter 8\recipe1\` *folder*

Invoking a WCF service without blocking the front UI

We can consume WCF services from various client applications and, in most cases, the WCF client consumer is a GUI application that needs to respond to front UI interactions as well as any background processing tasks. In such cases, if we need to call a long-running WCF service operation, it is important to make sure that the service invoking won't block the front UI interaction.

In this recipe, we will use a typical WinForm client application to demonstrate how we can consume a WCF service in GUI applications without impacting the front UI interaction.

How to do it...

WCF supports several means to achieve service operation invoking without blocking the front UI actions. Here we will introduce two methods to achieve this. The following screenshot shows the main window of the sample WinForm application.

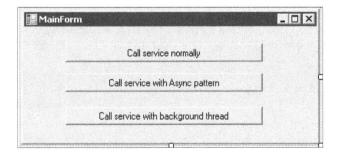

1. Call the service operation in the normal synchronous way.

   The client form contains three buttons, each of which demonstrates a service-invoking approach. The **Call service normally** button uses the standard synchronous method to invoke the WCF service (see following code snippet):

   ```
   private void btnSync_Click(object sender, EventArgs e)
   {
       TestProxy.DataServiceClient client =
                       new TestProxy.DataServiceClient();

       string data = client.GetData();

       MessageBox.Show(data);
   }
   ```

2. Call the service operation through asynchronous methods in the proxy class.

   The second **Call service with Async pattern** button shows the first approach to make service operation call without blocking the front UI. The following code snippet shows the button click function that uses the asynchronous method to invoke a WCF service.

   ```
   private void btnAsync_Click(object sender, EventArgs e)
   {
       TestProxy.DataServiceClient client = new
                       TestProxy.DataServiceClient();

       client.GetDataCompleted +=
        delegate(object src, TestProxy.GetDataCompletedEventArgs args)
        {
            MessageBox.Show(args.Result);
        };

       client.GetDataAsync();
   }
   ```

3. Call the service operation through a custom background thread.

   Now we come to another means to invoke the service operation as a background task. In this approach, we will manually spawn a .NET-managed thread and execute the service operation call code in the custom thread (see the `bthThread_Click` function):

   ```
   private void btnThread_Click(object sender, EventArgs e)
   {
       Thread th = new Thread(
               delegate()
   ```

```
        {
            TestProxy.DataServiceClient client =
                    new TestProxy.DataServiceClient();

            string data = client.GetData();

            MessageBox.Show(data);
        }
    );

    th.Start();
}
```

How it works...

In the sample WinForm client application, the first **Call service normally** button shows the normal way to invoke a WCF service operation synchronously. In such a case, if the service operation takes a long time to finish, the front UI interaction of the WinForm program will be totally frozen.

In the second **Call service with Async pattern** approach, we will switch to using the built-in **asynchronous** operation methods generated by the Visual Studio **Add Service Reference** option or the .NET **Svcutil.exe** tool to invoke the target service operations. Thus, the service operation call will be executed in a .NET thread pool thread. In this case, the execution of the service operation will not block the processing of the main UI thread of the WinForm application.

In the last case, the WCF service operation call is executed in the background. However, this time we are not using the thread from the .NET thread pool, but creating a custom background thread. The advantage of using a custom thread is that we can create as many such kinds of threads as possible, and as long as the operating system resource supports (unlike the .NET thread pool, which has a size limitation). The weakness of this approach is also obvious, that is, creating a custom thread is much more expensive than using a .NET thread pool thread. This is the trade-off we need to consider when choosing the proper approach to make a WCF service call in background mode.

See also

▶ *Complete source code for this recipe can be found in the* \Chapter 8\recipe2\ *folder*

Using throttling to control service concurrency

There are many facts in WCF which can impact the concurrency performance of a service. For example, the maximum number of instances that can be activated concurrently, the maximum number of sessions that can be active concurrently, and the maximum number of service operation calls that can be executed simultaneously. If configured incorrectly or in a bad manner, it is possible that our service might encounter a performance bottleneck or suffer a DOS attack in an unpredictable internet environment.

Fortunately, WCF also provides sufficient built-in configuration options for developers to control these concurrency-specific behaviors of the running service. This recipe will introduce the **Throttling** settings that WCF uses to achieve the task.

How to do it...

To control all those concurrency factors, we need to apply `ServiceThrottlingBehavior` on our target service on which we want to control the concurrency behaviors. `ServiceThrottlingBehavior` provides three properties:

- `maxConcurrentCalls`
- `maxConcurrentInstances`
- `maxConcurrentSessions`

By using these three properties, developers or service hosts can restrict the concurrency facets of a certain WCF service. The following table shows the detailed explanation of all the three properties in the MSDN library:

Attribute	Description
`maxConcurrentCalls`	A positive integer that limits the number of messages that currently process across a ServiceHost. Calls in excess of the limit are queued. Setting this value to `0` is equivalent to setting it to `Int32.MaxValue`. The default is `16`.
`maxConcurrentInstances`	A positive integer that limits the number of `InstanceContext` objects that execute at one time across a ServiceHost. Requests to create additional instances are queued and complete when a slot below the limit becomes available. The default is `Int32.MaxValue`.
`maxConcurrentSessions`	A positive integer that limits the number of sessions a ServiceHost object can accept.
	The service will accept connections in excess of the limit, but only the channels below the limit are active (messages are read from the channel).

WCF provides a convenient means for us to set the throttling properties through the `<serviceThrottling>` behavior element in the configuration file. As the following screenshot shows, we can set all `maxConcurrentCalls`, `maxConcurrentInstances`, and `maxConcurrentSessions` to 1 so that our service will only allow one client session and one service operation to be active (in execution mode) at the same time; and the server side will only create one and exactly one instance of the service class.

```
<behaviors>
  <serviceBehaviors>
    <behavior name="Throttled">
      <serviceThrottling
        maxConcurrentCalls="1"
        maxConcurrentSessions="1"
        maxConcurrentInstances="1"
      />
      <serviceMetadata
        httpGetEnabled="true"
        httpGetUrl=""
      />
    </behavior>
  </serviceBehaviors>
</behaviors>
</system.serviceModel>
</configuration>
```

How it works...

The `ServiceThrottlingBehavior` helps control those concurrency quotas (concurrent operation calls, instances, and sessions) of the hosting service. However, this is still not enough. We also need to select the appropriate `InstanceContextMode` and `ConcurrencyMode` for our service so that those throttling quotas work as expected.

For example, as the *Hosting a singleton instance service* recipe in this chapter demonstrates, by using `InstanceContextMode.Single`, the service will automatically restrict the number of service instances to one.

There's more...

For more information on `InstanceContextMode` and `ConcurrencyMode`, you can refer to the following MSDN library documents:

▸ InstanceContextMode Enumeration

http://msdn.microsoft.com/en-us/library/system.servicemodel.instancecontextmode.aspx

▸ ConcurrencyMode Enumeration

http://msdn.microsoft.com/en-us/library/system.servicemodel.concurrencymode.aspx

And you can get more detailed information about `ServiceThrottlingBehavior` at the following location:

▸ <serviceThrottling>

   `http://msdn.microsoft.com/en-us/library/ms731379.aspx`

See also

▸ *Hosting a singleton instance service*

Ensuring termination of a client session

Most WCF system bindings (such as NetTcpBinding and WSHttpBinding) support a session between the calling client and server. When the client side creates a new service proxy instance and invokes the service operation (or just opens the channel), there is a new session established between server and client. However, since WCF throttling adds a restriction on concurrent session numbers, if we keep instantiating new client proxies, the server will stop responding due to session exhaustion. Therefore, it is very important to take care of the session and make sure we properly terminate it after finishing the service invoking. This recipe will demonstrate the means to terminate the session appropriately.

How to do it...

WCF provides some useful properties in the `OperationContractAttribute` that can help control session initializing and terminating. If our service consumer will always adopt an expected and determined calling pattern and process, we can use `OperationContractAttribute.IsTerminating` to indicate that one of the service operations will help terminate the session after the client has invoked it. The following code snippet shows a sample service operation which utilizes the `IsTerminating` property:

```
[ServiceContract]
public interface IDataService
{
    [OperationContract(IsTerminating = true)]
    string GetData();
}
```

When the service client finishes invoking the `GetData` operation, the session between client and server will be terminated.

We can also use the famous try-catch-finally block to ensure the termination of a WCF session at the client side. For example, the `CallService` function shown next uses a `finally` block to ensure that the client proxy object is closed.

```
static void CallService()
{
   TestProxy.DataServiceClient client =
                      new TestProxy.DataServiceClient();

   try
   {
      Console.WriteLine(client.GetData());
   }
   finally
   {
      client.Close();
   }
}
```

How it works...

In the previous cases, we explicitly close the WCF client proxy object so as to ensure the termination of the client session. In some cases, where the server uses some connection-oriented transport protocol (such as NetTcpBinding), if we do not explicitly close the client proxy object (or ChannelFactory), the session will be implicitly terminated when the client application ends (since the session relies on the underlying physical TCP connection). However, for those connectionless protocols like HTTP, leaving the proxy unclosed will result in the session being alive until the session timeout quota is triggered.

There's more...

The sample code snippet directly closes the WCF client proxy object to ensure the termination of the session. However, sometimes there might occur some exceptions that can cause the proxy or underlying channel object to turn into a faulted state before we close it. Then, directly closing the proxy or channel object might raise an exception too. In such cases, we need to properly handle the potential exceptions and abort the proxy or channel object. The following code snippet shows the service operation call with proper exception handling:

```
static void CallServiceWithExceptionHandling()
{
   TestProxy.DataServiceClient client =
                      new TestProxy.DataServiceClient();
   try
   {
      // Making calls
      Console.WriteLine(client.GetData());

      // Close the proxy
```

```
        client.Close();
    }
    catch (TimeoutException timeEx)
    {
        client.Abort();
    }
    catch (FaultException faultEx)
    {
        client.Abort();
    }
    catch (CommunicationException commProblem)
    {
        client.Abort();
    }
}
```

More information about exception and fault handling in WCF can be found at the following location:

▸ Sending and Receiving Faults

   `http://msdn.microsoft.com/en-us/library/ms732013.aspx`

See also

▸ *Using throttling to control service concurrency*

▸ *Complete source code for this recipe can be found in the* `\Chapter 8\recipe4\` *folder*

Tuning WCF concurrency performance via Visual Studio testing tools

We have discussed WCF throttling settings which can help control the concurrency behavior of WCF services in the *Using throttling to control service concurrency* recipe of this chapter. However, WCF itself won't tell you what is the best or appropriate throttling setting for your service. It is the developer's or administrator's task to figure out the golden values for a specific WCF service.

In this recipe, you will be introduced to how we can utilize the Visual Studio 2010 testing components to help figure out the appropriate service-throttling settings for a WCF service.

The sample solution we use here consists of two projects—one is the WCF service project and the other is the Visual Studio test project. The following screenshot shows the solution structure in Visual Studio's **Solution Explorer**.

The WCF service project contains a very typical WSHttpBinding-based service that contains one service operation simulating a time-consuming task (as shown in the following code snippet):

```
[ServiceBehavior(
InstanceContextMode=InstanceContextMode.PerCall,
                ConcurrencyMode= ConcurrencyMode.Multiple)]
public class Service1 : IService1
{
    public string GetData(int value)
    {
        Thread.Sleep(1000 * 3);

        return string.Format("You entered: {0}", value);
    }
......
```

How to do it...

Here we will go through the complete steps of the sample testing case, which will cover not only how to create test items but also how we can analyze the test results of the test cases.

1. Create a Unit Test item for invoking the target service operation.

    The first thing we need to do is to create a unit test case to represent a simple WCF service operation call. Since the 2005 version, Visual Studio has provided many project templates and components for software testing. So in Visual Studio 2010, this can be done by creating a Unit Test item in Visual Studio.

The following code snippet shows the complete code logic of the sample `Unit Test` item in our sample solution:

```
[TestMethod]
public void TestMethod1()
{
    TestProxy.Service1Client client =
                        new TestProxy.Service1Client();

    string data = client.GetData(33);

    client.Close();
}
```

As we can see, the sample unit test function simply creates a new WCF service proxy instance and makes a single operation call against the target service.

2. Create a `Load Test` item based on the existing `Unit Test` item.

Given the unit test item, the next step is to create a `Load Test` (also one of the built-in test items) item in Visual Studio which will represent the main performance testing case in our sample solution. The following screenshot shows the Test Item creation wizard in Visual Studio 2010, which includes the **Load Test** item:

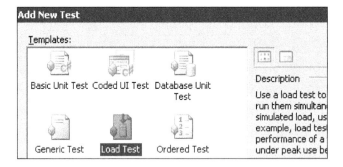

To make the `Load Test` fit our testing requirements, we need to do some adjustments on its properties. By using the Visual Studio **Properties** window, we can conveniently configure all the necessary testing properties. For our sample case, we will specify the following test settings on the `Load Test` item.

- The **Test Mix** value, which is pointing to the UnitTest method defined previously
- The **Run Settings** value, which includes the execute duration and max connection count

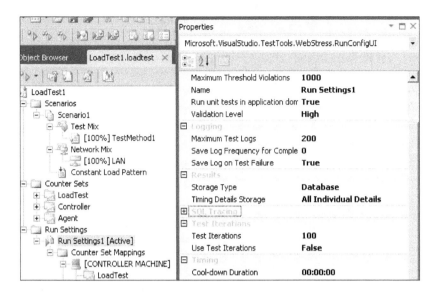

As shown in the previous screenshot, both the **Test Mix** and **Run Settings** items are displayed in the left tree view. And we can select either one to configure the detailed sub properties in the **Properties** window on the right.

3. Launch Load Test for collecting performance data.

   After configuring all the necessary testing properties, we can start Load Test through the Visual Studio **Test** menu item, as shown in the following screenshot.

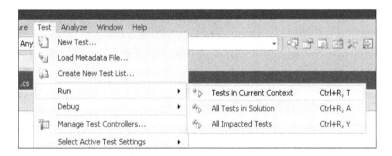

By choosing the **Tests in Current Context** menu item, Visual Studio will run all the available test items in the current test project one by one. For our sample case, tests to be run include the Load Test item and the Unit Test item. During the test execution period, the **Test Results** window will display the execution progress of each test item currently running.

4. Analyze the result through various test result views.

After a certain test item finishes running, we can review the test results using the **View Test Results Details** context menu over the selected test item (shown in the next screenshot).

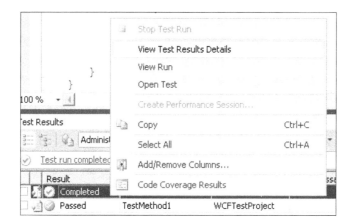

Now, here comes the most important and powerful part of the Visual Studio test harness—the test result reports. Visual Studio 2010 testing components provide several test results output formats that can let you select the preferred way to analyze the test result data. The next screenshot shows the toolbar for viewing test results. As we can see, there are four result formats available, including **Summary**, **Graphs**, **Tables**, and **Detail**.

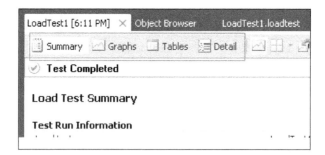

By clicking the particular tab on the toolbar, we are redirected to the corresponding page which shows the detailed test result information presented in the selected format. The following screenshot illustrates the **Summary** results view of our sample test case.

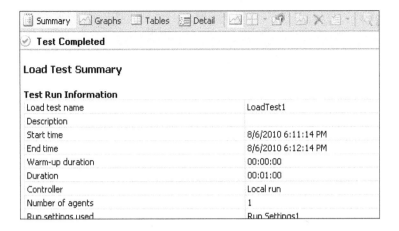

The following screenshot illustrates the **Graphs** results view of our sample test case.

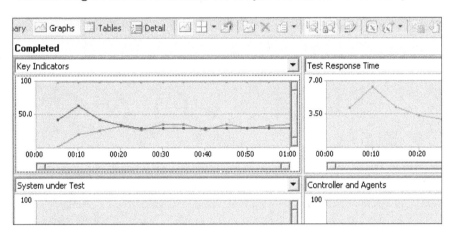

The graphical test result views are especially useful and important for performance tuning cases, since developers or testers can see the performance change or trend very conveniently from the visual output.

How it works...

In our sample service testing case, we use `Load Test` to measure the WCF service execution performance so as to adjust the throttling setting. If we feel the performance output of the test case is not quite good, enough then we need to adjust the service-throttling settings so as to tune the service performance behavior.

In real world performance-tuning scenarios, it is possible that we will have to change the throttling settings and run tests against the setting repeatedly so as to get closer to the appropriate setting values.

There's more...

The Visual Studio performance testing tools are much more powerful than what we showed in this recipe. For more information about the Visual Studio performance testing tools and results analysis, you can refer to the following articles in MSDN library.

> ▸ What's New for Testing
>
> `http://msdn.microsoft.com/en-us/library/bb385901.aspx`

> ▸ Monitoring and Analyzing a Load Test Result
>
> `http://msdn.microsoft.com/en-us/library/aa730850(VS.80).aspx`

See also

> ▸ *Using throttling to control service concurrency*
> ▸ *Complete source code for this recipe can be found in the* `\Chapter 8\recipe5\` *folder*

9
Extending WCF Runtime

In this chapter, we will cover:

- ▶ Using a custom `ServiceHost`
- ▶ Intercepting operation parameters in a strong-type manner
- ▶ Filtering operation requests based on message
- ▶ Generic operation error handling with `OperationInvoker`
- ▶ Altering an operation message via `MessageInspector`
- ▶ Building a custom `MessageEncoder`
- ▶ Centralizing authorization through a custom `ServiceAuthorizationManager`

Introduction

Sometimes, developers might want to not only utilize the built-in features of a certain application development platform, but also add custom extensibility into it. In such cases, the extensibility architecture of the application development platform is the most important and critical factor that determines whether customization demands of developers can be fully satisfied.

As a powerful and well-designed service development platform, WCF provides sufficient extension points so that the service developers can customize and extend certain parts of their service application based on the actual scenarios. This is benefited by the great architecture of WCF, which is well layered and enables developers to apply extensibility at the appropriate layer based on their service development requirements.

The following figure illustrates the major layers of the WCF architecture.

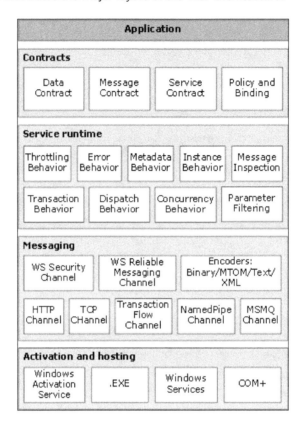

The WCF extension framework provides extension interfaces among the following parts:

- Extending ServiceHost and the Service Model layer
- Extending bindings
- Extending the Channel layer
- Extending security
- Extending the metadata system
- Extending encoders and serializers

In this chapter, we will use seven recipes to cover some common and useful extending scenarios in WCF service development. The first recipe will show how a custom ServiceHost works. The next five recipes will cover various cases in WCF binding, channel, and message extending. The last recipe uses a custom `ServiceAuthorizationManager` to demonstrate security extensions in a WCF service.

Using a custom ServiceHost

WCF provides a powerful and flexible configuration system that allows service developers or server administrators to configure service endpoints or hosting behaviors, either programmatically or declaratively (in app.config file). However, sometimes it is useful and important to find a proper means to configure a large amount of services in a common manner instead of manipulating each service individually. In such cases, a quite straightforward way is to create a custom ServiceHost and make all our service hosted with it.

How to do it...

In this recipe, we will use a DebugServiceHost (which ensures that IncludeExceptionDetails is enabled) sample to demonstrate how we can create a custom ServiceHost and use it to extend a WCF service.

1. Define a custom ServiceHost type.

    The first and most important thing to do is to create the custom ServiceHost type. Any custom ServiceHost type must be derived from either the ServiceHostBase or ServiceHost class under the System.ServiceModel.Activation namespace. The following code snippet shows the implementation of our sample ServiceHost type:

```
public class DebugServiceHost : ServiceHost
{
    public DebugServiceHost(Type serviceType, Uri[] baseAddresses)
                : base(serviceType, baseAddresses)
    { }

    protected override void ApplyConfiguration()
    {
        base.ApplyConfiguration();

        // Our custom configuration code

        ServiceDebugBehavior sdb =
            this.Description.Behaviors.Find<ServiceDebugBehavior>();
        if (sdb == null)
        {
            sdb = new ServiceDebugBehavior();
            this.Description.Behaviors.Add(sdb);
        }

        // Ensure exception detail is included in response
```

```
            sdb.IncludeExceptionDetailInFaults = true;
    }
}
```

The `DebugServiceHost` class is derived from the `ServiceHost` class and overrides the `ApplyConfiguration` method in which we find the `ServiceDebugBehavior` settings This ensures that the `IncludeExceptionDetails` option is enabled.

2. Add a custom `ServiceHostFactory` type for a IIS web hosting scenario.

   For WCF services that are hosted in IIS/WAS, we also need to implement a custom `ServiceHostFactory` that helps register our `ServiceHost` at the service activation point at runtime. The sample `DebugServiceHostFactory` type simply returns an instance of the `DebugServiceHost` type in the `GetServiceHost` method, shown as follows:

   ```
   // Custom ServiceHostFactory used for IIS/WAS hosting scenario
   public class DebugServiceHostFactory : ServiceHostFactory
   {
       protected override ServiceHost CreateServiceHost(Type
                           serviceType, Uri[] baseAddresses)
       {
           return new DebugServiceHost(serviceType, baseAddresses);
       }
   }
   ```

3. Apply the custom `ServiceHost` to the target WCF service.

   After defining the custom `ServiceHost` and `ServiceHostFactory` type, what we need to do is to apply the custom `ServiceHost` to the target services on which we want to apply the common customization. As an example, we use an IIS hosting scenario in which we need to apply the custom `ServiceHost` type in a `.svc` service extension file.

   The following screenshot shows a sample `.svc` file in which we have registered the sample `DebugServiceHostFactory` type.

   ```
   <%@ ServiceHost Language="C#" Debug="true"
     Service="WCFServiceApp.Service1"
     Factory="CustomLib.DebugServiceHostFactory, CustomLib"
   ```

How it works...

In WCF, each service will be activated through a `ServiceHost` instance. By default, WCF will use a default `ServiceHost` implementation for a given service and this `ServiceHost` simply reads the configuration from the `app.config` file when the service is requested for the first time. Therefore, if you have a large number of WCF services, which need to apply the same customization at service start-up or initializing time, it is a good idea to use a custom `ServiceHost` to inject the custom code logic.

In our sample service, the `DebugServiceHost` type overrides the `ApplyConfiguration` method in which it extracts the `ServiceDebugBehavior` instance and forces the `IncludeExceptionDetails` option to `true`. Also, our custom code is added after the `base.ApplyConfiguration` call; in this way, we can make sure the custom code logic will not be overwritten by the configuration setting in the `app.config` file.

See also

▸   *Complete source code for this recipe can be found in the* `\Chapter 9\recipe1\` *folder*

Intercepting operation parameters in a strong-type manner

WCF service operation calls are serialized into SOAP XML messages over wire, which gives us opportunity to intercept the message and manipulate it. However, this kind of interception is at the raw XML message level and is not quite convenient for inspecting or manipulating strong-typed operation parameters. In such cases, WCF provides built-in interfaces for developers to intercept the input and output parameters of the service operation call. For those services in which we want to inspect or modify the operation parameters, we can define a custom parameter inspector to achieve the task. In this recipe, we will demonstrate how we can use the parameter inspector to manipulate the parameters of incoming service operations.

How to do it...

The sample service will use a custom parameter inspector component to modify those string parameters passed in its operation calls. Let's go through the detailed steps:

1.   Create a custom type implementing the `IParameterInspector` interface.

    The first step is to define a custom type, which implements the `System.ServiceModel.Dispatcher.IParameterInspector` interface. WCF requires that each parameter inspector component implements this interface.

To implement the `IParameterInspector` interface, we just need to define two methods—`AfterCall` and `BeforeCall` (the following table shows their description in the MSDN library).

Name	Description
AfterCall	Called after client calls are returned and before service responses are sent.
BeforeCall	Called before client calls are sent and after service responses are returned.

Here is the complete definition of the custom parameter inspector type used in our sample service (see `StringParamValidator` in the following):

```
public class StringParamValidator : IParameterInspector
{
    #region IParameterInspector Members

    public void AfterCall(string operationName, object[] outputs,
                          object returnValue, object correlationState)
    {
        // Do nothing
    }

    public object BeforeCall(string operationName, object[] inputs)
    {
        // Validate string parameters
        for(int i=0;i<inputs.Length;++i)
        if (inputs[i] is string)
        {
            inputs[i] = "SafeWrapper[" + inputs[i] + "]";
        }

        return null;
    }

    #endregion
}
```

2. Install the custom parameter inspector on the target service operation.

   Now we come to the step for applying the custom parameter inspector to the sample service so that it can help intercept and modify the parameters of each operation call.

   To inject the custom parameter inspector, we can choose either to programmatically add it, or use `Attribute` to apply it declaratively. Here we use an `OperationBehavior` attribute to apply it in declaratively:

```
public class StringParamValidatorBehaviorAttribute : Attribute,
                    IOperationBehavior
{
    public void ApplyDispatchBehavior(OperationDescription
        operationDescription, DispatchOperation dispatchOperation)
    {
        StringParamValidator spv = new StringParamValidator();
        dispatchOperation.ParameterInspectors.Add(spv);
    }

}
```

StringParamValidatorBehaviorAttribute simply creates an instance of the StringParamValidator inspector and adds it into the target operation's ParameterInspectors collection.

Having the parameter inspector and OperationBehavior attribute defined, we can apply them on any WCF service operation we want to intercept parameters from. For our sample case, we will apply the StringParamValidator inspector to a simple test operation, which has two input parameters of string type (as the following screenshot shows).

```
[ServiceContract]
public interface IService1
{

    [OperationContract]
    [CustomLib.StringParamValidatorBehavior]
    string TestStringOperation(string str1, String str2);
```

With the StringParamValidatorBehavior attribute applied, whenever TestStringOperation is called, the corresponding input parameters will be processed by the StringParamValidator inspector component.

How it works...

There are many different extension interfaces in WCF extension architecture and the System.ServiceModel.Dispatcher.IParameterInspector interface is the one used for intercepting input and output parameters within each WCF service operation call.

Since our custom parameter inspector is applied at the server side (instead of the client proxy side), the BeforeCall method will go through all the input parameters and modify any input parameter of String type.

By using the WCF Test Client tool in the Windows SDK, we can quickly test the sample WCF service operation and check the response result. Here is the request and response data in the operation window of the WCF Test Client tool.

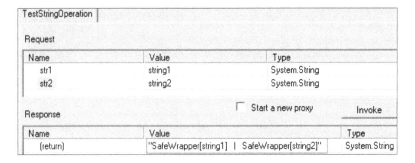

As the previous screenshot shows, the service correctly returns all the string parameters sent to the service and each of them has been changed the format defined in the `StringParamValidator` inspector.

See also

▸ *Using the WCF Test Client tool to test a service* in *Chapter 12*

▸ *Complete source code for this recipe can be found in the* `\Chapter 9\recipe2\` *folder*

Filtering operation requests based on message

WCF supports hosting multiple endpoints within a single service instance. At runtime, whenever a service request arrives, the WCF runtime needs to determine which endpoint (`EndpointDispatcher`) should be used to handle the request. This kind of request dispatching is processed through a filtering mechanism and there are some built-in filters that will help dispatch the requests to the proper endpoint. For example, there is a default `AddressFilter` instance associated with each endpoint which determines the request dispatching based on the request URL of the incoming request and the target endpoint's address. What's more powerful is that WCF also allows developers to create a custom filter to control the request dispatching based on their own requirement. In this recipe, we will illustrate how to use a custom `MessageFilter` to control service request dispatching.

How to do it...

Our sample case here will create a custom `MessageFilter` that demands a custom SoapHeader (carrying some culture information) from each request message and only messages that contain the correct header will be dispatched to the target endpoint.

1. Define a custom `MessageFilter` type.

   The first step is to create a custom `MessageFilter` type, which derives from the `System.ServiceModel.Dispatcher.MessageFilter` type. The `MessageFilter` abstract class contains two methods that need to be implemented. Both the `Match` methods are used to determine whether the incoming request message is matching the target service endpoint. In our sample `CultureHeaderFilter` (see the following code snippet), we will look up the `Headers` collection of the incoming message and try finding the message header with the name `culture`. If the expected culture header is not found, the message is determined as an invalid request message for the target endpoint.

   ```
   public class CultureHeaderFilter : MessageFilter
   {
       public CultureHeaderFilter()
       {}

       public override bool Match(System.ServiceModel.Channels.Message
                                  message)
       {
           // Look for the culture header
           int i = message.Headers.FindHeader("culture",
                           "urn:wcf:extension");

           return (i >= 0);
       }

       public override bool
               Match(System.ServiceModel.Channels.MessageBuffer buffer)
       {
           return Match(buffer.CreateMessage());
       }
   }
   ```

2. Create a custom `EndpointBehavior` class.

   Like other WCF extension components, `MessageFilter` can also be registered to a service endpoint through a custom behavior. Here we will define a custom `EndpointBehavior` to register the sample `CultureHeaderFilter`. The following code snippet shows the complete implementation of the custom `EndpointBehavior` and its corresponding `BehaviorExtension` type, which is used to register the `EndpointBehavior` in the service configuration file:

   ```
   public class CultureHeaderFilterEndpointBehavior :
                           IEndpointBehavior
   {
   ```

```csharp
        #region IEndpointBehavior Members
        public void ApplyDispatchBehavior(ServiceEndpoint endpoint,
                           EndpointDispatcher endpointDispatcher)
        {
            // Set AddressFilter to CultureHeaderFilter
            endpointDispatcher.AddressFilter =
                           new CultureHeaderFilter();
        }
        #endregion
    }


    public class CultureHeaderFilterEndpointBehaviorExtension :
                           BehaviorExtensionElement
    {
        public override Type BehaviorType
        {
            get { return typeof(CultureHeaderFilterEndpointBehavior); }
        }

        protected override object CreateBehavior()
        {
            return new CultureHeaderFilterEndpointBehavior();
        }
    }
```

3. Register the custom EndpointBehavior in the app.config file.

    After having the EndpointBehavior and BehaviorExtension type defined, we
    can register them within the app.config file of the target WCF service application.
    The following screenshot shows the <extensions> section within the web.config
    file of our sample service.

```xml
<extensions>
  <behaviorExtensions>
    <add name="cultureFilterBehavior"
         type="CustomLib.CultureHeaderFilterEndpointBehaviorExtension,
         />

  </behaviorExtensions>
</extensions>
/system.serviceModel>
```

4. Apply the custom `EndpointBehavior` onto the target WCF service.

    Finally, we come to the step for making our sample service use the custom `MessageFilter` component. This is done by applying the custom `CultureHeaderFilterEndpointBehavior` on the sample service endpoint.

    The following XML fragment screenshot shows the endpoint behavior configuration section of the sample service, which contains the `cultureFilterBehavior` element registered in the previous steps.

```
  <endpointBehaviors>
    <behavior name="customFilterBehavior">
      <cultureFilterBehavior/>
    </behavior>
  </endpointBehaviors>
</behaviors>

<services>
  <service name="WCFServiceApp.Service1" >
    <endpoint behaviorConfiguration="customFilterBehavior"
```

With all the previously mentioned types and configuration entries defined, the custom `CultureHeaderFilter` will start working when any incoming request arrives at the sample WCF service endpoint.

How it works...

In our sample service application, the `CultureHeaderFilter` component ensures that the request message contains a message header named `culture` (and corresponding namespace). If the client service proxy directly invokes the service operation without adding the custom message header, an `EndpointNotFoundException` will be returned to the client, as shown in the next screenshot.

```
C:\Windows\system32\cmd.exe
System.ServiceModel.EndpointNotFoundException: The message with To 'http://local
host:29789/Service1.svc' cannot be processed at the receiver, due to an AddressF
ilter mismatch at the EndpointDispatcher.  Check that the sender and receiver's
EndpointAddresses agree.

Server stack trace:
```

This exception indicates that the error is caused by an `AddressFilter` validation failure at the `EndpointDispatcher` of the target service endpoint. To resolve the problem, we can simply add a dynamic `culture` SOAP header into the operation request (as the following code snippet shows) so that the request will pass the filtering and reach the target endpoint:

```
TestProxy.Service1Client client =
                    new TestProxy.Service1Client();

using (OperationContextScope scope =
                    new OperationContextScope(client.InnerChannel))
```

```
{
    MessageHeader<string> cultureHeader = new
                    MessageHeader<string>("en-US");

    // Add the culture header into request
    OperationContext.Current.OutgoingMessageHeaders.Add(
                    cultureHeader.GetUntypedHeader("culture",
                    "urn:wcf:extension")
                    );

    client.GetData(11);
}
```

See also

▶ *Adding a dynamic SoapHeader into a message* in *Chapter 5*

▶ *Complete source code for this recipe can be found in the* `\Chapter 9\recipe3\` *folder*

Generic operation error handling with OperationInvoker

WCF provides a built-in interface called `IErrorHandler` for handling exceptions occurring within the WCF service operations processing pipeline. By using the `IErrorHandler` interface, you can capture those unhandled exceptions during service operation execution and return a customized `FaultException` object to the client.

However, if you feel `IErrorHandler` is not flexible or powerful enough, you can consider creating your own generic error-handling component, which can handle the exceptions occurring during the execution of certain WCF operations at the server side. In this recipe, we will demonstrate how to use the `IOperationInvoker` extension point to implement a custom operation error-handling component.

How to do it...

In the sample service, we will create a custom `OperationInvoker` and use it to intercept exceptions in each service operation call and log the exceptions into the Windows Event Log system.

1. Implement a custom `OperationInvoker` class.

   A WCF `OperationInvoker` can be created by implementing the `System.ServiceModel.Dispatcher.IOperationInvoker` interface. There are four methods that need to be defined in this interface:

Name	Description
AllocateInputs	Returns a System.Array of parameter objects.
Invoke	Returns an object and a set of output objects from an instance and set of input objects.
InvokeBegin	An asynchronous implementation of the Invoke method.
InvokeEnd	The asynchronous end method.

The Invoke method is the one in which we can intercept the operation call results and perform customization on them. Here we will create an ErrorHandlingInvoker class, which implements the IOperationInvoker interface and uses an Invoke member to capture the unhandled exceptions that occurred in the operation execution and log the error info into the server event log.

Since our sample ErrorHandlingInvoker only supports synchronous operation execution, we will focus on the Invoke and AllocateInputs interface members. The following code snippet shows the complete implementation of the ErrorHandlingInvoker type:

```
public class ErrorHandlingInvoker : IOperationInvoker
{
    private IOperationInvoker _baseInvoker = null;

    public ErrorHandlingInvoker(IOperationInvoker baseInvoker)
    {
        // Store the original default invoker
        _baseInvoker = baseInvoker;
    }

    #region IOperationInvoker Members

    public object[] AllocateInputs()
    {
        return _baseInvoker.AllocateInputs();
    }

    public object Invoke(object instance, object[] inputs,
                         out object[] outputs)
    {
        try
        {
            return _baseInvoker.Invoke(instance, inputs,
                          out outputs);
```

```
        }
        catch (Exception ex)
        {
            // Log the exception
            EventLog.WriteEntry(
                    "WCF ErrorHandling Invoker",
                    ex.ToString(),
                    EventLogEntryType.Error);

            outputs = new object[0];
            return string.Empty;
        }
    }
}
```

2. Define a custom `OperationBehavior` type.

    Like most other WCF extension components, we will also use a custom behavior
    to register it into the service runtime. Since the `OperationInvoker` component
    is operation oriented, we will implement a custom `OperationBehavior` for
    installing it. The following code snippet shows the main functionality of the custom
    `OperationBehavior` type used in our sample case:

```
public class ErrorHandlingOperationBehavior:
                    Attribute, IOperationBehavior
{
    #region IOperationBehavior Members

    public void ApplyDispatchBehavior(
                OperationDescription operationDescription,
                System.ServiceModel.Dispatcher.DispatchOperation
                dispatchOperation)
    {
        // Replace the default invoker with our custom
        ErrorHandlingInvoker
        ErrorHandlingInvoker errInvoker =
                new ErrorHandlingInvoker(dispatchOperation.Invoker);
        dispatchOperation.Invoker = errInvoker;
    }
    #endregion
}
```

In the `ApplyDispatchBehavior` member, we can find that the default `OperationInvoker` instance can be acquired from the `dispatchOperation` parameter of the `IOperationBehavior.ApplyDispatchBehavior` function. Our sample behavior class simply creates an `ErrorHandlingInvoker` instance to wrap the default `OperationBehavior` object and assign it to the `dispatchOperation` instance.

3. Apply the custom `OperationBehavior` type to the target service operations.

   The last step is to apply the custom `OperationBehavior` onto the target service operations. Here we will apply the `ErrorHandlingOperationBehavior` to the `GetData` operation in our sample service. The following code snippet shows the `ServiceContract` definition of the sample service, which contains the `GetData` operation:

   ```
   [ServiceContract]
   public interface IService1
   {
       [OperationContract]
       [CustomLib.ErrorHandlingOperationBehavior]
       string GetData(int value);


   }
   ```

How it works...

In the type constructor of our sample `OperationInvoker` class, we accept an `IOperationInvoker` instance and store it with a class member. This `IOperationInvoker` instance is the default operation invoker supplied by WCF runtime and our custom invoker class will use it to perform the real operation execution (refer to the `Invoke` method implementation above). The try-catch block will capture any exception that occurred during the operation execution and log it into the `Application` event source of the server Event Log system.

After applying the `ErrorHandlingOperationBehavior`, the WCF runtime will replace the default `OperationBehavior` of the `GetData` operation with our custom `ErrorHandlingInvoker`. If there is any exception thrown when the `GetData` operation code runs, the `ErrorHandlingInvoker.Invoke` method can capture it immediately. The following code snippet shows the `GetData` operation implementation in our sample service which will throw an `ArgumentException` based on the input parameter:

```
public class Service1 : IService1
{
    public string GetData(int value)
    {
```

```
        if (value < 0) throw new ArgumentException("Invalid Number!");

        return string.Format("You entered: {0}", value);
    }
......
```

As the code shows, the exception details will be logged into the Event Log system on the server machine. Here is a sample Event Log entry displayed in the Event Log viewer.

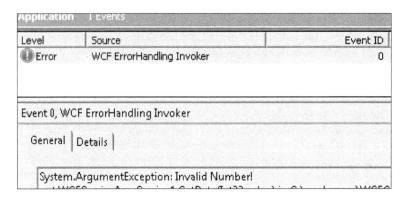

There's more...

In this recipe, the `ErrorHandlingInvoker` simply logs the error information. For real-world scenarios, we can add any other additional exception-handling code logic, such as rethrowing the exception or returning a custom data object as the return value.

In addition, `IOperationInvoker` provides a generic intercepting point of WCF service operation execution. We can use it to achieve more advanced extension functionalities such as implementing AOP-like patterns for multiple service operations.

▶ IErrorHandler Interface

   `http://msdn.microsoft.com/en-us/library/system.servicemodel.dispatcher.ierrorhandler.aspx`

See also

▶ *Complete source code for this recipe can be found in the* `\Chapter 9\recipe4\` *folder*

Altering operation messages via MessageInspector

In this chapter, we have covered many WCF extension components that can intercept the service operation calls, including `OperationInvoker`, `ParameterInspectors`, and `MessageFilter`. Each of them focuses on a certain point within the entire WCF operation execution process. This recipe will introduce another extension component, `MessageInspector`, which can help intercept the entire SOAP message of each WCF operation call.

How to do it...

In our sample scenario, we have a WCF service that contains an operation that returns a list of `ProductItem` objects (each of which contains a `Name` and an `Amount` property). The `ServiceContract` and related data types are shown in the following code snippet:

```
[ServiceContract]
public interface IDataService
{
    [OperationContract]
    List<ProductItem> GetProductList();
}

[DataContract(Namespace="")]
public class ProductItem
{
    [DataMember]
    public string Name { get; set; }
    [DataMember]
    public int Amount { get; set; }
}
```

And, we will create a custom `MessageInspector` to intercept the underlying SOAP response message of each `GetProductList` operation call and inject an additional `ProductItem` record, which represents the `Total Amount` of all the ProductItems returned.

1. Define a custom `MessageInspector` type.

    The first thing to do is to create a custom `MessageInspector` type. WCF supports `MessageInspector` at both server and client side with two different interfaces—`System.ServiceModel.Dispatcher.IDispatchMessageInspector` and `System.ServiceModel.Dispatcher.IClientMessageInspector`. For our case, as we need to intercept the SOAP response message at the WCF client, we will implement the `IClientMessageInspector` interface in our sample `MessageInspector` type.

As the following table shows, there are two operation members in the `IClientMessageInspector` interface—the `AfterReceiveReply` operation, which can help intercept the response message returned from the server side, and the `BeforeSendRequest`, which can help intercept the request message sent out from the client.

Name	Description
AfterReceiveReply	Enables inspection or modification of a message after a reply message is received, but prior to passing it back to the client application.
BeforeSendRequest	Enables inspection or modification of a message before a request message is sent to a service.

The sample `MessageInspector` implements the `AfterReceiveReply` method and modifies the original `Message` object returned from the service. The new `Message` instance will contain an additional `ProductItem` element at the end of the `ProductItem` list. The complete code logic of the custom `MessageInspector` class is shown in the following code snippet:

```
public class SumMessageInspector : IClientMessageInspector
{
    #region IClientMessageInspector Members

    public void AfterReceiveReply(ref
                      System.ServiceModel.Channels.Message reply,
                      object correlationState)
    {
        reply = GetTransformedMessage(reply);
    }

    Message GetTransformedMessage(Message oldMsg)
    {
        MessageBuffer mb = oldMsg.CreateBufferedCopy(int.MaxValue);
        Message newMsg = mb.CreateMessage();

        var reader = newMsg.GetReaderAtBodyContents().ReadSubtree();
        XElement bodyElm = XElement.Load(reader);

        var items = bodyElm.Descendants("ProductItem");
        int totalAmount = 0;
        foreach (var item in items)
        {
```

```
                totalAmount += int.Parse(item.Element("Amount").Value);

        }


        var products = items.First().Parent;
        products.Add(
                new XElement("ProductItem",
                new XElement("Amount", totalAmount),
                new XElement("Name", "TotalItems")
                )
                );
        reader.Close();
        newMsg.Close();

        MemoryStream ms = new MemoryStream();
        bodyElm.Save(ms);
        ms.Position = 0;

        var xmlreader = XmlDictionaryReader.CreateTextReader(
                ms, new XmlDictionaryReaderQuotas());

        newMsg = Message.CreateMessage(oldMsg.Version,
                oldMsg.Headers.Action, xmlreader);
        newMsg.Headers.CopyHeadersFrom(oldMsg.Headers);
        newMsg.Properties.CopyProperties(oldMsg.Properties);

        return newMsg;
    }

}
```

2. Create a custom `EndpointBehavior` type.

   Since our custom `SumMessageInspector` is only used at the WCF client, we just implement a custom `EndpointBehavior` class (for injecting the `MessageInspector` into the client runtime). The following code snippet shows the complete implementation of the `SumInspectorBehavior` class:

```
public class SumInspectorBehavior : IEndpointBehavior
{
    #region IEndpointBehavior Members

    public void ApplyClientBehavior(ServiceEndpoint endpoint,
                    ClientRuntime clientRuntime)
```

```
    {
        clientRuntime.MessageInspectors.Add(
                new SumMessageInspector());
    }
}
```

3. Register the custom `EndpointBehavior` in the service client.

   Now, we need to apply the custom `MessageInspector` to our sample WCF service client. This time, we will use the programmatic way to install the `MessageInspector` instead of the declarative approach (which we have used in other recipes in this chapter).

   Since the client application uses **ChannelFactory** to consume the WCF service, we directly inject the custom `SumInspectorBehavior` object into the `Behaviors` collection of the client endpoint (see the `CallService` function in the following code snippet):

```
private static void CallService()
{

    ChannelFactory<WCFServiceApp.IDataService> cf =
                new ChannelFactory<WCFServiceApp.IDataService>(
                        binding,
                        svc_url);
    cf.Endpoint.Behaviors.Add(
                new CustomLib.SumInspectorBehavior());

    WCFServiceApp.IDataService dataproxy = cf.CreateChannel();

    foreach (var item in dataproxy.GetProductList())
    {
        Console.WriteLine("Name: {0}, Amount: {1}", item.Name,
                item.Amount);
    }
}
```

As the `CallService` function demonstrates, the custom `SumMessageInspector` instance is injected via the `SumInspectorBehavior`, which is added into the `Endpoint.Behaviors` collection during the construction of the WCF ChannelFactory instance.

How it works...

In our sample service, since we only want to alter the response messages sent from the server side (in the client application), we have only implemented the `AfterReceiveReply` method of the `IClientMessageInspector` interface (leave the `BeforeSendRequest` method not implemented). In case you want to perform any message modification before the operation call sent from the client service stack, you should implement the `BeforeSendRequest` method.

The console client application uses ChannelFactory to consume the WCF service and displays all the `ProductItem` records returned in the `GetProductList` operation call. By using WCF message logging, we can capture the original SOAP message returned from the server side. The following XML fragment shows the response SOAP message captured from the sample service.

```
<s:Body>
  <GetProductListResponse xmlns="http://tempuri.org/">
    <GetProductListResult xmlns:i="http://www.w3.org/200
      <ProductItem xmlns="">
        <Amount>11</Amount>
        <Name>Product1</Name>
      </ProductItem>
      <ProductItem xmlns="">
        <Amount>22</Amount>
        <Name>Product2</Name>
      </ProductItem>
      <ProductItem xmlns="">
        <Amount>33</Amount>
        <Name>Product3</Name>
      </ProductItem>
```

As you can see, the service operation call corresponding to the message (see the previous screenshot) contains three `ProductItem` objects. However, since the `SumMessageInspector` injects a new `ProductItem` (with the *Total Amount* calculated from all the existing `ProductItem` objects), the final output of the client application shows four records including the **Total Amount** item at the bottom (which is shown in the following console output screenshot).

```
C:\Windows\system32\cmd.exe
Name: Product1, Amount: 11
Name: Product2, Amount: 22
Name: Product3, Amount: 33
Name: TotalItems, Amount: 66
Press any key to continue . . .
```

In real-world WCF application development scenarios, we can use `MessageInspector` to achieve many more message-level tasks, such as validating message content, transforming messages, and so on.

See also

▸ *Using ChannelFactory to consume a WCF service* in *Chapter 5*

▸ *Using built-in tracing and message logging* in *Chapter 12*

▸ *Complete source code for this recipe can be found in the* `\Chapter 9\recipe5\` *folder*

Building a custom MessageEncoder

MessageInspector can intercept the underlying messages of WCF service operation calls. However, this is not the only way for intercepting and customizing messages in a WCF service. In WCF extension architecture, there is another powerful component called `MessageEncoder`, which can also perform customization on the underlying messages of WCF service operation calls.

In this recipe, we will demonstrate how we can use a custom MessageEncoder to alter the raw message of a WCF service operation.

How to do it...

The sample service will use a custom `MessageEncoder` component to customize the SOAP XML content of each service operation call. The entire process will be as follows:

▸ Create a custom `MessageEncoder` type

▸ Create a custom `MessageEncoderFactory` type

▸ Create a custom `EncoderBindingElement` type for registering the encoder in the `BindingElement` stack

▸ Inject the custom `EncoderBindingElement` into the target service endpoint

Let's look at each of these steps in detail.

1. Create a custom `MessageEncoder` type.

    First, we will define a custom `Encoder` type derived from the `System.ServiceModel.Channels.MessageEncoder` base type. The `MessageEncoder` type contains several virtual functions related to message reading/writing, as shown in the following table.

Name	Description
`ReadMessage(ArraySegment<Byte>, BufferManager, String)`	When overridden in a derived class, reads a message from a specified stream.
`ReadMessage(Stream, Int32, String)`	When overridden in a derived class, reads a message from a specified stream.

Name	Description
WriteMessage(Message, Stream)	When overridden in a derived class, writes a message to a specified stream.
WriteMessage(Message, Int32, BufferManager, Int32)	When overridden in a derived class, writes a message of less than a specified size to a byte array buffer at the specified offset.

The ReadMessage function is responsible for deserializing the raw data obtained from the transport layer into the WCF message object. The WriteMessage function on the contrary will focus on serializing WCF Message object into its raw content at the transport layer. For our sample case, we will only deal with *Buffered* transfer mode (regardless of *Streaming* mode). Therefore, we only need to implement the ReadMessage/WriteMessage pairs that accept the ArraySegment<byte> type as parameter. The following code snippet shows the main implementation of the sample CustomEncoder class:

```
public class CustomEncoder : MessageEncoder
{

    public override Message ReadMessage(ArraySegment<byte> buffer,
                BufferManager bufferManager, string contentType)
    {
        byte[] msgContents = new byte[buffer.Count];
        Array.Copy(buffer.Array, buffer.Offset, msgContents, 0,
                msgContents.Length);
        bufferManager.ReturnBuffer(buffer.Array);

        MemoryStream stream = new MemoryStream(msgContents);

        XmlReader reader = XmlReader.Create(stream);
        XElement elm = XElement.Load(reader);
        reader.Close();

        var msgElm = elm.Descendants().First();
        XmlReader msgReader = msgElm.CreateReader();

        return Message.CreateMessage(msgReader, int.MaxValue,
                this.MessageVersion);
    }
    public override Message ReadMessage(Stream stream, int
                maxSizeOfHeaders, string contentType)
    {
        return this.innerEncoder.ReadMessage(stream,
                maxSizeOfHeaders, contentType);
```

```
      }

      public override ArraySegment<byte> WriteMessage(Message
                  message, int maxMessageSize,
                  BufferManager bufferManager, int messageOffset)
      {
         MemoryStream stream = new MemoryStream();
         XmlWriter writer = XmlWriter.Create(stream,
                  new XmlWriterSettings());
         writer.WriteStartElement("CustomEnvelope", "");
         message.WriteMessage(writer);
         writer.WriteEndElement();
         writer.Close();

         byte[] messageBytes = stream.GetBuffer();
         int messageLength = (int)stream.Position;
         stream.Close();

         int totalLength = messageLength + messageOffset;
         byte[] totalBytes = bufferManager.TakeBuffer(totalLength);
         Array.Copy(messageBytes, 0, totalBytes, messageOffset,
                  messageLength);

         ArraySegment<byte> byteArray =
                  new ArraySegment<byte>(
                  totalBytes, messageOffset, messageLength
                  );
         return byteArray;
      }
   }
```

As the `ReadMessage` and `WriterMessage` methods have shown, our sample encoder will add a custom wrapper XML element around the default WCF message content.

2. Create a custom `MessageEncoderFactory` type.

   A `MessageEncoderFactory` type is always required for activating a certain `MessageEncoder` instance. Therefore, the next step is to define a custom `MessageEncoderFactory` type. Building the `EncoderFactory` type is quite straightforward since the only important member to implement is the `MessageEncoder` property, which will be called by WCF runtime so as to obtain the `Encoder` instance. Here we simply return a `CustomEncoder` instance in our sample implementation (see the code of the `CustomEncoderFactory` type displayed as follows):

```
public class CustomEncoderFactory : MessageEncoderFactory
{

    public override MessageEncoder Encoder
    {
        get { return new CustomEncoder(......); }
    }
}
```

3. Create a custom `EncoderBindingElement` type for registering the encoder in `BindingElement` stack.

Having the `MessageEncoder` and `MessageEncoderFactory` types defined, we still need to define a custom `EncoderBindingElement` type which will represent a `BindingElement` to be used within a WCF service binding (like BasicHttpBinding, WSHttpBinding, or CustomBinding). The following code snippet shows the main section of the sample `EncoderBindingElement` type:

```
public class CustomEncoderBindingElement :
                   MessageEncodingBindingElement
{

    public override MessageEncoderFactory
                  CreateMessageEncoderFactory()
    {
        return new CustomEncoderFactory(this,
                    innerBindingElement.CreateMessageEncoderFactory()
                    );
    }

     public override IChannelFactory<TChannel>
            BuildChannelFactory<TChannel>(BindingContext context)
    {
        context.BindingParameters.Add(this);
        return base.BuildChannelFactory<TChannel>(context);
    }

    public override IChannelListener<TChannel>
            BuildChannelListener<TChannel>(BindingContext context)
    {
        context.BindingParameters.Add(this);
        return base.BuildChannelListener<TChannel>(context);
    }
}
```

4. Inject the custom `EncoderBindingElement` into the target service endpoint.

Finally, we can use code to build a `CustomBinding` containing our custom `EncoderBindingElement` type (see the `GetCustomBinding` function shown as follows):

```
static Binding GetCustomBinding()
{
    var cb = new CustomBinding(
                new CustomEncoderBindingElement(
                new TextMessageEncodingBindingElement()),
                new HttpTransportBindingElement()
                {
                    TransferMode = TransferMode.Buffered
                }
            );
    return cb;
}
```

Any WCF service that wants to use the custom `MessageEncoder` needs to use this `CustomBinding` (obtained from the `GetCustomBinding` function) for the service endpoints it contains.

How it works...

In the previous sample `CustomEncoderBindingElement` type, there is a `MessageEncoderFactory` property which is responsible for providing an instance of the `MessageEncoderFactory` type. However, the remaining two methods (`BuildChannelFactory` and `BuildChannelListener`) look a bit strange here. Actually, both of the methods are responsible for registering the custom `EncoderBindingElement` type into the `Encoder` list of the underlying WCF Channel. The runtime will ignore the custom encoder without having the custom `EncoderBindingElement` added in the `BindingContext.BindingParameters` collection.

By using the custom encoder class, the WCF runtime will call into the `ReadMessage` and `WriteMessage` implementation at the same time the `Message` object of a certain service operation call comes in or goes out of the Channel.

In our sample test service, the `CustomBinding` uses plain HttpTransportBindingElement so that we can use the Fiddler tool to capture the request and response data over the wire. Here is the request message that has been altered by the `CustomEncoder`.

Headers	TextView	WebForms	HexView	Auth	Raw	XML	

```
<?xml version="1.0" encoding="utf-8"?><CustomEnvelope><s:Envelope
xmlns:s="http://schemas.xmlsoap.org/soap/envelope/"><s:Body><Add xmlns="http://tempuri.o
</lv><rv>5</rv></Add></s:Body></s:Envelope></CustomEnvelope>
```

The next screenshot shows the response message of the sample service. We can find that the serialized message content is obviously different from a standard SOAP message, since there is an additional `<CustomEnvelope>` element at the root.

Transformer	Headers	TextView	ImageView	HexView	WebView	Auth	Caching

Raw	XML

```
<?xml version="1.0" encoding="utf-8"?><CustomEnvelope><s:Envelope xmlns:a="http://www.w3.org/2005/0{
xmlns:s="http://www.w3.org/2003/05/soap-envelope"><s:Header><a:Action s:mustUnderstand="1">
http://tempuri.org/ICalcService/AddResponse</a:Action><a:RelatesTo>urn:uuid:1ea5062c-90a9-4ad2-9ea6-{
</a:RelatesTo></s:Header><s:Body><AddResponse xmlns="http://tempuri.org/"><AddResult>8</AddResult>
</AddResponse></s:Body></s:Envelope></CustomEnvelope>
```

In addition, compared with `MessageInspector`, `MessageEncoder` gives you the opportunity to alter the message in its serialized format, while `MessageInspector` lets you alter the WCF message in a strong-type manner. Or, we can say that `MessageEncoder` intercepts the operation message at the Transport layer, while `MessageInspector` still processes the message at the WCF service level.

There's more...

In this recipe, we have defined a custom `EncoderBindingElement` for registering the custom `MessageEncoder` into the WCF Binding element stack, which requires that the `CustomBinding` be created programmatically. Alternatively, we can also create a `ConfigurationSectionHandler` so that the custom `MessageEncoderBindingElement` can be injected declaratively in the `app.config` file. For detailed information on using Configuration Handler for `MessageEncoder` registering, you can refer to the following MSDN article:

- Message Encoding Binding Configuration Handler

  `http://msdn.microsoft.com/en-us/library/ms751486.aspx`

See also

- *Altering an operation message via MessageInspector*
- *Capturing a WCF request/response message via the Fiddler tool* in *Chapter 12*
- *Complete source code for this recipe can be found in the* `\Chapter 9\recipe6\` *folder*

Centralizing authorization through a custom ServiceAuthorizationManager

Authorization plays a very important role in service security. By adopting proper authorization policies and rules, we can control who can access which part of the functions exposed in a particular WCF service.

WCF provides several means to perform operation authorization, such as role-based and claim-based authorization. These built-in authorization means will work well for most cases, since the authenticated client identity will be used for determining the authorization result. However, sometimes we will need to apply some custom code logic for service operation authorization.

In this recipe, we will demonstrate how we can use the `ServiceAuthorizationManager` to implement custom service access authorization.

How to do it...

Among all the available custom authorization approaches, using a custom `ServiceAuthorizationManager` is a very simple and clear one. Our sample case will use a custom `ServiceAuthorizationManager` to control the operation access based on an HTTP header in the request message. Let's take a look at the detailed steps to implement this solution:

1. Define a custom `ServiceAuthorizationManager` type.

    The first thing we need to do is create a custom implementation of the `System.ServiceModel.ServiceAuthorizationManager` class. This is the built-in base type for other concrete `ServiceAuthorizationManager` classes.

    Our sample `ServiceAuthorizationManager` class simply overrides the `CheckAccessCore` method and detects whether there is a **User-Agent** HTTP header there. If the header is not found, the service operation access will fail. The following code snippet shows the complete implementation of the `CheckAccessCore` method in our sample `ServiceAuthorizationManager` class:

```
public class CustomAuthManager : ServiceAuthorizationManager
{
    protected override bool CheckAccessCore(
                OperationContext operationContext)
    {

        HttpRequestMessageProperty httpProps =
                OperationContext.Current.IncomingMessageProperties
                [HttpRequestMessageProperty.Name]
                as HttpRequestMessageProperty;
```

```
        string userAgent = httpProps.Headers["User-Agent"];

        if (string.IsNullOrEmpty(userAgent)) return false;
        return true;
    }
}
```

2. Apply the custom `ServiceAuthorizationManager` in the server application.

   What makes the custom `ServiceAuthorizationManager` approach very convenient is that the steps to apply it in the target service are quite simple and straightforward. What we need to do is specify the custom `ServiceAuthorizationManager` type in the `<serviceAuthorization>` behavior. The following fragment shows how the sample `ServiceAuthorizationManager` is registered in the service behavior configuration entry.

```
<serviceBehaviors>
  <behavior>
    <!-- register the custom AuthorizationManager -->
    <serviceAuthorization
      serviceAuthorizationManagerType="CustomLib.CustomAuthManager,
                        />
```

   After applying the custom `ServiceAuthorizationManager` type, whenever a certain service operation of the target server is invoked, the `CheckAccessCore` method of the custom `ServiceAuthorizationManager` instance will be invoked so as to determine the authorization result, based on our own code logic.

How it works...

The `ServiceAuthorizationManager` type contains several methods that can be overridden. For typical cases, we only need to override the `CheckAccessCore` method of the `ServiceAuthorizationManager` base class. This method is called by the WCF runtime every time a service operation is requested by the client.

In the previous sample `CheckAccessCore` implementation, we used a User-Agent HTTP header to determine the service operation access control result. This forces the service client caller to supply a User-Agent header in the operation request (see the `CallService` function shown as follows):

```
static void CallService()
{
    TestProxy.Service1Client client = new TestProxy.Service1Client();
    using (OperationContextScope scope = new
                    OperationContextScope(client.InnerChannel))
    {
```

```
HttpRequestMessageProperty httpProps =
                    new HttpRequestMessageProperty();
httpProps.Headers["User-Agent"] = "Test Client";

OperationContext.Current.OutgoingMessageProperties
                    [HttpRequestMessageProperty.Name] = httpProps;
Console.WriteLine(client.GetData(11));

        }
    }
```

In real-world service development scenarios, we can apply various kinds of service authorization code logic such as using a database for an access control rules repository or even calls to other Web Services for access control information. Anyway, no matter how the authorization details are implemented, the `ServiceAuthorizationManager` opens a straight and convenient door for common service authorization-extending requirements.

See also

> ▸ *Authorizing through declarative role-based access control* in *Chapter 7*

> ▸ *Complete source code for this recipe can be found in the* `\Chapter 9\recipe7\` *folder*

10

RESTful and AJAX-enabled WCF Services

In this chapter, we will cover:

- ▶ Building a self-hosted REST service
- ▶ Using an auto-generated Help page
- ▶ Mapping URL suffix to operation parameters
- ▶ Applying `OutputCache` in a REST service
- ▶ Implementing a file download via REST endpoint
- ▶ Consuming a WCF service from a ASP.NET AJAX client
- ▶ Accessing a remote REST service in an AJAX client

Introduction

Though by default a WCF service will use SOAP XML and WSDL for service transferring and description, it is no longer the only means. There is another service style called, **REST** (**Representational State Transfer**), which is becoming more and more popular in the distributed service development area. In REST service programming, every service can expose its service operations or other public resources through a URI. And in most cases, the URI is just a standard HTTP URL string so that the REST service client can consume it through standard HTTP GET/POST requests. This really makes it very simple and convenient to consume a REST service.

To align the popularity of the RESTful service trend, WCF starts providing REST service programming support from version 3.5, which gets further enhanced in version 4.0.

In this chapter, we will go through the REST-oriented features in WCF programming, especially focusing on how we can leverage the WCF REST programming model to build REST-style services and how we can consume REST services using different kinds of client applications like the ASP.NET AJAX scripting client.

Building a self-hosted REST service

Since a REST-style WCF service provides an endpoint that is accessible through standard HTTP GET/POST requests, it is quite common and reasonable to host a REST service in an ASP.NET web application (via a `.svc` file). However, we can also use any .NET-managed application to host a WCF REST service out of an IIS server.

In this recipe, we will demonstrate how to use a console application to host a WCF REST service.

How to do it...

Creating a self-hosted REST service is quite similar to a standard WCF service, but with some minor differences. Let's take a look at the detailed steps here:

1. Define the `ServiceContract` for the REST service.

    The first thing to do is define a `ServiceContract` for our sample REST service. Here we will use a very typical interface as the `ServiceContract` of the sample REST service (see the following code snippet):

    ```
    [ServiceContract(Namespace="WCF.REST")]
    public interface IDataService
    {
        [OperationContract]
        [WebGet(ResponseFormat= WebMessageFormat.Json)]
        SimpleData GetData();
    }

    [DataContract]
    public class SimpleData
    {
        [DataMember]
        public string StringValue { get; set; }
        [DataMember]
        public bool BoolValue { get; set; }
        [DataMember]
        public int IntValue { get; set; }
    }
    ```

The `IDataService ServiceContract` only contains a single operation `GetData` that will return a custom type instance. It is worth noticing that the `GetData` has an additional `WebGetAttribute` applied on it. This attribute indicates that this service operation needs to be consumed through a HTTP GET request. There is also a corresponding `WebInvokeAttribute` for a HTTP POST request.

2. Add REST-specific configuration entries into the `app.config` file.

Having the `ServiceContract` type defined, the next step is to apply the appropriate service and endpoint configuration for our REST service. For a standard WCF REST service, the configuration includes two main parts; it is necessary to apply the following two configuration settings:

- Configure the REST service endpoint with WebHttpBinding
- Add the `<webHttp/>` behavior element in the endpoint behavior collection

The following configuration fragment shows the endpoint behavior with the `<webHttp/>` behavior element applied.

```
<system.serviceModel>
    <behaviors>
        <endpointBehaviors>
            <behavior name="RESTEndpointBehavior" >
                <webHttp/>
            </behavior>
```

And, the previous endpoint behavior needs to be linked to the target endpoint in the sample service. Here is the complete service endpoint configuration, which includes both the WebHttpBinding- and the WebHttp-enabled endpoint behavior.

```
<services>
    <service name="RESTServiceConsoleApp.DataService">
        <endpoint address="" behaviorConfiguration="RESTEndpointBehavior"
                  binding="webHttpBinding"
                  contract="RESTServiceConsoleApp.IDataService">
        </endpoint>
        <host>
            <baseAddresses>
                <add baseAddress="http://localhost:1111/RESTDataService/"
```

3. Start up the ServiceHost for the REST service.

The last step is to start up the ServiceHost for our sample REST service. The `RunService` function shows the service hosting code, in which a standard WCF ServiceHost instance is initialized and started:

```
private static void RunService()
{
    using (WebServiceHost host = new
                        WebServiceHost(typeof(DataService)))
```

```
    {
        host.Open();
        Console.WriteLine("REST service started...");
        Console.ReadLine();
    }
}
```

As you can see, the entire service hosting code logic looks similar to standard WCF self-hosted cases. However, the difference here is that we have used a host of the `System.ServiceModel.Web.WebServiceHost` type, which is dedicated for hosting REST style-services.

How it works...

After the sample REST service starts running, we can launch a web browser and consume the service by typing the endpoint address in the browser address bar. The following screenshot shows the data (returned by the `GetData` function) displayed in the web browser.

A WCF REST service supports two built-in response message content types for operation return value—XML and JSON. By default, XML is used if we do not explicitly set a response message format for REST service operations. In case we need to manually control the response format, we can change it through the `ResponseFormat` property of `WebGetAttribute` or `WebInvokeAttribute` (shown in the following code snippet):

```
[OperationContract]
[WebGet(ResponseFormat= WebMessageFormat.Json)]
SimpleData GetData();
```

In addition, it is very convenient to capture the underlying messages of a WCF REST service as they are transferred over the HTTP protocol. The next screenshot shows the captured response message of the `GetData` operation, which uses JSON as response message format.

```
Raw    XML
HTTP/1.1 200 OK
Content-Length: 60
Content-Type: application/json; charset=utf-8
Server: Microsoft-HTTPAPI/2.0
Date: Thu, 22 Jul 2010 09:48:47 GMT

{"BoolValue":true,"IntValue":11,"StringValue":"test string"}
```

See also

▸ *Capturing a WCF request/response message via the Fiddler tool* in *Chapter 12*

▸ *Complete source code for this recipe can be found in the* \Chapter 10\recipe1\ *folder*

Using an auto-generated Help page

Unlike SOAP-based WCF services, REST services use normal HTTP GET/POST requests for service communication. Therefore, a WSDL-based service metadata document is not that useful for describing a WCF REST service and the REST service clients will not use any pre-generated proxy class for consuming the REST service operations. In other words, for REST service client consumers, some service operation description information, like the operation endpoint address and message/parameter syntax, will be much more important than WSDL document or SOAP message format. Fortunately, in WCF 4.0 there is a *Help page* feature which can help a WCF REST service automatically provide a service description page to client consumers.

In this recipe, we will show you how the Help page feature can simplify the process of consuming a WCF REST service.

How to do it...

To demonstrate the WCF 4.0 Help page feature, we will use a typical REST service that contains two service operations with different method signatures and REST-specific settings. Let's have a look at the detailed steps to use Help page.

1. Define the ServiceContract of the REST service:

   The sample ICalcService ServiceContract contains two operations—Add, which uses the HTTP GET method, while the Subtract operation uses the HTTP POST method. The following code snippet shows the complete sample ServiceContract:

```
[ServiceContract]
public interface ICalcService
{
    [OperationContract]
    [WebGet(BodyStyle=WebMessageBodyStyle.Wrapped)]
    int Add(int lv, int rv);
    [OperationContract]
```

```
[WebInvoke(BodyStyle=WebMessageBodyStyle.Wrapped)]
int Subtract(int lv, int rv);
}
```

2. Turn on Help page in the service endpoint configuration.

   The next step is to enable the Help page feature, which is not enabled by default. This can be done by setting the `helpEnabled` attribute to `true` under the `<webHttp>` behavior element of the target service endpoint behavior. The following screenshot shows the endpoint and behavior configuration of the sample REST service.

```
<service name="WCFRESTService.CalcService">
  <endpoint address="" behaviorConfiguration="RESTEndpoint"
            binding="webHttpBinding"
            contract="WCFRESTService.ICalcService" />
</service>
services>
ehaviors>
<endpointBehaviors>
  <behavior name="RESTEndpoint">
    <webHttp helpEnabled="true" />
  </behavior>
```

3. Make sure `WebServiceHostFactory` is used when using an IIS host.

   This is an optional step and only required when the REST service is hosted in an IIS web application. Since our sample WCF REST service is hosted in a web application (instead of a self-hosting application), we need to make sure the `WebServiceHostFactory` type is used as the `Factory` in the `.svc`. This is necessary for the WCF REST programming model to take effect.

```
<%@ ServiceHost Language="C#" Debug="true" Service="WCFRESTService
Factory="System.ServiceModel.Activation.WebServiceHostFactory" %>
```

4. Access the Help page through the service base address.

   After having the service and behaviors configured correctly, we can visit the base address of the target service (the `.svc` file in our sample service) in the web browser. The browser will show you the service description page, which will lead you to the auto-generated Help page. Here is the Help page generated in our sample REST service.

avorites   Operations at http://localhost:7732/CalcService.svc

Operations at http://localhost:7732/CalcServi

This page describes the service operations at this endpoint.

Uri	Method	Description
Add	GET	Service at http://localhost:7732/CalcService.svc/Add?lv={LV}&rv={RV}
Subtract	POST	Service at http://localhost:7732/CalcService.svc/Subtract

The Help page will show all the service operations available within the currently selected service endpoint, including basic properties such as operation URI, HTTP protocol method, and brief description.

How it works...

In the default entry point of the auto-generated Help page, each operation description row has a hyperlink that points to the detailed information page of the corresponding service operation. The detailed page will provide a sample **Url** syntax for invoking the REST service operation (including placeholders for all the operation parameters). The following screenshot shows the sample detailed information page for the Add operation of the sample REST service.

Reference for http://localhost:7732/CalcS

Url: http://localhost:7732/CalcService.svc/Add?lv={LV}&rv={RV}

HTTP Method: GET

Message direction	Format	Body
Request	N/A	The Request body is empty.
Response	Unknown	Cannot infer schema. The Response body is wrapped.

See also

▶ *Complete source code for this recipe can be found in the* \Chapter 10\recipe2\ *folder*

Mapping URL suffix to operation parameters

Since WCF REST services use normal HTTP GET/POST for operation invocation, all the operation-wide data, like parameters and return value, are encapsulated in a HTTP message body or request header. And for WCF REST operations based on HTTP GET, the parameters are directly embedded in the URL string. By default, HTTP GET-based REST operations will use a **query string** for carrying input parameters. However, in real-world REST service scenarios, it is more common that we need to use more user-friendly URLs instead of the auto-generated query-string-based syntax so that the client consumers can call the REST service operations more conveniently.

In this recipe, we will demonstrate how we can use the UriTemplate feature of a WCF REST service to define a custom URL template for service operation.

How to do it...

We will continue to use the `CalcService` service as our example here, since the calculation operations are quite good for demonstrating the `UriTemplate` feature:

1. Apply `UriTemplate` on the REST service operations.

   Let's have a look at the `ServiceContract` definition first. This version of `CalcService` contains two `Add` operations with different URL syntax. One of them uses a standard query string for passing the input parameters, while the other uses a URL suffix to carry input parameters.

   Here is the complete `ServiceContract` definition of the sample `CalcService`:

   ```
   [ServiceContract]
   public interface ICalcService
   {
       [OperationContract]
       [WebGet(UriTemplate="Add?lv={lv}&rv={rv}")]
       int Add_ParamsInQueryString(string lv, string rv);

       [OperationContract]
       [WebGet(UriTemplate = "Add({lv},{rv})")]
       int Add_ParamsInUrlSuffix(string lv, string rv);
   }
   ```

   As you can see, the `ICalcService` type contains two service operations—`Add_paramsInQueryString` and `Add_ParamsInUrlSuffix`. The key point here is that both operations have applied a custom `UriTemplate` property through `WebGetAttribute`. The URL syntax of each operation is defined in `WebGetAttribute`.

2. Invoke the REST operation with the customized URL syntax.

   Now we can try using the customized URL syntax to call the REST operation defined in our `CalcService`. Since the `Add_ParamsInUrlSuffix` operation adopts a user-friendly URL template, we can invoke this operation in a web browser through a very simple and clear URL as follows:

   ```
   Http://servername:port/CalcService.svc/Add(1,3)
   ```

   The following screenshot shows the response data of the operation invoked through the above URL.

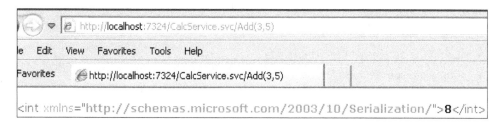

How it works...

In the previous sample service, the `UriTemplate` property is used by service developers to customize the URL format of a particular REST service operation. As the sample `OperationContract` shows, we can use a relative URL in the `UriTemplate` property and include operation parameters as part of the URL string. At runtime, each individual parameter can be identified through the `{param name}` style placeholder in the request URL of the service operation. The `Add_ParamsInQueryString` method uses a standard query string to carry its input parameters, while the `Add_ParamsInUrlSuffix` method carries input parameters directly in the URL suffix.

By using the Help page feature, we can get the URL syntax of the two sample operations, as shown in the following screenshot:

Operations at http://localhost:7324/CalcService.

This page describes the service operations at this endpoint.

AddParamsInQueryString

Uri	Method	Description
Add	GET	Service at http://localhost:7324/CalcService.svc/Add?lv={LV}&rv={RV}
Add({lv},{rv})	GET	Service at http://localhost:7324/CalcService.svc/Add({LV},{RV})

AddParamsInUrlSuffix

There's more...

The sample service operations define the two input parameters of the `Add` operation as `System.String` type, though they're actually used as `Integer` values. This is because the current `UriTemplate` of the WCF REST service operation only supports the string type for multiple parameter placeholders defined in one operation. So for any non-string type parameters, we need to manually parse them into their actual types within the operation code.

In addition, for more guidelines and restrictions on using the `UriTemplate` feature, you can refer to the following MSDN reference:

- UriTemplate and UriTemplateTable

  http://msdn.microsoft.com/en-us/library/bb675245.aspx

See also

> ▶ *Using the auto-generated Help page*
>
> ▶ *Complete source code for this recipe can be found in the* \Chapter 10\recipe3\ *folder*

Applying OutputCache in a REST service

In WCF REST service development, we will often encounter some cases in which we will return certain data that is very expensive to generate or is not frequently changed. For such REST service operations, WCF 4.0 adopts the OutputCache feature in ASP.NET web application platform so that the response of WCF REST service operations can also be cached at the server side according to some user-defined cache profile settings.

In this recipe, we will show you how to use the OutputCache feature in a WCF REST service.

How to do it...

The following steps will guide you in how to apply a simple OutputCache profile (which makes the operation response be cached for 30 seconds) onto a sample REST service:

1. Define an OutputCache profile.

   The REST service in WCF 4.0 directly takes advantage of the OutputCache functionality of ASP.NET runtime. So, we need to define a cache profile through the ASP.NET <outputCacheSettings> configuration entries. The following configuration fragment shows the sample cache profile that will cache the service response for 30 seconds.

   ```
   <outputCacheSettings>
     <outputCacheProfiles>
       <add name="CacheFor30Seconds"
            duration="30"
            varyByParam="None"
            enabled="true"/>

     </outputCacheProfiles>
   </outputCacheSettings>
   </caching>
   /system.web>
   ```

2. Apply the OutputCache profile to the target service operation.

   After defining the cache profile, we need to apply it on our WCF REST service. The OutputCache profile can be applied at individual operation level. For our sample REST service, we will apply the cache profile on the GetData operation as shown in the following code snippet.

```
[OperationContract]
[WebGet]
[AspNetCacheProfile("CacheFor30Seconds")]
string GetData();
```

As you can see, the `System.ServiceModel.Web.`
`AspNetCacheProfileAttribute` type is used for applying the `OutputCache`
profile on WCF service operations.

2. Turn on the ASP.NET Compatibility mode in the service environment.

So far, the sample `CacheFor30Seconds` cache profile has been applied onto the
`GetData` service operation. However, this is still not sufficient for the `OutputCache`
to work. Since the `OutputCache` is an ASP.NET feature, we need to enable
`AspNetCompatibility` mode in the hosting web application of the REST service.
There are two settings required for the ASP.NET Compatibility mode to be enabled.

One is to mark the REST service type with the
`AspNetCompatibilityRequirementsMode.Allowed` attribute (see the following
code snippet).

```
[AspNetCompatibilityRequirements(
RequirementsMode=AspNetCompatibilityRequirementsMode.Allowed
)]
public class DataService : IDataService
{
```

The other is to turn on the `AspNetCompatibility` mode in the `web.config` file of
the hosting web application (see the configuration fragment).

```
<system.serviceModel>
  <serviceHostingEnvironment
    aspNetCompatibilityEnabled="true"
```

How it works...

Now, we have done all the things necessary for making `OutputCache` work in a WCF
REST service. For our sample service, whenever the `GetData` operation is newly called, its
response content will be cached for 30 seconds (based on the cache profile applied) so that
sequential operation calls will get processed much more quickly.

There's more...

The ASP.NET `OutputCache` profile supports more advanced cache options, such as caching by file, by HTTP headers, or even by custom code logic. For more information on the ASP.NET `OutputCache` profile, you can refer to the following MSDN document:

- add Element for outputCacheProfiles for caching

  `http://msdn.microsoft.com/en-us/library/ms228300.aspx`

See also

- *Hosting a HTTP service with a ASP.NET-compatible context* in *Chapter 3*
- *Complete source code for this recipe can be found in the* `\Chapter 10\recipe4\` *folder*

Implementing file download via REST endpoint

WCF REST services by default convert the response content of service operations into either XML or JSON format. However, these two formats are definitely not the only formats we can use for responses of REST operations. By customizing the `OperationContract` of a service operation, we can make the operation return any arbitrary format of data, such as image, text, ZIP package, or even raw binary files.

In this recipe, we will use a custom REST service that returns files to client consumers as an example to demonstrate how we can use a REST service endpoint to return data in a customized format.

How to do it...

To return custom format data in a WCF REST service, the most important thing is designing the `ServiceContract` and `OperationContract` to support the response of arbitrary binary format. This can be achieved by changing the return value to `System.IO.Stream` type, which is a magic type through which the operation code can return any kind of data content to the client.

The `IFileService` type shows the sample REST `ServiceContract`, which defines a `GetFile` operation that will return file content based on the filename and extension in the request parameters.

```
[ServiceContract]
public interface IFileService
```

```
    {
        [OperationContract]
        [WebGet(UriTemplate="GetFile/{filename}/{ext}")]
        Stream GetFile(string filename, string ext);
    }
```

In our sample REST service, we will simply return some data read from the files on the local disks. Here is the complete code of the GetFile operation implementation:

```
    [AspNetCompatibilityRequirements
    (RequirementsMode=AspNetCompatibilityRequirementsMode.Allowed)]
    public class FileService : IFileService
    {
        public Stream GetFile(string filename, string ext)
        {
            string filepath =
                Path.Combine(HttpContext.Current.Server.MapPath("~/Files/")
                ,filename+"."+ext);
            if (!File.Exists(filepath)) throw new
                ArgumentException("Invalid filename---\"" +
                filepath + "\"");
            WebOperationContext.Current.OutgoingResponse.ContentType =
                "application/octet-stream";
            return File.OpenRead(filepath);
        }
    }
```

The GetFile method simply constructs the absolute file path and returns the FileStream object to the client.

How it works...

Since the sample FileService exposes the GetFile operation through the HTTP GET method, we can directly use a web browser to invoke it so as to download files. The next screenshot shows the response data of the GetFile operation (in this case, it returns an image file).

In the sample operation, we use the `WebOperationContext.Current.OutgoingResponse.ContentType` property to set the content type of the response. This is helpful when the service consumer will proactively interpret the content type of the service response.

Also, the `application/octet-stream` content type used here is a generic value for raw binary data. In real scenarios, we can specify other, more concrete values, such as text/XML or image/JPEG, as the content type value based on what we want to be returned in our REST operations.

See also

▶ *Using the auto-generated Help page*

▶ *Complete source code for this recipe can be found in the* `\Chapter 10\recipe5\` *folder*

Consuming a WCF service from an ASP.NET AJAX client

Nowadays, more and more web application development platforms have adopted AJAX features so as to provide rich client-side interaction and user experience in browser-based applications. ASP.NET AJAX is one of the representatives of the AJAX-enabled web application development platform. One cool feature of ASP.NET AJAX is that it can use script code to invoke XML Web Services within the hosting web application. As a unified service development platform, WCF also provides support for building services that can be consumed by an ASP.NET AJAX client.

In this recipe, we will demonstrate how to build an ASP.NET AJAX-enabled WCF service and consume it from an ASP.NET web page.

How to do it...

In the sample case, we will build both a WCF service and an ASP.NET web page, and host them in the same web application:

1. Create an AJAX-enabled WCF service.

   Let's create the WCF service first. The sample WCF service has a simple `ServiceContract` that contains an authentication method, as the following code snippet shows:

   ```
   [ServiceContract(Namespace="AccountService", Name="AccountSVC")]
   public interface IAccountService
   {
   ```

```
[OperationContract]
[WebGet]
bool ValidateUser(string username, string password);
}
```

2. Add AJAX-specific settings into the service configuration.

    Since our sample service needs to be consumed by an ASP.NET AJAX client, the next step is to add some AJAX-specific configuration settings so as to make the service AJAX-enabled. There are two settings necessary here—making the service endpoint use WebHttpBinding, and adding the <enableWebScript> behavior element into the service endpoint behavior. The following XML fragment shows the service endpoint and behavior configuration of our sample authentication service.

```
<system.serviceModel>
  <services>
    <service name="WebApplication.AccountService">
      <endpoint address="" behaviorConfiguration="AJAXEndpoint"
                binding="webHttpBinding"
                contract="WebApplication.IAccountService"/>
    </service>
  </services>
  <behaviors>
    <endpointBehaviors>
      <behavior name="AJAXEndpoint">
        <webHttp />
        <enableWebScript/>
      </behavior>
```

3. Create an ASP.NET web page to consume the WCF service through AJAX script.

    As we have made the WCF service AJAX-ready, we will now turn to the client-side ASP. NET web page, in which we will use AJAX script to consume the WCF service. The sample ASP.NET page is a very typical user login page, which contains some standard ASP.NET user login controls. Here is the main UI of the sample web page.

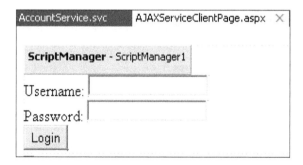

The textbox control in the page is used for collecting user credentials and the **Login** button is used for executing the AJAX scripts. There is also a `ScriptManager` control in the page, which has defined the path to the target WCF service we will invoke in the page. The following screenshot shows the complete definition of the `ScriptManager` control.

```
<form id="form1" runat="server">
<div style="margin-left:auto;margin-right:auto">
    <div id="divLogin">
        <asp:ScriptManager ID="ScriptManager1" runat="server">
            <Services>
                <asp:ServiceReference Path="~/AccountService.svc" />
            </Services>
        </asp:ScriptManager>
```

4. Add script code for invoking the WCF service operations.

   Since we have referenced the WCF service endpoint in the `ScriptManager` control, Visual Studio will help retrieve the scripts (auto-generated by the AJAX-enabled WCF service). It is time to add the AJAX script codes for invoking the WCF service. Following is the complete AJAX script code we have used in the sample web page.

```
<script type="text/javascript">
    function OnLogin() {
        var username = document.getElementById("txtUsername").value;
        var password = document.getElementById("txtPassword").value;

        var as = new AccountService.AccountSVC();
        as.ValidateUser(username, password,    /*function parameters*/
                    OnComplete,     /*operation finish callback */
                    OnError,        /*operation error callback */
                    null);      /* context object */
    }

    function OnComplete(result) {
        if (result == true) alert("Login Succeeded!");
        else alert("Login failed!");
    }

    function OnError(result) {
        alert(result.get_message());
    }
```

As the `OnLogin` script function shows, the AJAX-enabled WCF service provides a script prototype for the target service. With this script prototype, we can create a WCF service proxy in script code and invoke the service operations on it. As AJAX uses an async calling pattern, we have defined two callback functions here for handling the return value or potential error of the service call.

How it works...

In the sample web page, the `ScriptManager` control plays a very important role, as any ASP. NET page that utilizes the AJAX feature should add a `ScriptManager` control as the first server control within the page form.

It is interesting how the ASP.NET client page gets the script prototypes and helper scripts for calling the WCF service. By using Fiddler, we can capture all the HTTP traffic between the ASP. NET page and the WCF service. As the traffic records show (see the next screenshot), the ASP. NET page will always send requests to the AJAX-enabled WCF service to download the helper scripts at the initial stage.

When we click the **Login** button in our sample page to invoke the service, the callback function will raise the alert dialog which displays the returned validation result from the sample authentication service. The following screenshot shows the web page window (after calling the sample WCF service).

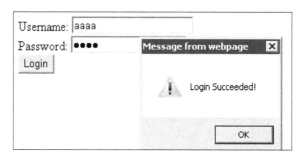

There's more...

It is worth noticing that so far the ASP.NET AJAX framework only allows web pages to invoke WCF services or XML Web Services hosted in the same web application (local services). This limitation is due to the **XSS (Cross-site scripting)** protection consideration. In the following *Accessing a remote REST service in an AJAX client* recipe, we will discuss how to use web script to access a WCF REST service hosted in a remote web application.

See also

▶ *Accessing a remote REST service in an AJAX client*

▶ *Complete source code for this recipe can be found in the* \Chapter 10\recipe6\ *folder*

Accessing a remote REST service in an AJAX client

As we have discussed in the *Consuming a WCF service from an ASP.NET AJAX client* recipe, ASP.NET AJAX script can consume a WCF REST service (with webScript behavior enabled) through the ScriptManager control. However, this kind of AJAX script client can only consume WCF services that are hosted in the same web application as the Web pages. Trying to access a remote WCF service through the ASP.NET AJAX script will not work. Don't worry, we have found some alternative ways to work around this problem.

In this recipe, we will demonstrate a very simple way to call a remote WCF REST service in an ASP.NET web page via jQuery-based AJAX script.

How to do it...

Since XSS protection prevents AJAX scripts from sending HTTP POST requests to a remote service host, the solution we will demonstrate here is to use AJAX script to consume a remote WCF REST service through the HTTP GET method.

1. Configure the target WCF REST service to open HTTP GET-based endpoints.

   The first step is to make the service operation on the sample WCF REST service using the HTTP GET verb. The following code snippet shows the complete definition of the sample REST service operation:

   ```
   [ServiceContract]
   public interface IDataService
   {
       [OperationContract]
       [WebGet(UriTemplate="GetData?val={value}",
                   ResponseFormat=WebMessageFormat.Json)]
       string GetData(int value);

   ......
   ```

   The hosting and configuration parts of the sample REST service here are exactly the same as what we have discussed in the *Building a self-hosted REST service* recipe of this chapter.

2. Import a jQuery script component in to the client web page.

   In the sample web page here, we will leverage the jQuery AJAX component to simplify the HTTP GET request processing. jQuery is an open source AJAX library that contains lots of handy AJAX script components and interfaces that can help simplify the AJAX tasks in a web page. To use jQuery in an ASP.NET web page, we need to import the jQuery script resources at the page header (see the following page fragment).

```
<html xmlns="http://www.w3.org/1999/xhtml">
<head runat="server">

    <script type="text/javascript" src="Scripts/jquery-1.4.1.js"></scri
    <script type="text/javascript" src="Scripts/jquery-1.4.1-vsdoc.js">
```

3. Invoke HTTP GET-based service operations using the jQuery API.

   Finally, we can start using the jQuery API to consume the remote REST service operations. In this sample page, we use the jQuery $.ajax function to invoke the remote REST service operations. The complete jQuery function is shown in the following code snippet:

```
function CallRemoteService() {
    var inputVal = $("#txtInput").val();

    $.ajax({
        type: "GET",
        url: "http://localhost:33309/DataService.svc/GetData?val="
        + inputVal,
        data: "{}",
        contentType: "application/json; charset=utf-8",
        dataType: "json",
        success: function (returnData) {

            alert(returnData);

        }
    });
}
```

There's more...

The restriction on calling remote WCF services (or Web Services) in the client script is due to the famous XSS issue. For more information about XSS security vulnerability and protection, you can refer to the following page on Wikipedia:

▶ Cross-site scripting

   http://en.wikipedia.org/wiki/Cross-site_scripting

See also

▸ *Building a self-hosted REST service*

▸ *Using the auto-generated Help page*

▸ *Complete source code for this recipe can be found in the* \Chapter 10\recipe7\ *folder*

11
Interoperability

In this chapter, we will cover:

- ▸ Building a WS-I Basic Profile 1.1 compatible service
- ▸ Consuming an ASMX Web Service from a WCF client
- ▸ Accessing a WCF service via the .NET `WebRequest` component
- ▸ Consuming a WCF service with a raw MSMQ program
- ▸ Using a WCF service in Microsoft Office

Introduction

For a distributed service programming platform, it is quite common to communicate with different kinds of heterogeneous platforms at either the server side or client side. Therefore, WCF has opened many existing interfaces for interoperating with non-WCF or non-.NET framework platforms.

In this chapter, we will use five recipes to demonstrate some useful interoperability scenarios in WCF service development, including building a WS-I BP 1.1 conformed service, interoperating with XML Web Service, plain HTTP client, and MSMQ client, along with consuming WCF service from Office client.

Building a WS-I Basic Profile 1.1 compatible service

WS-I Basic Profile includes a series of service specifications for defining XML Web Services, which can interoperate with other heterogeneous service programming platforms.

In this recipe, we will demonstrate how to configure a WCF service to be compatible with the 1.1 version of WS-I Basic Profile.

Getting ready

It would be helpful if you can get some general understanding about the WS-I Basic Profile and its latest version. Here is the WS-I Basic Profile page on Wikipedia:

- WS-I Basic Profile

  http://en.wikipedia.org/wiki/WS-I_Basic_Profile

How to do it...

The sample case here uses a WCF service containing some service operations that return different data objects (including primitive type and custom complex type). We will look at the steps to make the service become WS-I Basic Profile 1.1 compatible:

1. Define the `ServiceContract`.

   The first thing to do is define a standard request/reply pattern-based `ServiceContract` (see the following code snippet).

   ```
   [ServiceContract]
   public interface IService1
   {

       [OperationContract]
       string GetData(int value);

       [OperationContract]
       CompositeType GetDataUsingDataContract(CompositeType
               composite);
   }
   ```

2. Adjust the BasicHttpBinding with Basic Profile 1.1 compatible settings.

   The next step is to set up a proper binding that is compatible with WS-I Basic Profile 1.1. In WCF, the BasicHttpBinding is the best choice, since BasicHttpBinding is the built-in binding for a plain HTTP scenario and doesn't contain those WCF-specific features (such as message security or reliable message). Here we will build the sample binding based on the BasicHttpBinding. The following screenshot shows the Basic Profile 1.1 compatible binding used in our sample service.

```
<bindings>
  <basicHttpBinding>
    <binding name="basicProfile1.1"
             messageEncoding="Text"
    >
      <security mode="None"></security>
    </binding>
  </basicHttpBinding>
```

   As you can see, the sample binding is using `Text` as the `messageEncoding` type.

3. Ensure metadata generation in the service behavior.

   In the end, we need to enable metadata publishing so that the proper WSDL of the service will be generated. The following fragment shows the service behavior which has turned on metadata generation.

```
<behaviors>
  <serviceBehaviors>
    <behavior>
      <serviceMetadata httpGetEnabled="true" />
```

How it works...

To verify that the service does conform to WS-I Basic Profile 1.1, we can get the WSDL document of the service and use a validation tool to compare it. Or, we can also use the WCF Test Client tool to try invoking the sample service operation and validating the underlying SOAP messages (shown in the following screenshot).

```
ce Projects                              GetDataUsingDataContract
/localhost:33845/Service1.svc
Service1 (BasicHttpBinding_IService1)    Request
  GetData()
  GetDataUsingDataContract()             <s:Envelope xmlns:s="http://schemas.xmlsoap.org/soap/envelope/">
config File                                <s:Header>
                                             <Action s:mustUnderstand="1" xmlns="http://schemas.microsoft.cor
                                           </s:Header>
                                           <s:Body>
                                             <GetDataUsingDataContract xmlns="http://tempuri.org/">
                                               <composite xmlns:d4p1="http://schemas.datacontract.org/2004/0
                                                 <d4p1:BoolValue>false</d4p1:BoolValue>
                                                 <d4p1:StringValue i:nil="true" />
```

See also

▸ *Using the WCF Test Client tool to test a service* in *Chapter 12*

▸ *Complete source code for this recipe can be found in the* `\Chapter 11\recipe1\` *folder*

Consuming an ASMX Web Service from a WCF client

As a unified distributed communication platform, WCF can help developers build standard SOAP XML-based Web Services so that traditional XML Web Service clients can consume it. Likewise, it is also quite convenient to use WCF-based client applications for consuming traditional XML Web Services.

In this recipe, we will show you how to consume a traditional ASMX Web Service from a WCF-based client application.

How to do it...

We will use a simple ASMX Web Service as an example here. The complete steps for consuming the sample service are as follows:

1. Create the sample ASMX Web Service.

   The sample ASMX Web Service contains a single operation that returns some string data. The complete definition of the Web Service is shown in the following code snippet.

```
[WebService(Namespace = "http://tempuri.org/")]
[WebServiceBinding(ConformsTo = WsiProfiles.BasicProfile1_1)]
public class TestWebService : System.Web.Services.WebService
{

    [WebMethod]
    public string GetData()
    {
        return "Hello World";
    }

}
```

2. Generate the proxy class in the WCF client application.

Now, we come to the step for creating the service proxy class against the target ASMX Web Service. To do so, we can use the Visual Studio **Add Service Reference** command option. Like generating a proxy against a standard WCF service, we need to get the WSDL document (metadata) of the target ASMX Web Service first. The Visual Studio **Add Service Reference** command will generate a proxy class based on the retrieved metadata. The next screenshot shows the **Add Service Reference** dialog in which we input the metadata document address of the sample ASMX Web Service.

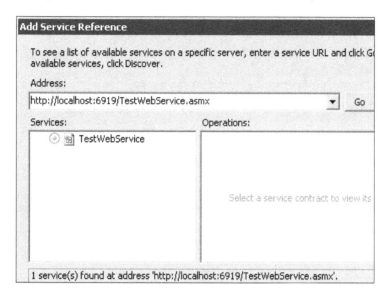

3. Call the ASMX Web Service methods with generated proxy class.

After generating the proxy types, we can use them to consume the target Web Service just as we did when calling a standard WCF service operation (see the `CallASMXService` function):

```
private static void CallASMXService()
{
    ASMXProxy.TestWebServiceSoapClient client =
                    new ASMXProxy.TestWebServiceSoapClient();

    Console.WriteLine(client.GetData());
}
```

How it works...

As we can see, the process of generating the client proxy against an ASMX Web Service is almost the same as a standard WCF service. By looking into the generated proxy code, we can find that the WCF proxy generation engine will create a `System.ServiceModel.ClientBase<T>` derived type as the main service proxy class (see the following code snippet):

```
[System.Diagnostics.DebuggerStepThroughAttribute()]
[System.CodeDom.Compiler.GeneratedCodeAttribute("System.ServiceModel"
                , "4.0.0.0")]
public partial class TestWebServiceSoapClient :
    System.ServiceModel.ClientBase<TestClient.ASMXProxy.
TestWebServiceSoap>,
    TestClient.ASMXProxy.TestWebServiceSoap {

    public TestWebServiceSoapClient() {
    }
......
```

In the `app.config` file of the client application, there also exists the endpoint and binding configurations, which are associated with the proxy class. The following XML fragment shows the endpoint and binding configuration section in the WCF client application's `app.config` file.

```
<bindings>
    <basicHttpBinding>
        <binding name="TestWebServiceSoap" closeTimeout="00:01:00" openTimeou
            receiveTimeout="00:10:00" sendTimeout="00:01:00" allowCookies="fa
            bypassProxyOnLocal="false" hostNameComparisonMode="StrongWildcard
            maxBufferSize="65536" maxBufferPoolSize="524288" maxReceivedMessa
            messageEncoding="Text" textEncoding="utf-8" transferMode="Buffere
            useDefaultWebProxy="true">
            <readerQuotas maxDepth="32" maxStringContentLength="8192" maxArra
            <security mode="None">...</security>
        </binding>
    </basicHttpBinding>
</bindings>
<client>
    <endpoint address="http://localhost:6919/TestWebService.asmx"
        binding="basicHttpBinding" bindingConfiguration="TestWebServiceSoap"
        contract="ASMXProxy.TestWebServiceSoap" name="TestWebServiceSoap" />
```

As the `<binding>` section shows, a traditional ASMX Web Service is using a plain HTTP transport layer, which does not adopt any security protection settings at either the transport or message layer. Also, WCF-specific features like `ReliableMessage` and Transaction are not used here, either.

▶ *Creating a typed service client* in *Chapter 4*

▶ *Complete source code for this recipe can be found in the* \Chapter 11\recipe2\ *folder*

Accessing a WCF service via the WebRequest component

Sometimes, it is required that our WCF service be called by some client platform which can only issue plain HTTP GET/POST requests. Or, in .NET framework-based applications, we sometimes might need to use WebRequest components (under *the* System.Net namespace) to consume XML Web Services or WCF services.

In this recipe, we will demonstrate how to use a .NET WebRequest component to consume an HTTP-based WCF service.

How to do it...

Here we will use a HttpWebRequest component to retrieve some simple text data from a standard WCF service application. Let's take a look at the steps to achieve this:

1. Set up the WCF service application.

   The sample service here is a very simple one that contains one operation that accepts an input parameter and returns a string value. The following code snippet shows the service implementation.

```
public class Service1 : IService1
{
    public string GetData(int value)
    {
        return string.Format("You entered: {0}", value);
    }
}
```

Like those XML Web Service-compatible services, we need to make the sample WCF service use BasicHttpBinding (which doesn't involve many WCF-specific features) so that the `WebRequest`-based client can correctly consume it. The following XML fragment shows the service and endpoint configuration of the sample service.

```
<services>
  <service name="WCFHttpService.Service1">
    <endpoint address=""
              binding="basicHttpBinding"
              contract="WCFHttpService.IService1">

    </endpoint>
  </service>
</services>
```

2. Call the target WCF service operation with `WebRequest` code.

   The most important step is at the client side where we will need to instantiate the `WebRequest` component, and issue a WCF operation call and process a response through it. The overall code flow of the `WebRequest`-based operation call is divided into the following four parts:

   ❑ Creating a `WebRequest` instance with the target endpoint URL

   ❑ Initializing the HTTP properties and request content

   ❑ Sending the request and waiting for a response

   ❑ Reading the response content

   The `CallServiceWithWebRequest` function shows the complete code of the `WebRequest` client:

```
static void CallServiceWithWebRequest()
{
    var soapRequest =
          @"<s:Envelope
              xmlns:s='http://schemas.xmlsoap.org/soap/envelope/'>
              <s:Body>
                <GetData xmlns='http://wcf.test.org/'>
                    <value>11</value>
                </GetData>
              </s:Body>
            </s:Envelope>";

    var bytes = Encoding.UTF8.GetBytes(soapRequest);

    WebRequest request =
          WebRequest.Create("http://localhost:6950/Service1.svc");
    request.Method = "POST";
```

```
request.ContentType = "text/xml; charset=utf-8";
request.Headers.Add("SOAPAction", "GetData");


var requestStream = request.GetRequestStream();
requestStream.Write(bytes, 0, bytes.Length);
requestStream.Close();

// Get the response.
WebResponse response = request.GetResponse();

var responseStream = response.GetResponseStream();
var reader = new StreamReader(responseStream);
Console.WriteLine(reader.ReadToEnd());

reader.Close();
responseStream.Close();
response.Close();
}
```

As you can see, the `WebRequest` type contains some built-in properties for setting those well-known HTTP headers such as **Content-Type** and **Method**, and we can also add other special headers through the `Headers` collection.

For a HTTP POST request, we can get a reference to the request `Stream` object and write the request content (the SOAP XML message in our sample case) into it.

After the HTTP requests get issued, we can try retrieving the response data through the `GetResponse` method. When the response arrives, we can open the response `Stream` object and read the response content from it.

How it works...

In our `WebRequest`-based client, we directly compose the request message through an XML fragment and also manually add the HTTP headers into the request. Someone might wonder how we can get the proper SOAP XML message format of a particular WCF service and what kinds of HTTP headers are necessary.

Well, there are several useful means that can help us get the SOAP XML message of the WCF service when hosting over the HTTP protocol. If the service is not secured at the message layer, we can use the Fiddler tool to capture the SOAP XML message at the transport layer (including the HTTP headers). Here is a sample screenshot showing the captured HTTP message of our sample WCF HTTP service.

Another way is to use the WCF message logging feature, which can also help capture the SOAP XML message at either the server side or client side.

See also

▸ *Capturing a WCF request/response message via the Fiddler tool* in *Chapter 12*

▸ *Using built-in tracing and message logging* in *Chapter 12*

▸ *Complete source code for this recipe can be found in the* \Chapter 11\recipe3\ *folder*

Consuming a WCF service with a raw MSMQ program

WCF provides built-in NetMsmqBinding for developing services over the MSMQ transport layer. However, the NetMsmqBinding totally encapsulates the underlying details of the MSMQ programming layer so that a developer only needs to focus on the WCF service programming model and object model. This is good for pure WCF applications; however, for some scenarios where the client side is a legacy MSMQ program, the NetMsmqBinding will not work and we will need a means to make the WCF service interoperable with the raw MSMQ API-based client.

In this recipe, we will demonstrate how to use the WCF MsmqIntegrationBinding to make a WCF service work correctly with a raw MSMQ (System.Messaging)-based client application.

How to do it...

Unlike most sample cases used in other recipes, here we will build the client application first and then generate a WCF service application to interoperate with the client. Here are the detailed steps:

1. Create a raw MSMQ-based client application.

   First, let's have a look at the MSMQ client application so as to understand how the client side will deliver the data to the server side. In our sample case, the MSMQ client uses the .NET `System.Messaging` namespace components to perform raw MSMQ message delivering. The following code snippet shows the complete MSMQ message-sending function of the client application:

```
static void Run()
{

    MessageQueue queue = null;
    MessageQueueTransaction trans = null;
    try
    {
        queue = new MessageQueue();
        queue.Path = Constants.QUEUE_PATH;
        queue.DefaultPropertiesToSend.Recoverable = true;

        trans = new MessageQueueTransaction();
         trans.Begin();

        MyOrder order = new MyOrder();
        order.ID = DateTime.Now.Ticks.ToString();
        order.Name = "Order_" + order.ID;

        Message msg = new Message(order);


        queue.Send(msg, trans);
        trans.Commit();
    }
    catch (Exception ex)
    {
        trans.Abort();
    }
    finally
    {
        queue.Close();
```

```
    }
        Console.WriteLine("message sent..");
}
```

As you can see, the raw MSMQ client uses a `System.Messaging.Message` object to encapsulate the request message and the message includes a `MyOrder` type instance, which is the business data object in the sample application scenario. The `MyOrder` type is a very typical business data type, which contains some primitive data fields (as shown in the following code snippet):

```
[DataContract(Namespace =
                "http://Microsoft.ServiceModel.Samples")]
public class MyOrder
{
    [DataMember]
    public string ID;

    [DataMember]
    public string Name;
}
```

Also, as our sample service scenario uses a transactional queue physically, the client code uses a `MessageQueueTransaction` to represent the transaction to ensure the delivery of the message data.

2. Define the WCF service to interoperate with the MSMQ client.

    Now that we have the raw MSMQ-based client code logic defined, the next step is to build a WCF service that can interoperate with the raw MSMQ client. For the server side, it is important that we define a proper `ServiceContract`. The following code snippet shows the sample `ServiceContract` used here:

```
[ServiceContract(Namespace =
                "http://Microsoft.ServiceModel.Samples")]
[ServiceKnownType(typeof(MyOrder))]
public interface IOrderProcessor
{
    OperationContract(IsOneWay = true, Action = "*")]
    void SubmitPurchaseOrderInMessage(MsmqMessage<MyOrder> msg);
}
```

3. Set up the ServiceHost for the WCF service.

    With the `ServiceContract` defined, we can start configuring the endpoint and service so as to set up the ServiceHost. In the sample service application, we will construct the ServiceHost and related configuration in code instead of using the `app.config` file. The complete service hosting code logic of the sample WCF service is shown in the following code snippet:

```
static void Main()
{
    //init queue
    if (!MessageQueue.Exists(Constants.QUEUE_PATH))
                MessageQueue.Create(Constants.QUEUE_PATH, true);

    //init wcf host via code
    Uri baseUri = new Uri("http://localhost:7878/msmqsvc");
    using (ServiceHost host = new
                ServiceHost(typeof(OrderProcessorService),baseUri))
    {
        //add metadata behavior
        ServiceMetadataBehavior smb = new
                ServiceMetadataBehavior(){ HttpGetEnabled=true};
        host.Description.Behaviors.Add(smb);

        //add service endpoint
        MsmqIntegrationBinding binding = new
            MsmqIntegrationBinding(MsmqIntegrationSecurityMode.None);
        host.AddServiceEndpoint(typeof(ClassLib.IOrderProcessor),
        binding, "msmq.formatname:DIRECT=OS:" +
            Constants.QUEUE_PATH);

        host.Open();
......
    }
}
```

As the **highlighted code** shows, instead of using the NetMsmqBinding, we use the MsmqIntegrationBinding, which is the binding designed for working with a raw MSMQ programming model.

How it works...

In our sample WCF service application, there are two key points that make the ServiceContract interoperable with a MSMQ client. One is the IsOneWay property of the OperationContract. As MSMQ is a one-way communication component, the WCF service also needs to define the corresponding service operation as one-way style. Another point is the input parameter type; here we use the generic type System.ServiceModel. MsmqMessage<T>, which is dedicated for a service operation that is mapping to a raw MSMQ client request, and the generic parameter represents the data object that will be carried through the MSMQ message.

See also

▶ *Complete source code for this recipe can be found in the* \Chapter 11\recipe4\ *folder*

Using a WCF Service in Microsoft Office

One interesting and useful interoperate scenario of WCF service development is how to consume a WCF service from a Microsoft Office client such as Word, Excel, or Outlook. Currently, there are several possible solutions for WCF service consumption in an Office client, which include:

▶ Creating a .NET client proxy and exposing it as a COM object

▶ Using the XML HTTP component to consume the WCF service over plain HTTP in VBA code

▶ Directly using VSTO and .NET-managed code to consume WCF services

In this recipe, we will demonstrate a different approach for consuming a simple WCF service in a Microsoft Office client, which utilizes the *WCF service moniker* component.

How to do it...

The sample service here will use Office Excel as an example to demonstrate the client-side service-consuming ability in Microsoft Office. Let's take a look at the detailed steps to build the sample application:

1. Create a sample WCF service.

   As Office clients do not have a rich .NET object model, like standard .NET client applications, we will generally not use an Office client to consume very complicated WCF services. Our sample service here contains a very simple operation that accepts an integer and returns a string value (see the IService1 contract type):

   ```
   [ServiceContract(Namespace="http://wcf.test.org")]
   public interface IService1
   {
       [OperationContract]
       string GetData(int value);
   }
   ```

   The IService1 service is hosted through BasicHttpBinding with a mex endpoint opened (as shown in the following configuration fragment). This is important for the Office client.

```
<service name="SimpleWCFService.Service1">
    <endpoint address=""
            binding="basicHttpBinding"
            bindingNamespace="http://wcf.test.org"
            contract="SimpleWCFService.IService1" />

    <endpoint address="mex" binding="mexHttpBinding"
            contract="IMetadataExchange" />

    <host>
        <baseAddresses>
            <add baseAddress="http://localhost:8734/Service1/" />
        </baseAddresses>
    </host>
</service>
```

2. Add VBA code in Excel to consume the WCF service.

Now let's move to the Office client; we will use Excel 2010 as the example here. The most common programming interfaces in Microsoft Office client applications is the VBA macro. In the sample case here, we will also use the VBA code for service consuming. We can open the VBA Macro editor (shown in the following screenshot) through the **Developer** ribbon.

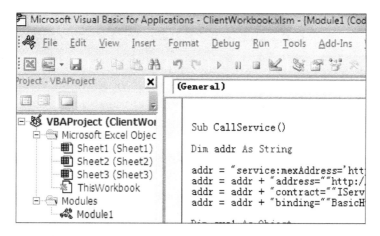

In the VBA editor, we can define a custom macro function for consuming the WCF service via WCF Service Moniker. The `CallService` function in the following code snippet shows the complete VBA code for our sample Excel workbook:

```
Sub CallService()

Dim addr As String

addr = "service:mexAddress='http://localhost:8734/Service1/mex',"
addr = addr + "address=""http://localhost:8734/Service1/"","
```

```
addr = addr + "contract=""IService1"", contractNamespace=""http://
wcf.test.org"","

addr = addr + "binding=""BasicHttpBinding_IService1"",
bindingNamespace=""http://wcf.test.org"""

Dim svc1 As Object
Set svc1 = GetObject(addr)
MsgBox svc1.GetData(11)

End Sub
```

The macro first composes a URL string, which consists of the following parts:

- ▸ Service metadata address
- ▸ Service endpoint address
- ▸ ServiceContract information
- ▸ Endpoint binding information

The entire URL string is used as input parameter in the `GetObject` function call, which returns a COM-based proxy object created by the Service Moniker object. Here is the output screen of the Excel workbook after calling the `GetData` sample operation.

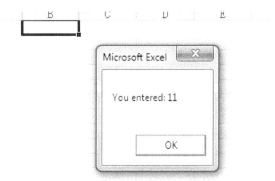

How it works...

In the sample Office VBA function, we have used a component called *WCF service moniker*, which is provided by WCF for integrating WCF service into COM-based client applications. The WCF service moniker can obtain the definition of a particular WCF service's `ServiceContract` in the form of a WSDL document, through the use of the `wsdl` parameter or through Metadata Exchange, using the `mexAddress` parameter.

The next screenshot shows the WSDL document of our sample service. As we can see, it contains the Binding name, Contract name, and namespace information.

```
<wsdl:definitions name="Service1" targetNamespace="http://tempuri.org/" xmlns:wsdl="http://
  xmlns:soapenc="http://schemas.xmlsoap.org/soap/encoding/" xmlns:wsu="http://docs.
  xmlns:xsd="http://www.w3.org/2001/XMLSchema" xmlns:soap12="http://schemas.xmls
  xmlns:wsa="http://schemas.xmlsoap.org/ws/2004/08/addressing" xmlns:wsp="http://s
  xmlns:wsap="http://schemas.xmlsoap.org/ws/2004/08/addressing/policy" xmlns:wsaw
  xmlns:msc="http://schemas.microsoft.com/ws/2005/12/wsdl/contract" xmlns:wsa10="h
  xmlns:wsx="http://schemas.xmlsoap.org/ws/2004/09/mex" xmlns:wsam="http://www.v
  <wsdl:import namespace="http://wcf.test.org" location="http://localhost:8734/Service1/
  <wsdl:types />
  <wsdl:service name="Service1">
  - <wsdl:port name="BasicHttpBinding_IService1" binding="i0:BasicHttpBinding_IService1"
      <soap:address location="http://localhost:8734/Service1/" />
```

See also

▶ *Complete source code for this recipe can be found in the* \Chapter 11\recipe5\
   folder

12
Diagnostics

In this chapter, we will cover:

- ▸ Using the WCF Test Client tool to test a service
- ▸ Capturing a WCF request/response message via Fiddler tool
- ▸ Using built-in tracing and message logging
- ▸ Debugging in a Windows service host
- ▸ Creating a custom Visual Studio Debugger Visualizer for WCF debugging
- ▸ Using `PerformanceCounters` for WCF service monitoring

Introduction

In WCF service development, we often need to troubleshoot applications so as to figure out some problems or unexpected behaviors. Therefore, good diagnostic means will greatly improve the troubleshooting experience and simplify the problem-resolving process.

WCF provides many built-in mechanisms and components for service application diagnostics and troubleshooting, together with some other general troubleshooting tools and best practices. In this chapter, we will introduce some useful WCF diagnostic means and tools that can help developers perform common troubleshooting and problem solving in WCF development.

Using the WCF Test Client tool to test a service

When developing a WCF service, we always need to test the service operations frequently during the coding stage. Normally, we can create a console project, generate a WCF client proxy, and invoke the service operations through the proxy class. However, this still seems a bit inconvenient and wastes much time on repeating the proxy generation and client-side invoking code. Fortunately, from WCF 3.5, there comes a useful tool with Visual Studio that can help simplify WCF service testing. This is the **WCF Test Client** tool.

In this recipe, you will learn how to use the WCF Test Client tool to perform an ad hoc test on WCF services.

How to do it...

The WCF Test Client tool is one of the tools provided by Visual Studio that can be found within the Visual Studio installation folder, such as `C:\Program Files\Microsoft Visual Studio 10.0\Common7\IDE`.

Let's take a look at the detailed steps to use this tool:

1. Launch the WCF Test Client tool from the command line.

   For your convenience, you can use the Visual Studio Command Prompt to launch it from the command line (shown in the following screenshot) instead of going to the installation path of the tool.

   The main interface of the WCF Test Client tool is a WinForm that contains three menus—**File**, **Tools**, and **Help**.

2. Add a reference to a particular WCF service (to be tested).

   To test a particular WCF service, we simply go through the **File | Add Service** menu item, which will show a popup dialog for us to give the metadata location of the target service.

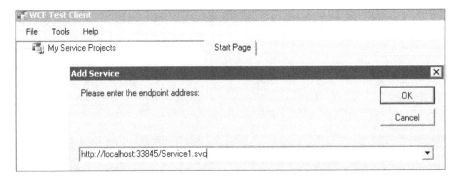

3. Select a service operation and invoke it through the test user interface.

   After we add a certain WCF service, the left panel will display the WCF service information. We can find the service operations and service configuration file displayed in a hierarchical structure in the panel.

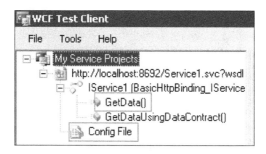

Clicking on the **Config File** node shows the content of the auto-generated client configuration file (containing the `System.ServiceModel` fragment of the service endpoint). The following screenshot shows the client configuration of a sample WCF service generated in the WCF Test Client tool.

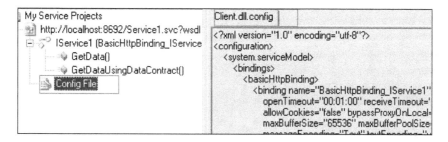

If we want to test a particular service operation, we just double-click the node with the operation name so that the right panel will show the main interface for us to invoke the operation. The following screenshot shows the operation testing interface for a sample operation called `GetDataUsingDataContract`, which receives and returns a composite data object.

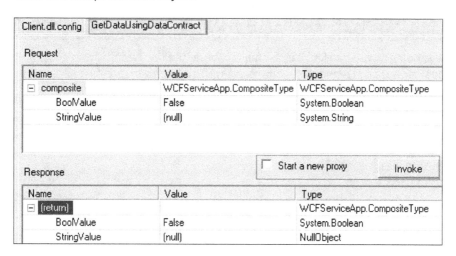

The screenshot also displays the testing result (the response data of the testing operation). As you can see, the test tool allows developers to input test values for not only primitive types, but also complex types. For the sample operation `GetDataUsingDataContract`, the WCF Test Client uses a WinForm `PropertyView` like a window for displaying and editing its input parameters and return value.

After assigning the proper parameters, we can use the **Invoke** button to actually call the target service operation, and the return value will be shown in the bottom view if the service operation call succeeds.

There's more...

Though it is quite convenient to use the WCF Test Client tool for simple service testing cases, there still exists some limitations here. For example, since the WCF Test Client tool is using WSDL/metadata to generate a test client proxy dynamically, it will not work for REST services that do not provide WSDL/metadata or SOAP-based endpoints. Also, for those WCF services in which we have applied custom extension components (such as `MessageInspector`, `MessageEncoder`, and so on), the WCF Test Client cannot help either, since it doesn't allow us to inject extension components like a standard client application. If you hit these kinds of limited cases, it is still recommended to create a standard .NET client application for service testing.

See also

 ▸ *Complete source code for this recipe can be found in the* `\Chapter 12\recipe1\` *folder*

Capturing WCF request/response messages via Fiddler tool

When developing a WCF service, it is useful to capture the underlying messages of service operations (request and response). There are several different means for capturing service operation messages in WCF service applications.

In this recipe, we will introduce how we can use the **Fiddler** tool to capture the underlying messages issued by a WCF service (or client proxy) over the HTTP transport protocol.

How to do it...

Fiddler is a free web debugging tool that can help analyze network communication data over the HTTP transport layer such as the message/data issued by Internet Explorer, WinINet components, or .NET `WebRequest` components. Here we will demonstrate the detailed steps to use Fiddler to inspect the messages of a locally deployed WCF service application:

1. Get the Fiddler tool installed on the local machine.

   First, we need to install Fiddler on the target machine where we want to capture messages. You can get the Fiddler tool at its official site (`http://www.fiddler2.com/fiddler2/`).

   After successfully installing Fiddler, we can switch it on and it will start to automatically listen for any HTTP traffic over the local network, since it is working like a web proxy on the installed machine.

2. Use a Fiddler reserved address for capturing the localhost traffic.

   One thing worth noticing is that Fiddler by default does not capture the network data issued through a localhost address. In case we want to capture the HTTP data sent against an `http://localhost`-based service endpoint, we need to explicitly change the localhost host name to `ipv4.fiddler`, which is a reserved name for a local machine in the Fiddler tool. The following code snippet shows how we can use this reserved host name in a standard WCF service client application:

```
static void CallService()
{
    TestProxy.Service1Client proxy =
                    new TestProxy.Service1Client();

    proxy.Endpoint.Address = new EndpointAddress(
            http://ipv4.fiddler:8799/Service1.svc"
            );

    string data = proxy.GetData(11);
}
```

3. Inspect the captured HTTP messages in Fiddler.

   Here we use the previous WCF service client code as an example; after the client proxy invokes the operation, we can view the captured messages in Fiddler through the **Web Sessions** window.

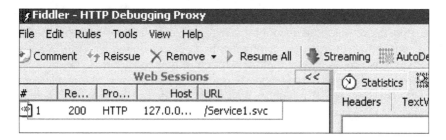

By double-clicking the specific session item in the Session window, we can continue to view the detailed message information (such as the message headers and content of request and response) of each session. The following screenshot shows the detailed message information of a sample service operation call displayed in Fiddler.

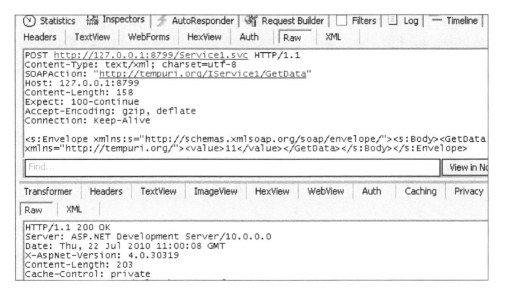

As you can see, the detailed information is presented in multiple views such as TextView, WebForms, HexView, Raw, XML, and so on. We can choose any of them to inspect the HTTP message content or headers based on the purpose of our analysis.

See also

> ▸ *Complete source code for this recipe can be found in the* \Chapter 12\recipe2\ *folder*

Using built-in tracing and message logging

As WCF developers, we will often encounter some general exceptions or errors (such as "underlying connection closed .....", "communication object is in faulted state", "security exception...") from which we cannot quite determine what is really wrong. Or, in some cases, we might want to have a look at how the WCF runtime is transforming the service operation calls into data messages under the hood. Well, WCF provides a built-in event-tracing and message-logging functionality that can help simplify such general error troubleshooting.

In this recipe, we will demonstrate how we can leverage the tracing and message-logging feature in WCF service development.

How to do it...

You can enable WCF tracing and message logging either by editing the `app.config` file directly, or by using the **WCF Service Configuration Editor** option. Here we will show you the steps for using the **WCF Service Configuration Editor** tool.

1. Open the `app.config` file through the WCF Service Configuration Editor tool.

    The **WCF Service Configuration Editor** tool is also provided by Windows SDK for .NET Framework. If you have Visual Studio 2008 or 2010 installed, you can directly launch it through the **Tools** menu.

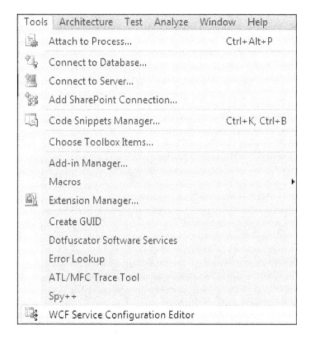

    Within the **WCF Service Configuration Editor**, we can use the **File | Open | Config File** menu (shown in the next screenshot) to open the `app.config` file of a particular .NET framework application in which we run the WCF service or client code.

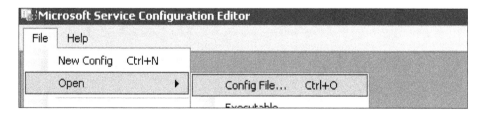

2. Turn on the **Tracing** and **MessageLogging** settings in the WCF **Diagnostics** configuration section.

After opening the `app.config` file, we can start configuring the WCF diagnostics settings by selecting the **Diagnostics** node on the left, which in turn displays two buttons on the right panel. These two buttons are used by developers to enable the **Tracing** and **MessageLogging** features, as shown in the following screenshot.

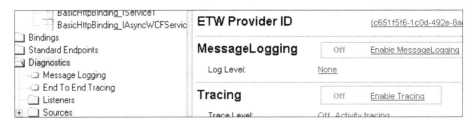

By default, both **Tracing** and **MessageLogging** options are disabled. After we turn them on, the corresponding XML configuration fragment should be added in the `app.config` file (as shown in the following configuration fragment).

```
    <sharedListeners>
        <add initializeData="c:\workspace\wcf\callbackservicesln\con
            type="System.Diagnostics.XmlWriterTraceListener, System,
            name="ServiceModelTraceListener" traceOutputOptions="Tim
            <filter type="" />
        </add>
    </sharedListeners>
</system.diagnostics>
<system.serviceModel>
  <diagnostics>
    <messageLogging  logMalformedMessages="true"
                     logMessagesAtTransportLevel="True"
                     />
```

3. Run the WCF service application or client consumer application.

Now, with the Tracing and MessageLogging configuration settings enabled, we can start our WCF service or client application so that the WCF runtime will record the service processing activities and operation messages into some log files with the `.svclog` file extension.

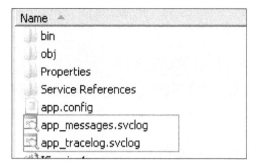

4. Open the `.svclog` file and inspect the log entries.

    Double-clicking on the `.svclog` files will automatically launch the **WCF Service Trace Viewer** tool (also provided by Windows SDK for .NET Framework) to display the data in the log files. Here is a sample screenshot of the **WCF Service Trace Viewer** tool, which has opened a particular tracing file.

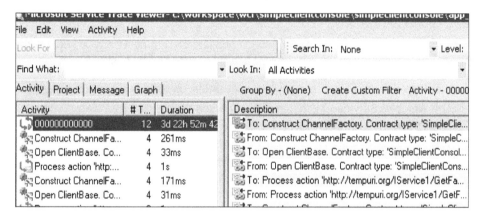

    WCF Service Trace Viewer will display trace and message entries, in both graphical and text formats, so that service developers can conveniently view them the way they prefer.

How it works...

WCF tracing and message logging features are also based on the diagnostics and tracing mechanism provided in the .NET framework infrastructure. Therefore, if you're already familiar with the standard .NET framework tracing and logging components and settings, you will find it more straightforward to configure the WCF tracing and message logging options in the `app.config` file rather than using the GUI tool.

Tracing and message logging features are very useful for common WCF error probing and troubleshooting. Now, if you encounter any unexpected error and cannot figure out what is happening during WCF service development or testing, just turn on the tracing and message logging and let them tell you what has happened.

Debugging in a Windows service host

Sometimes when developing WCF services that are hosted in a Windows Service application, we might find that it is not quite convenient to debug the service code. Though we can use WCF tracing or message logging to perform some verbose-level troubleshooting, in some cases it is still necessary to have a debugger (like Visual Studio) to do step-through code debugging against the service source code.

In this recipe, we will demonstrate how you can use Visual Studio to perform source-code debugging against a WCF service hosted in a Windows Service application.

Getting ready

Before we start debugging the Windows Service application that hosts a WCF service, there are several things we need to get ready. Here is a quick list to go through:

- ▶ Windows Service should already be successfully compiled and set up
- ▶ The Windows Service EXE image should be compiled either as a Debug version or a Release version with debugging information (symbols)
- ▶ The developer needs to log on using a user account that has sufficient permission to debug the target Windows Service running account, preferably using the admin account

How to do it...

Now, let's take a look at the steps to debug the WCF service hosted in a Windows Service. The sample WCF service and Windows Service application are created through the Visual Studio built-in Windows Service project template and have been installed into the Windows Service collection on the test server machine:

1. Start the Windows Service host application.

   The first step is to start the Windows Service application that hosts the WCF service in Windows **Service Configuration Manager**. Here is a sample screenshot, which shows the service list in Windows **Service Configuration Manager**.

We can start a specific Windows Service by selecting the Start option in the right-click context menu.

2. Attach the target Windows Service process in the Visual Studio IDE.

    Now let's attach the debugger to the debugee service application. To attach a running process, we need to start the Visual Studio 2010 IDE and choose the **Debug** menu. Then, within the sub menus under it, select the **Attach to Process** option (see, next screenshot).

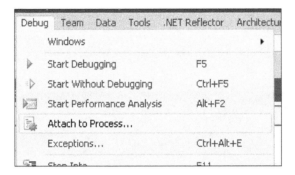

The **Attach to Process** option will launch a dialog in which we can choose the target process to debug. We can also apply some detailed debugging options in the dialog. Here we just pick the process corresponding to the target Windows Service application and click on the **Attach** button to start the debug session.

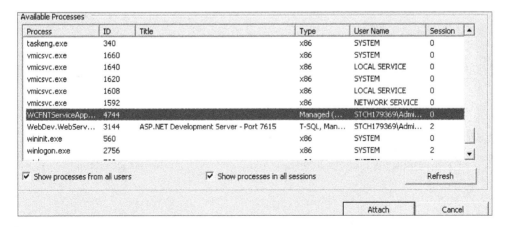

3. Invoke the target service operation so as to debug into the source code.

   After the Windows Service process has been successfully attached, we can use a client proxy to invoke particular service operations and the Visual Studio debugger will break into the code based on the breakpoints we have added in the service source code.

```
public class TestService : ITestService
{
    public void DoWork()
    {
        // Do some work here

        Debug.WriteLine("DoWork is called...");
    }
}
```

See also

▶ *Complete source code for this recipe can be found in the* \Chapter 12\recipe4\ *folder*

Creating a custom Visual Studio Debugger Visualizer for WCF debugging

Starting from Visual Studio 2005, developers can create some debugger assistant components called **Debugger Visualizers** to help better inspect the data values during source-code debugging. For example, developers can create some custom visualizers for inspecting picture content when debugging through code that deals with **Image** objects. In this recipe, we will illustrate how you can leverage the Debugger Visualizer to enhance WCF service code-debugging by creating a custom Debugger Visualizer.

How to do it...

In our sample case, we will create a custom Visual Studio Debugger Visualizer for inspecting service endpoint information of a particular ServiceHost object:

1. Define the custom Debugger Visualizer type.

   First, let's create a custom Debug Visualizer type. Visual Studio 2010 provides a built-in item template for creating Debug Visualizer (see following screenshot). We can simply create the custom Debugger Visualizer through this project template.

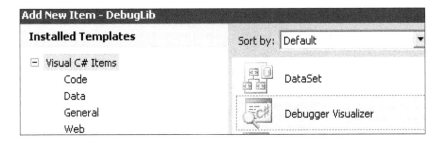

Another way is by simply adding a reference to the `Microsoft.VisualStudio.DebuggerVisualizers.dll` assembly and creating a class deriving from the `Microsoft.VisualStudio.DebuggerVisualizers.DialogDebuggerVisualizer` type. In our sample case, we will go through the second approach and create a normal class library project to hold the custom Debugger Visualizer type.

The following code snippet shows the definition of the sample Debugger Visualizer type together with a `VisualizerObjectSource` derived type that will help perform data serializing tasks against the target object of the visualizer:

```csharp
// Visualizer for ServiceHost type
public class ServiceHostVisualizer : DialogDebuggerVisualizer
{
    protected override void Show(IDialogVisualizerService
            windowService, IVisualizerObjectProvider objectProvider)
    {
        string svcHostData = objectProvider.GetObject() as string;

        if (svcHostData != null) MessageBox.Show(svcHostData);

    }
}

// ObjectSource class for serializing the target object into
custom data
public class ServiceHostVisualizerObjectSource :
        VisualizerObjectSource
{

    public override void GetData(object inObject, Stream outStream)
    {
        if (inObject != null && inObject is ServiceHostBase)
        {
            var svcHost = inObject as ServiceHostBase;
```

```
StringBuilder sb = new StringBuilder("Endpoints in
    ServiceHost:\n");
foreach (var ep in svcHost.Description.Endpoints)
{
   sb.AppendFormat("Address:{0}, Binding:{1},
        Contract:{2}\n",
        ep.Address, ep.Binding, ep.Contract
        );
}

BinaryFormatter bf = new BinaryFormatter();
bf.Serialize(outStream, sb.ToString());
   }
  }
 }
```

As you can see, the `ServiceHostVisualizerObjectSource` type simply queries out all the endpoints within the `ServiceHost` object (passed into the visualizer at debugging time) and dumps them into a string. And the visualizer will pull out the string from the associated object context and print them.

2. Apply debugging options and restrictions on the custom Debugger Visualizer.

   In addition to the visualizer and `ObjectSource` types, we need to add an additional assembly-level attribute of the `System.Diagnostics.DebuggerVisualizer` type so as to indicate that the custom visualizer is targeting the `ServiceHost` type. This attribute can be added in any source code file within the same project of the custom Debugger Visualizer. For simplicity, we will put it in the source code file of the custom Debugger Visualizer type. The next screenshot shows the attribute declaration for our sample `ServiceHostVisualizer` type.

   ```
   [assembly: System.Diagnostics.DebuggerVisualizer(
   typeof(DebugLib.ServiceHostVisualizer),
   typeof(DebugLib.ServiceHostVisualizerObjectSource),
   Target = typeof(System.ServiceModel.ServiceHostBase),
   Description = "My WCF ServiceHost Visualizer")]
   ```

3. Install the Debugger Visualizer into Visual Studio.

   After creating the visualizer types, the next step is to install it into the Visual Studio Visualizer collection so that the next time you launch the Visual Studio debugger to debug WCF service code, the custom Visualizer will be loaded and used. The good news is that installing a custom Debugger Visualizer into Visual Studio is quite simple and straightforward. What we need to do is simply copy the .NET assembly containing the custom Debugger Visualizer types into the following locations:

❑ Visual Studio install path: `\Microsoft Visual Studio 10.0\`
`Common7\Packages\Debugger\Visualizers`

❑ `My Documents\Visual Studio 2010\Visualizers`

The following screenshot shows the Visual Studio install path on the test machine
where we have put our custom `ServiceHostVisualizer` assembly.

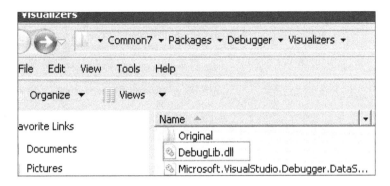

4. Launch a Visual Studio debugging session and use the custom Debugger Visualizer.

Now, we can launch the Visual Studio Debugger and debug into our WCF service
code. You can choose a `ServiceHost` type variable and find a zoom icon (see
the next screenshot) beside it. By clicking the zoom icon, Visual Studio will use our
custom `ServiceHost` Visualizer to inspect the `ServiceHost` instance under
debugging.

```
static void Main(string[] args)
{
    using(ServiceHost host = new ServiceHost(typeof(Service1)))
    {
        host.Open();
            host    {System.ServiceModel.ServiceHost}
✔ My WCF ServiceHost Visualizer
        Console.WriteLine("service started ....");
        Console.ReadLine();
```

In our sample case, the `ServiceHostVisualizer` will dump out all the service endpoints within the `ServiceHost` instance. The following screenshot shows the endpoint list displayed by the `ServiceHostVisualizer` in our sample application during debugging.

There's more...

There is more information about how to develop custom Visual Studio Debugger Visualizers in the MSDN reference. You can find them at the following location:

▶ Visualizers

   `http://msdn.microsoft.com/en-us/library/zayyhzts.aspx`

Also, for real-world Visualizer samples, there are many existing Visualizer projects on the CodePlex site (`http://www.codeplex.com/site/search?query=visualizer`)

See also

▶ *Complete source code for this recipe can be found in the* `\Chapter 12\recipe5\` *folder*

Using PerformanceCounters for WCF service monitoring

PerformanceCounters are very useful components on Windows operating systems for application/service performance monitoring. WCF has provided plenty of built-in PerformanceCounters to help developers or administrators monitor the application performance and health more conveniently.

In this recipe, we will demonstrate how we can enable the WCF PerformanceCounters for a given WCF service application and monitor the values of specific WCF PerformanceCounters.

How to do it...

Now, let's have a look at the detailed steps for utilizing the built-in PerformanceCounters in a WCF service application:

1. Turn on PerformanceCounters in the service diagnostics setting.

   By default, WCF PerformanceCounters are not enabled so as not to involve additional performance hits for WCF service runtime. However, it is quite straightforward to turn on the PerformanceCounters for a given WCF application; we just need to set the `<diagnostics performanceCounters />` attribute to one of the following values:

   - `Off`: Performance counters are disabled.
   - `ServiceOnly`: Only performance counters relevant to this service are enabled.
   - `All`: Performance counters can be viewed at runtime.
   - `Default`: A single performance counter instance, `_WCF_Admin`, is created. This instance is used to enable the collection of SQM data for use by the infrastructure.

   The following XML fragment shows the configuration setting for turning on the PerformanceCounters in a WCF service's configuration file.

```
<system.serviceModel>
    <diagnostics  performanceCounters="" >
                                              Off
                                              ServiceOnly
                                              All
                                              Default
```

2. Use the Windows Reliability and Performance Monitor tool to monitor the PerformanceCounters.

   After the PerformanceCounters have been enabled in the WCF service application, we can use the Windows Reliability and Performance Monitor tool to look up the values of certain WCF PerformanceCounters. Performance Monitor is a GUI component of the Windows operating system and the file of this tool is located in the Windows system folder at `\Windows\System32\perfmon.exe`.

But in most cases, we will start it by simply typing `perfmon.exe` in the command line. After the Performance Monitor is launched, we can select the **Performance Monitor** node on the left panel to view existing PerformanceCounters. The following screenshot shows the main user interface of the Performance Monitor tool.

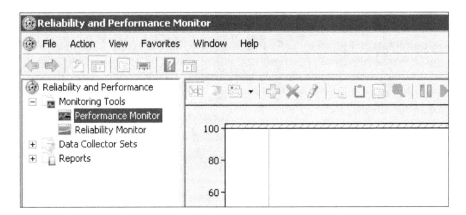

If the WCF PerformanceCounters you want to monitor are not originally added into the Graphic view, we can add it through the **Add Counters** dialog (as shown in the next screenshot). WCF has scoped all the built-in PerformanceCounters to three different levels:

- Service level
- Endpoint level
- Operation level

If you have multiple versions of .NET framework installed (such as .NET Framework 3.5 and 4.0) on the host machine, you will also find multiple versions of PerformanceCounters for each WCF PerformanceCounter category (shown in the following screenshot).

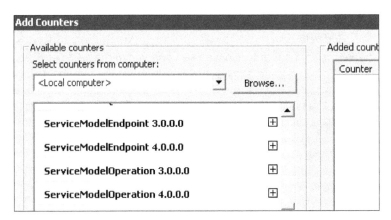

By expanding a particular counter category, we can further look into the detailed individual PerformanceCounters of each category. The following screenshot shows the detailed PerformanceCounter items listed under the **ServiceModelService 4.0.0.0** category.

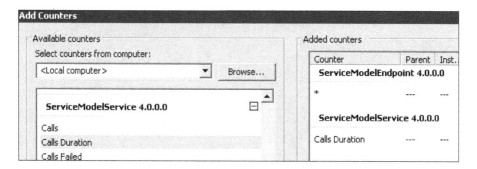

Now, having all these built-in PerformanceCounters available, WCF service developers and administrators can choose the proper counter combination so as to get the required performance statistics of the target WCF service applications.

13

Miscellaneous WCF Development Tips

In this chapter, we will cover:

- ▶ Creating test X.509 certificates for WCF Service
- ▶ Managing X.509 certificates installed on service machine
- ▶ Building an RSS feed service
- ▶ Building a routing service
- ▶ Registering WCF components manually in IIS server

Introduction

Having gone through various aspects of WCF development, there are still some other useful tips left. As there is no definite category for these individual tips, I will share these tips with you here as a miscellaneous collection.

In this chapter, we will go through five recipes that cover some tools and configuration tips for WCF development. For example, we will cover how to generate and manage X.509 certificates for testing scenarios. Also, a typical example about the new service routing feature will be provided in the last recipe.

Creating test X.509 certificates for WCF Service

When dealing with message or transport layer security in WCF service development, it is quite often possible that we will need to get some X.509 certificates for tests in development environment. For a production environment, we can obtain X.509 certificates from some well-know, public certificate authorities such as VeriSign, Inc. Then, how can we generate some temporary certificates for testing scenarios at development time?

In this recipe, we will go through several simple and handy means for creating X.509 certificates used at WCF service development time.

How to do it...

We will demonstrate two very common means for creating test X.509 certificates on Windows development environment. One is using the Windows operating system's built-in *Windows Certificate Service* and the other is using the `makecert.exe` tool provided in .NET framework SDK.

1. Use Windows Certificate Services.

   If in your development environment there is a Windows 2000, 2003, or 2008 server machine which has Certificate Service installed and running, then using Windows Certificate Service to create test X.509 certificate is a very convenient means.

   Microsoft Windows Certificate Service is a built-in feature of server operating system and you can turn on it through the **Add/Remove Windows Components/Features** option in Control Panel if the service is not already installed. Windows Certificate Service supports requesting and issuing X.509 certificates through a web page-based interface, which is quite easy for users to access. The following screenshot shows the default page of the Windows Certificate Service web interface.

If you want more control over the detailed properties of the certificate you want to generate, the Certificate Service provides an **Advanced Certificate Request** view for users to specify customized certificate request parameters (see the **Advanced Certificate Request** form shown as follows).

2. Use `makecert.exe` tool.

Another very common and useful means for creating a test X.509 certificate is using the `makecert.exe` tool. `makecert.exe` is a command line tool provided by Microsoft for developers to create test certificates that can be used for testing purpose. `makecert.exe` is available, if you have .NET framework SDK installed on the development machine. You can directly go to the .NET framework SDK installation folder such as `C:\Program Files\Microsoft SDKs\Windows\v7.0\Bin`.

To invoke the `makecert.exe` tool, you can use Visual Studio command prompt console in which you can directly use the `makecert.exe` command.

In order to create a certificate with this tool, the following arguments must be used:

- ❑ `-sr`: Store location. It can be `LocalMachine` or `CurrentUser`.
- ❑ `-ss`: Store folder. It can take different values but these are probably the most common, `My` (Personal) or `Trusted` (Trusted folder).
- ❑ `-n`: Certificate distinguished name. It is very important to choose a right name for the certificate, as it will be used to identify it (this name is also used to look for the certificate).

For example, the following command uses `makecert.exe` to create an X.509 certificate with `MyTestCertificate` as subject name and is stored in `LocalMachine` root location and `My` store folder.

```
makecert.exe -sr LocalMachine -ss My -n CN=MyTestCertificate
```

Here is another `makecert` command that creates a self-signed certificate, specifies a subject name of `"CN=MyCompany"`, specifies start and ending validity periods, places the certificate in the `LocalMachine | My` store, specifies and exchanges key, and makes the private key exportable.

```
makecert -sr LocalMachine -ss my -r -pe -n "CN=My Company" -b
01/01/2005 -e 01/01/2010 -sky exchange
```

There's more...

For more information about Windows Certificate Services, you can refer to the following references:

- Certificate Services

  `http://msdn.microsoft.com/en-us/library/aa376539(VS.85).aspx`

- Building an Enterprise Root Certification Authority in Small and Medium Businesses

  `http://technet.microsoft.com/en-us/library/cc875810.aspx`

This recipe only covers two typical examples of using `makecert.exe` tool. You can get complete syntax and command options of `makecert.exe` tool on the following page:

- Certificate Creation Tool (Makecert.exe)

  `http://msdn.microsoft.com/en-us/library/bfsktky3(VS.80).aspx`

Managing X.509 certificates installed on service machine

In addition to how to generate test X.509 certificates, another thing WCF developers might also be interested in is how we can manage the X.509 certificates already installed on a certain Windows machine.

In this recipe, we will demonstrate three common means for looking up and viewing certificate information on a given machine.

How to do it...

Now, let's take a detailed look at the certificate management means one by one.

1. Use certificates **MMC** snap-in.

   The first and the most commonly used means is using the certificates MMC snap-in to lookup certificates. **MMC (Microsoft Management Console)** is a component of Windows 2000, and later Windows NT-based operating systems that provides system administrators and advanced users with a flexible interface to configure and monitor the system.

Here are the detailed steps for opening the certificates MMC snap-in component for looking up certificates:

- ❑ Open a command prompt window.

- ❑ Type mmc and press the _Enter_ key. (Note that to view certificates in the local machine store, you must be in the Administrator role)

- ❑ On the **File** menu, click **Add/Remove Snap In**.

- ❑ Click on **Add**. In the **Add Standalone Snap-ins** dialog box, select **Certificates** (shown in the next screenshot).

- ❑ Click on **Add**. In the certificates snap-in dialog box, select **Computer** account (for LocalMachine store) and click on **Next**. Optionally, you can select **My User** account for CurrentUser store.

- ❑ In the **Select Computer** dialog box, click on **Finish**.

- ❑ In the **Add Standalone Snap-in** dialog box, click on **Close**.

- ❑ On the **Add/Remove Snap-in** dialog box, click on **OK**.

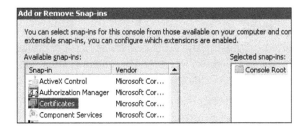

After successfully adding the certificates MMC snap-in, we can start exploring the certificates within the selected certificate stores and sub stores. The following screenshot shows the main certificate management window in the MMC snap-in.

The certificate stores are displayed in a hierarchical layout in the left panel of the management window.

Double-clicking on a certain certificate item in the right panel will display a pop-up dialog to show the detailed information and properties of the selected certificate.

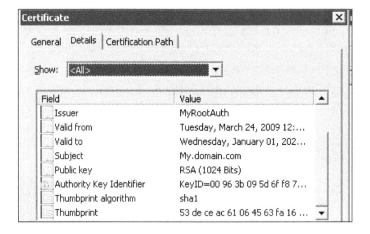

2. Use Certmgr.exe tool.

Certmgr.exe (Certificate Manager Tool) is a very useful tool provided by .NET framework SDK for managing the X.509 certificates on Windows machines. Though we might often use Certmgr.exe to install or remove certificates, it is also quite good at looking up and viewing certificates installed in the certain stores on a machine.

We can simply launch Certmgr.exe in the .NET framework command line prompt, just like `makecert.exe`. To use Certmgr.exe for certificate looking up, we normally need to specify three parameters in the command. They are:

- `-c`: Indicates that the command will display certificates in the specified location.

- `-r`: Specifies the root store location (either `LocalMachine` or `CurrentUser`).

- `-s`: Specifies the sub store name.

For example, the following command will display all the certificates contained in the `LocalMachine` | `My` store.

```
certmgr -c -r localmachine -s my
```

By executing the command, a list of certificates with detailed information will be dumped in the command line console (shown in the following screenshot).

3. Use **Windows PowerShell**.

   Microsoft Windows PowerShell is a new command line shell and scripting technology that helps IT professionals or developers achieve greater control and productivity over Windows operating system.

   If PowerShell is available on the WCF development machine, it is quite convenient to check certificate information via it. PowerShell can let you explore certificates on machine through a directory-based structure. For example, we can query out all the certificates existing in the `LocalMachine` | `My` store using the following PowerShell command:

   ```
   ls cert:\LocalMachine\My
   ```

   The following command window shows the certificate list output from the previous command in PowerShell console.

Also, we can apply additional pipeline commands so as to further format the query result in PowerShell. For example, by using `Format-List` method together with the `ls` query, we can display each certificate with a detailed information view. The following screenshot shows a sample detailed information list of the queried certificates using the `Format-List` command option.

```
Select Administrator: Windows PowerShell
PS C:\> ls cert:\localmachine\my | Format-List


Subject       : CN=
Issuer        : CN=
Thumbprint    : EEFB5EE92D20963FB420BDD1808703EBC5589E9F
FriendlyName  :
NotBefore     : 10/29/2009 2:20:20 AM
NotAfter      : 10/27/2019 2:20:20 AM
Extensions    : {System.Security.Cryptography.Oid, System.Se

Subject       : CN=My.domain.com
Issuer        : CN=MyRootAuth
Thumbprint    : 53DECEAC61064563FA168ACB00D910D0CB12C4B0
FriendlyName  :
NotBefore     : 3/24/2009 12:00:00 AM
NotAfter      : 1/1/2020 12:00:00 AM
Extensions    : {System.Security.Cryptography.Oid}
```

There's more...

More information on how to use Certmgr.exe tool can be found at the following MSDN reference:

▶ Certificate Manager Tool (Certmgr.exe)

```
http://msdn.microsoft.com/en-us/library/e78byta0(VS.80).aspx
```

Building an RSS feed service

Nowadays, **Syndication** (commonly known in the form of RSS or ATOM feeds) is widely used over the Internet for websites or personal blogs to expose or integrate data and resource through a highly interoperable format.

Ever since .NET framework 3.5, WCF has added support for building Syndication service through standard WCF service development framework. We can build either an RSS (or an ATOM) or even a custom feed service by creating a WCF service and operations.

In this recipe, we will show you how to build a simple RSS 2.0 feed through WCF Syndication feature.

How to do it...

Here are the detailed steps to create the sample RSS 2.0 feed.

1. Define a `ServiceContract` for the RSS feed service.

    The first thing to do for building a WCF feed service is to define a `ServiceContract` with operations that will return feed data. WCF provides a well-defined Syndication object model to support this, what we need to do is simply define a service operation that will return an instance of `SyndicationFeedFormatter` type or its derived types. The `ISimpleRSSFeed` interface shows the `ServiceContract` of the sample RSS feed service.

    ```
    [ServiceContract]
    [ServiceKnownType(typeof(Rss20FeedFormatter))]
    public interface ISimpleRSSFeed
    {
        [OperationContract]
        [WebGet]
        SyndicationFeedFormatter MainFeed();
    }
    ```

    As we can see, the `MainFeed` operation returns a `SyndicationFeedFormatter` object and we have applied `ServiceKnownType` to indicate that the actual return object will be an `Rss20FeedFormatter` (for RSS 2.0 feed format) instance. WCF Syndication feature is based on REST programming model. Therefore, we can set the operation as `WebGet` enabled so that the feed service operation can be consumed through HTTP GET protocol by any WebRequest-enabled client such as Internet Explorer browser.

2. Implement the `ServiceContract` with WCF Syndication classes.

    The following code snippet shows the complete implementation of the sample `SimpleRSSFeed` service.

    ```
    public class SimpleRSSFeed : ISimpleRSSFeed
    {
        public SyndicationFeedFormatter MainFeed()
        {
            SyndicationFeed feed = new SyndicationFeed("WCF development
                    Feed", "This is a feed for WCF development", new
                    Uri("http://wcfserver/feedservice/mainfeed"));
            feed.Authors.Add(new SyndicationPerson("steven@test.org"));
            feed.Categories.Add(new SyndicationCategory("WCF"));
            feed.Categories.Add(new SyndicationCategory("Coding"));
            feed.Description = new TextSyndicationContent("This is a
                    feed about WCF development");
    ```

```
            SyndicationItem item1 = new SyndicationItem(
                    "WCF Addressing",
                    "This is the content for WCF Addressing",
                    new Uri("http://wcfserver/Content/addressing"),
                    "item1",
                    DateTime.Now);

            SyndicationItem item2 = new SyndicationItem(
                    "WCF Contract",
                    "This is the content for WCF Contract",
                    new Uri("http://wcfserver/Content/contract"),
                    "item2",
                    DateTime.Now);

            SyndicationItem item3 = new SyndicationItem(
                    "WCF Binding",
                    "This is the content for WCF Binding",
                    new Uri("http://wcfserver/Content/binding"),
                    "item3",
                    DateTime.Now);

            List<SyndicationItem> items = new List<SyndicationItem>();

            items.Add(item1);
            items.Add(item2);
            items.Add(item3);

            feed.Items = items;

            return new Rss20FeedFormatter(feed);
        }
    }
```

The `MainFeed` function is quite straightforward, it simply creates a `SyndicationFeed` object which represents the entire RSS feed. Then it adds several `SyndicationItem` objects into the `Items` collection. Each `SyndicationItem` object represents a certain feed item within the entire RSS feed output. The `MainFeed` function returns an `Rss20FeedFormatter` object so that the `SyndicationFeed` object will be serialized into RSS 2.0 format. In case you would like to use Atom 1.0 format, you can switch the formatter to `Atom10FeedFormatter` type.

3. Apply proper endpoint configuration for the RSS feed service.

   In addition to the feed service definition, we also need to make sure the service and endpoint is properly configured in the `app.config` file. For our sample RSS feed service, we will expose it through WebHttpBinding at an HTTP location. The following fragment shows the configuration section of the sample RSS 2.0 service.

```
<service name="FeedService.SimpleRSSFeed">
    <endpoint address=""
                binding="webHttpBinding"
                  contract="FeedService.ISimpleRSSFeed">
    </endpoint>

    <host>
        <baseAddresses>
            <add baseAddress="http://wcfserver:7771/FeedService/"/>
```

4. Access the RSS feed service through web browser.

   Finally, after the RSS feed service gets started, we can simply launch a web browser and consume the feed service by typing the endpoint and operation URL in the address bar. The following screenshot shows the feed output of the sample RSS 2.0 feed service in IE.

There's more...

For more information about the Syndication service support in WCF, you can refer to the following MSDN document:

 ▸ WCF Syndication

   http://msdn.microsoft.com/en-us/library/bb412202.aspx

See also

 ▸ *Complete source code for this recipe can be found in* \Chapter 13\recipe3\ *folder*

Building a routing service

There is one interesting scenario in WCF service development, which is to build an intermediate routing service between the client consumers and the backend real service. This is quite useful for many cases, for example, the backend service machine might not be directly accessible from client consumers or the service provider might want to add additional routing logic so as to differentiate the service requests from various client consumers.

Though building routing service is supported ever since WCF in .NET Framework 3.x, the new routing service feature in WCF 4.0 makes it rather easy to create our own WCF routing service.

This recipe will demonstrate how to create a WCF 4.0 routing service that routes service operation requests based on the request message content.

How to do it...

The sample routing service here will help route the service operation requests received from client consumers to the target real service at backend server. Here are the detailed steps to build it.

1. Setup the backend service.

    Let's have a look at the backend service which will actually process the operation requests from client consumers. The real service is a very standard WCF service, which contains a single operation returning a string value (see `IDataService ServiceContract`).

    ```
    [ServiceContract]
    public interface IDataService
    {
        [OperationContract]
        string GetData();
    }
    ```

    The backend service is hosted with BasicHttpBinding at a certain HTTP endpoint location (see the service configuration fragment shown as follows).

    ```xml
    <service name="BackEndService.DataService">
      <endpoint address=""
                binding="basicHttpBinding"
                contract="BackEndService.IDataService" />
        <host>
          <baseAddresses>
            <add baseAddress="http://localhost:8732/BackEndService/"
          </baseAddresses>
    ```

2. Create a service host for routing service.

   Now, we come to steps for setting up the routing service. Let's take a look at how we can host a routing service first. The hosting code of the routing service is quite straightforward, which looks like a normal WCF service (see following code snippet).

```
static void Main(string[] args)
{
    try
    {
        using (ServiceHost router = new
                        ServiceHost(typeof(RoutingService)))
        {
            router.Open();
            Console.WriteLine("Routing Service started at: {0}",
                            router.BaseAddresses[0]);
            Console.ReadLine();
        }
    }
    catch (Exception ex)
    {
        Console.WriteLine(ex.ToString());
    }
}
```

   As you can see, the only difference from a normal WCF service is that we use the `System.ServiceModel.Routing.RoutingService` class as the service type. This is when we are initializing the `ServiceHost`. `RoutingService` class, which is a new type added in .NET framework 4.0 for hosting routing service.

3. Add routing settings in the configuration file of routing service.

   But how does the routing function work when the hosting code of the routing service is so simple. The answer is the configuration of the routing service in which we have put all the routing rules.

   The following fragment shows the service configuration of the sample routing service.

```xml
<service behaviorConfiguration="routingServiceBehavior"
    name="System.ServiceModel.Routing.RoutingService">
  <host>
    <baseAddresses>
      <add baseAddress="http://localhost:7001/routingservice/" />
    </baseAddresses>
  </host>
  <endpoint address=""
            binding="basicHttpBinding"
            name="RequestReplyRoutingEndpoint"
            contract="System.ServiceModel.Routing.IRequestReplyRouter" />
```

As you can see, the routing service defines an endpoint that uses the same BasicHttpBinding as the backend service. And the Contract used here is of `System.ServiceModel.Routing.IRequestReplyRouter` type, which means the routing endpoint is for processing requests with **Request/Reply** message exchange pattern.

In addition to the Contract, there is another important part within the routing service configuration—the behavior it uses. The WCF 4.0 routing service needs to configure a `<routing>` behavior element in the `serviceBehavior`. The `<routing>` behavior will specify a `filterTableName`, which points to the routing table configuration. The following XML fragment shows the `serviceBehavior` used for the sample routing service, which points to a routing table named `ActionRoutingTable`.

```
<serviceBehaviors>
  <behavior name="routingServiceBehavior">
    <routing filterTableName="ActionRoutingTable" />
```

Now, the last configuration setting is the routing table configuration, which is also defined within the `<system.serviceModel>` section (shown in the following fragment).

```
<routing>
  <filters>
    <filter name="ActionFilter" filterType="Action"
            filterData="http://tempuri.org/IDataService/GetData" />

    <filter name="DefaultFilter" filterType="MatchAll" />
  </filters>
  <filterTables>
    <filterTable name="ActionRoutingTable">
      <add filterName="ActionFilter" endpointName="TargetEndpoint"/>
    </filterTable>

    <filterTable name="DefaultRoutingTable">
      <add filterName="DefaultFilter" endpointName="TargetEndpoint" />
    </filterTable>
  </filterTables>
</routing>
<system.serviceModel>
```

The routing table consists of two parts—filters and filter tables. Each filter table represents a routing table instance that is referenced in the routing service behavior. In each filter table, we can add single or multiple routing rules each of which requires a `filterName` and an `endpointName`. The `filterName` points to the filter defined in `<filters>` collection and `endpointName` points to the target client endpoints configured in the routing service.

How it works...

At runtime, when the routing service validates the routing table (when a request comes and needs routing), it will go through each rule and if the filter of the rule matches, the corresponding endpoint will be used to forward the incoming request message.

In our sample routing service, the routing table uses a filter that will forward the requests based on its **SOAP Action** value in the message. Therefore, only the message that has **Action** which matches the target backend service, will get forwarded.

Also, the sample routing service will only forward operations with Request/Reply message exchange pattern. In addition to the Request/Reply pattern, there are another three patterns also supported by the WCF 4.0 service routing. The following table shows all four kinds of routing contracts currently supported.

Contract	Shape	Channel shape
ISimplexDatagramRouter	SessionMode = SessionMode. Allowed	IInputChannel -> IOutputChannel
	AsyncPattern = true	
	IsOneWay = true	
ISimplexSessionRouter	SessionMode = SessionMode. Required	IInputSessionChannel -> IOutputSessionChannel
	AsyncPattern = true	
	IsOneWay = true	
IRequestReplyRouter	SessionMode = SessionMode. Allowed	IReplyChannel -> IRequestChannel
	AsyncPattern = true	
IDuplexSessionRouter	SessionMode=SessionMode. Required	IDuplexSessionChannel -> IDuplexSessionChannel
	CallbackContract=typeof (ISimplexSession)	
	AsyncPattern = true	
	IsOneWay = true	
	TransactionFlow(TransactionFlowOption. Allowed)	

There's more...

In addition to Action-based filters, there are many other supported filter types such as XPath filter, address Filter, custom filter, and so on. You can get the complete filter types from the following MSDN reference:

▸ Filtering

http://msdn.microsoft.com/en-us/library/ms731081.aspx

▶ *Complete source code for this recipe can be found in* \Chapter 13\recipe4\ *folder*

Registering WCF components manually in IIS server

When hosting WCF in IIS web server, it is required that the WCF-specific modules and application script mappings are installed. By default, after installing .NET framework 3.x or 4.0, those WCF extension modules and script mappings will be installed in the IIS server automatically. However, in some cases where the server environment has become corrupt or cleaned, we might need to manually install the WCF components.

In this recipe, we will demonstrate how to manually register the WCF extension components on a development machine.

How to do it...

.NET framework provides a built-in tool for configuring WCF components on a given machine. This tool is called ServiceModelReg.exe, which is included in the .NET framework tools. For computers that have .NET framework version 3.0 or later installed, you can find this tool in the framework installation folder C:\Windows\Microsoft.NET\Framework\v4.0.30319.

In common cases, we can directly launch the ServiceModelReg.exe within the Visual Studio command line prompt or use the absolute path to the ServiceModelReg.exe tool. By executing ServiceModelReg.exe with /? option, we can get the help document of the tool (see command line output shown next).

To register the WCF component in the IIS server on the machine, we can use the following command:

```
ServiceModelReg.exe /i
```

Or, if we want to repair an existing installation of the WCF service model extensions, we can use the /r option like:

```
ServiceModelReg.exe /r
```

There's more...

For more options on the ServiceModelReg.exe tool, you can refer to the following MSDN reference:

▶ ServiceModel Registration Tool (ServiceModelReg.exe)

```
http://msdn.microsoft.com/en-us/library/ms732012(VS.90).aspx
```

Index

Thank you for buying
Microsoft Windows Communication Foundation 4.0
Cookbook for Developing SOA Applications

About Packt Publishing

Packt, pronounced 'packed', published its first book "*Mastering phpMyAdmin for Effective MySQL Management*" in April 2004 and subsequently continued to specialize in publishing highly focused books on specific technologies and solutions.

Our books and publications share the experiences of your fellow IT professionals in adapting and customizing today's systems, applications, and frameworks. Our solution-based books give you the knowledge and power to customize the software and technologies you're using to get the job done. Packt books are more specific and less general than the IT books you have seen in the past. Our unique business model allows us to bring you more focused information, giving you more of what you need to know, and less of what you don't.

Packt is a modern, yet unique publishing company, which focuses on producing quality, cutting-edge books for communities of developers, administrators, and newbies alike. For more information, please visit our website: www.PacktPub.com.

About Packt Enterprise

In 2010, Packt launched two new brands, Packt Enterprise and Packt Open Source, in order to continue its focus on specialization. This book is part of the Packt Enterprise brand, home to books published on enterprise software – software created by major vendors, including (but not limited to) IBM, Microsoft and Oracle, often for use in other corporations. Its titles will offer information relevant to a range of users of this software, including administrators, developers, architects, and end users.

Writing for Packt

We welcome all inquiries from people who are interested in authoring. Book proposals should be sent to author@packtpub.com. If your book idea is still at an early stage and you would like to discuss it first before writing a formal book proposal, contact us; one of our commissioning editors will get in touch with you.

We're not just looking for published authors; if you have strong technical skills but no writing experience, our experienced editors can help you develop a writing career, or simply get some additional reward for your expertise.

**WCF 4.0 Multi-tier Services
Development with LINQ to Entities**

**WCF 4.0 Multi-tier Services
Development with LINQ to
Entities**

ISBN: 978-1-849681-14-8   Paperback: 348 pages

Build SOA applications on the Microsoft platform with
this hands-on guide updated for VS2010

1. Master WCF and LINQ to Entities concepts by
    completing practical examples and applying them
    to your real-world assignments

2. The first and only book to combine WCF and LINQ
    to Entities in a multi-tier real-world WCF service

3. Ideal for beginners who want to build scalable,
    powerful, easy-to-maintain WCF services

**Applied Architecture Patterns
on the Microsoft Platform**

**Applied Architecture Patterns
on the Microsoft Platform**

ISBN: 978-1-849680-54-7   Paperback: 544 pages

An in-depth scenario-driven approach to architecting
systems using Microsoft technologies

1. Provides an architectural methodology for choosing
    Microsoft application platform technologies to meet
    the requirements of your solution

2. Examines new technologies such as Windows
    Server AppFabric, StreamInsight, and Windows
    Azure Platform and provides examples of how they
    can be used in real-world solutions

3. Written by a distinguished team of specialists in
    the Microsoft space

Please check **www.PacktPub.com** for information on our titles

Microsoft Silverlight 4 Data and Services Cookbook

ISBN: 978-1-847199-84-3   Paperback: 476 pages

Over 85 practical recipes for creating rich, data-driven business applications in Silverlight

1. Design and develop rich data-driven business applications in Silverlight

2. Rapidly interact with and handle multiple sources of data and services within Silverlight business applications

3. Understand sophisticated data access techniques in your Silverlight business applications by binding data to Silverlight controls, validating data in Silverlight, getting data from services into Silverlight applications and much more!

Microsoft Silverlight 4 Data and Services Cookbook

Over 85 practical recipes for creating rich, data-driven business applications in Silverlight

Gill Cleeren   Kevin Dockx   [PACKT] enterprise

Refactoring with Microsoft Visual Studio 2010

ISBN: 978-1-849680-10-3   Paperback: 372 pages

Evolve your software system to support new and ever-changing requirements by updating your C# code base with patterns and principles

1. Make your code base maintainable with refactoring

2. Support new features more easily by making your system adaptable

3. Concepts are presented in a comfortable one-on-one, pair-programming style

Refactoring with Microsoft Visual Studio 2010

Evolve your software system to support new and ever-changing requirements by updating your C# code base with patterns and principles

Peter Ritchie   [PACKT] enterprise

Please check **www.PacktPub.com** for information on our titles

Microsoft Windows Workflow Foundation 4.0 Cookbook

ISBN: 978-1-849680-78-3   Paperback: 255 pages

Over 70 recipes with hands-on, ready to implement solutions for authoring workflows

Microsoft Windows Workflow Foundation 4.0 Cookbook

1. Customize Windows Workflow 4.0 applications to suit your needs

2. A hands-on guide with real-world illustrations, screenshots, and step-by-step instructions

3. Explore various functions that you can perform using WF 4.0 with running code examples

4. A hands-on guide with real-world illustrations, screenshots, and step-by-step instructions

Microsoft Enterprise Library 5.0

ISBN: 978-1-849680-90-5   Paperback: 272 pages

Develop Enterprise applications using reusable software components of Microsoft Enterprise Library 5.0

Microsoft Enterprise Library 5.0

1. Develop Enterprise Applications using the Enterprise Library Application Blocks

2. Set up the initial infrastructure configuration of the Application Blocks using the configuration editor

3. A step-by-step tutorial to gradually configure each Application Block and implement its functions to develop the required Enterprise Application

Please check **www.PacktPub.com** for information on our titles

Microsoft Azure: Enterprise Application Development

ISBN: 978-1-849680-98-1   Paperback: 217 pages

Straight talking advice on how to design and build enterprise applications for the cloud

1. Build scalable enterprise applications using Microsoft Azure

2. The perfect fast-paced case study for developers and architects wanting to enhance core business processes

3. Packed with examples to illustrate concepts

4. Written in the context of building an online portal for the case-study application

Microsoft Azure: Enterprise Application Development

Straight-talking advice on how to design and build Enterprise applications for the cloud

Richard J. Dudley
Nathan Duchene

Microsoft Silverlight 4 Data and Services Cookbook

ISBN: 978-1-847199-84-3   Paperback: 476 pages

Over 80 practical recipes for creating rich, data-driven business applications in Silverlight

1. Design and develop rich data-driven business applications in Silverlight

2. Rapidly interact with and handle multiple sources of data and services within Silverlight business applications

3. Understand sophisticated data access techniques in your Silverlight business applications by binding data to Silverlight controls, validating data in Silverlight, getting data from services into Silverlight applications and much more!

Microsoft Silverlight 4 Data and Services Cookbook

Gill Cleeren   Kevin Dockx

Please check **www.PacktPub.com** for information on our titles

www.ingramcontent.com/pod-product-compliance
Lightning Source LLC
LaVergne TN
LVHW062307060326
832902LV00013B/2084